Process Metaphysics and

Hua-yen Buddhism

Bibliotheca Indo-Buddhica Series No. 146

Process Metaphysics and Hua-yen Buddhism

A CRITICAL STUDY OF CUMULATIVE PENETRATION VS. INTERPENETRATION

STEVE ODIN

The Stony Brook Center for Religious Studies
State University of New York at Stony Brook

SRI SATGURU PUBLICATIONS
A DIVISION OF
INDIAN BOOKS CENTRE
DELHI-INDIA

Published by :
Sri Satguru Publications
Indological and Oriental Publishers
A Division of
Indian Books Centre
40/5, Shakti Nagar,
Delhi-110007
(INDIA)

First Indian Edition : Delhi, 1995

ISBN 81-7030-424-5

PRINTED IN INDIA

To Sung-bae Park

In a certain sense, everything is everywhere at all times.

Alfred North Whitehead
Science and the Modern World

Contents

Preface

In this study I have attempted to establish an East-West dialogue between Whiteheadian process metaphysics and Hua-yen Buddhism at a generalized level of speculative discourse within the unity of a syncretic harmonization pattern. On the one side, this dialogue involves a sustained critique of the Hua-yen doctrine of "interpenetration" from the standpoint of Whiteheadian process theory, which argues for what I have called in this work a doctrine of "cumulative penetration." On the other side, this dialogue attempts to develop Whiteheadian process theory as a *hermeneutical framework* which enables us to radically reinterpret Hua-yen Buddhist thought patterns in contemporary Western terms. However, in addition to the Whiteheadian framework, I have also incorporated several other Western hermeneutical systems which are useful for interpreting Hua-yen Buddhist modes of thought such as linguistic analysis, descriptive phenomenology, dialectical discourse and depth-psychology, although always within the context of advancing the Whitehead/Buddhist dialogue, and always within the specific context of the critical problematic generated by this dialogue as a dialectical tension, namely, the problem which I have termed "interpenetration" vs. "cumulative penetration."

In that this work essentially represents my reflections while in graduate school for philosophy at SUNY Stony Brook, I have a special debt of gratitude to those with whom I have studied during the preparation of this manuscript. I would at this time like to gratefully acknowledge Professor David A. Dilworth whose encyclopedic East-West scholarship and expertise in both Whitehead and Hua-yen Buddhism were a major source of inspiration for this study; Professor Justus Buchler, a giant in the field of systematic metaphysics; Professor Thomas J. Altizer, one of the first to explore the Whitehead/Buddhist dialogue; Professor

Antonio T. deNicolas who helped me to shift into a multiplicity of new frameworks in my study of Eastern texts; Professor Walter Watson for his valuable critical suggestions concerning this project; Professors Christopher George, Christopher Chappel and Richard A. Gard of the Institute for Advanced Studies in World Religions for their great assistance; Professors Don Ihde and Edward S. Casey from whom I acquired the phenomenological perspectives employed here; Professor Sung-bae Park who made possible my specialized study of East Asian Buddhism as a Post-Doctoral Fellow at the SUNY at Stony Brook Center for Religious Studies; and especially, Professor Robert C. Neville, who has truly been my mentor throughout both undergraduate and graduate school, and from whom I have learned more about speculative philosophy than I can express. I would also like to offer my great respect and gratitude to Hua-yen master Hsüan Hua, Abbot of Tathāgata Monastery, who kindly granted me an extended stay at Dharma Realm University in the City of Ten Thousand Buddhas at Talmage California for purposes of research. And finally, I would like to thank Jaya for proofreading the final version of this work as well as for bringing so much happiness to my life during these years of graduate study.

STEVE ODIN

Abbreviations

Works by Alfred North Whitehead

1) *Adventures of Ideas.* New York: Macmillan Co., 1967 .... AI
2) *Concept of Nature.* Cambridge: Cambridge University Press, 1971 .... CN
3) *Modes of Thought.* New York: Macmillan Co., 1968 .... MT
4) *Process and Reality.* Corrected Edition, ed. by David Ray Griffin and Donald W. Sherburne. New York: Macmillan Co., 1978 .... PR
5) *Religion in the Making.* New York: Macmillan Co., 1960 .... RM
6) *Science and the Modern World.* New York: Macmillan Co., 1967 .... SMW

PROLOGUE

Ŭisang's Ocean Seal of Hua-yen Buddhism

The celebrated "Ocean Seal" (*haein do*) composed by Priest Ŭisang (625–702), the First Patriarch of Korean Hua-yen Buddhism, has been acclaimed by many Chinese, Korean and Japanese patriarchs alike as being the most masterful distillation and condensation of Hua-yen (Kor. *Hwaŏm;* Jap. *Kegon*) Buddhist thought. The Ocean Seal is included in Ŭisang's one extant literary work, written in 668 A.D. while studying in China, entitled the *Hwaŏm ilsŭng pŏpkye do* (Chi. *Hua-yen i ch'eng fa-chieh tu*) or "Diagram of the *Dharmadhātu* according to the Hua-yen One Vehicle," which also contains a concise autocommentary on the seal.[1] Ŭisang's Ocean Seal encapsulates the inmost heart-mind of the Hwaŏm or Hua-yen metaphysical vision, which the indigenous tradition calls the "round" (*wŏn*) or "all-embracing" view, in a poem composed of only 210 Chinese characters, arranged in 30 verses of 7 characters each, with 4 sides, 4 corners and 54 angles, which is concentrically patterned like a winding maze, thus forming a beautiful Buddhist maṇḍala or "mystic circle," both beginning and ending at the center of the diagram. In some of the traditional *kyo* or "scriptural study" monasteries throughout Korea, Ŭisang's Ocean Seal has been awarded as a kind of diploma or certificate of achievement for monks who had successfully completed their course of study within the temple, thus indicating the great esteem accorded to the seal in the heritage of Korean Hwaŏm Buddhism. Ŭisang's Ocean Seal is still regularly chanted in Korean Buddhist monasteries (such as the famous *Haeinsa* or Ocean Seal Temple in *Kyŏngnam,* Korea), as an efficacious *dhāraṇī* or "mystic hymn" having *mantric* power, with the ultimate intent of eliciting the supreme Hwaŏm visionary experience of *haein sammae* or "Ocean-Seal-Samādhi," which itself includes the contemplative envisagement of *li-shih-wu-ai* or the "non-obstructive interpenetration of universal-principle with particular-phenomena" as well as *shih-shih-wu-ai* or the "non-obstructive interpenetration of particular-phenomena with particular-phenomena. Indeed, in his autocommentary on the seal Ŭisang even speaks of *li-li-hsiang-chi* or the "mutual identification of universal-principles with universal-principles," an enigmatic statement which is unique amongst Hua-yen doctrinal formulations.[2] Thus, due to the mysteries of *li-shih-wu-ai* and *shih-shih-wu-ai,* it is said that Buddhas absorbed in Ocean-Seal-Samādhi see all dharmas both near and far of the past, present and future without obstruction; they instantly travel to all Buddhalands the number of dustmotes without obstruction; they accomplish all inconceivable miracles according to their wish without obstruction; they emanate waves of immeasurable compassion and joy to all sentient beings without obstruction; they pervade all lands and seas without obstruction; they emit clouds of radiance and orbs with satellite orbs of rainbow lights throughout all ten worlds of the dharma-realm without obstruction; they adorn all Pure Lands and heavenly abodes with a rain of lotus flowers without obstruction; and this multiplied to infinity.

According to Ŭisang's maṇḍala diagram, in Ocean-Seal-Samādhi (*haein sammae*) one enters the "primordial realm" (*ponje*) of *dharmadhātu,* described as "round, interpenetrating and non-dual" (*wŏllyung mui sang*), "unmoving but originally still" (*pudong bonrae jok*), "nameless, formless and without (distinctions)," (*mumyong musang cholilch'e*), "extremely profound, subtle and sublime" (*shimshim kŭkmimyo*), and "not attached to self-nature but manifested according to (causal) conditions" (*pulsu jasŏng suyŏnsŏng*), such that "One is in All and Many is in One" (*il jung'ilch'e dajung'il*) as well as "One is identical to All and Many is identical to One" (*il jŭg'ilche da jŭg'il*); thus, "in one particle of dust is contained the ten directions" (*ilmijnjung hamshibang*) and "incalculably long eons are identical to a single thought-instant" (*muryang wonkŏp chŭgilnyŏm*), whereupon "particular-phenomena and universal-principle are completely merged without distinction" (*isa myŏng'yon mubunbyŏl*) and "*saṃsāra* and *nirvāṇa* are always harmonized together" (*saensa yŏlban sanggonghwa*), although these interfusing and mutually identical realms " are not confused or mixed but function separately" (*ingbul japnan kyŏkpyŏlsŏng*). Then, from the fountainhead of Ocean-Seal-Samādhi, unimaginable miracles abundantly overflow "according to one's wishes" (*yŏi*), raining down in a "shower of jewels" (*ubo*), so as to fill all of "empty space" (*hogong*), bestowing waves of blessings of compassionate-grace to all sentient beings throughout *saṃsāra* in proportion to their capacities. Thus, in concordance with the "round-sudden" (*wŏndon*) teachings of Hwaŏm Buddhism concerning "original enlightenment" (*pongak*) and "sudden awakening" (*tono*), "the moment one begins to aspire with their heart, instantly perfect enlightenment (is attained) (*chobalshimshi pyŏnjŏngak*), so that "he who practices (contemplation), returns to the primordial realm"(*haengja hwanbonje*), adorning the *dharmadhātu* with the "inexhaustible treasure" (*mujinbo*) of *dhāraṇī* like a "palace of jewels" (*silbojŏn*). Finally, one comes to repose in the "real world and bed of the middle way" (*silche chung dosang*), which is the ancient and primordial realm named "Buddha" (*pul*). Due to its marvelously concise and synoptic character, there is perhaps a no more simple and direct method of introducing the key teachings of Hua-yen Buddhism than through Ŭisang's "Ocean Seal" or "Diagram of the *dharmadhātu*," a translation of which has been provided in the next few pages, accompanied by several excerpts from his autocommentary as well as a short biography of Ŭisang's life as extracted from an account recorded in Iryon's *Sanguk Yusa*.[3]

As indicated above, the seventh-century monk Ŭisang (625-702) of the Unified Silla Dynasty is recognized as the First Patriarch of Korean Hwaŏm Buddhism. Ŭisang's father was Hin-sin and his family name was Kim. He became an ordained monk at the age of twenty-nine and resided at Hwangpok Temple. Soon afterward he departed on a journey to T'ang China to pursue advanced studies in Buddhist doctrine accompanied by his friend Wŏnhyo (617-686). Wŏnhyo himself finally became a great master of Hwaŏm doctrine and undisputably the most highly esteemed figure in the history of Korean Buddhism. But when Ŭisang and Wŏnhyo arrived at Liaotung they were somehow mistaken for Silla spies by the Koguryo border guards and detained for ten days, after which they were allowed to return home. Again, on a second attempt to visit China, Ŭisang and Wŏnhyo were forced to take refuge in a small hut during a thunderstorm. The following morning, Wŏnhyo realized that he had in fact slept overnight in a tomb and drunk water from a skull, mistaking it in the dark for a gourd, thereupon becoming filled with nausea. Yet, at this moment, Wŏnhyo is said to have experienced Sudden Enlightenment (*tono*), realizing instantaneously that all discriminated entities are "mind-only," since in the nocturnal darkness, a gourd and skullcap or a crypt and house are ultimately the same. Consequently, Wŏnhyo relinquished his lifelong plans of pilgrimage to China, remaining in Korea as a towering yet eccentric figure, spending the last years of his life as a shamanistic wanderer, dancing all throughout the nation while beating a drum and wearing a mask, chanting a song-poem he had composed named *wu-ai ke* (Kor. *mu-ae ga*), meaning "Song of Non-Obstruction" (*wu-ai* or "non-obstruction" being the key technical term of Hwaŏm Buddhism, synonymous with "interpenetration" or "interinclusiveness"), while everywhere inspiring the masses to chant Amitābha Buddha's name and to long for Pure Land. Whereas Ŭisang later completed his journey to China in 650 A.D., eventually returning to Korea to become the highly acclaimed First Patriarch of Korean Hwaŏm Buddhism.

Upon his arrival at Yangchow in the Middle Kingdom of China, the Chinese military governor honored Ŭisang with a grand reception. Several days after, Ŭisang visited the monk Chih-yen (602-688), the Second Patriarch of Chinese Hua-yen and teacher of Fa-tsang (643-712), the celebrated Third Patriarch. The previous night, Chih-yen had foreseen Ŭisang's visitation in an auspicious dream wherein he envisioned a great tree growing in the Haedong (Silla) province of Korea, whose branches covered all of China, at the top of which was a phoenix nest filled with jewels radiating a blinding light. Waking in wonderment and awe, Chih-yen awaited in anticipation until Ŭisang knocked at his door, receiving his guest with a special ceremony stating, "In a dream last night I awaited your coming." The two then discussed the mysteries of the Hwaŏm Sūtra long into the evening, whereupon Chih-yen declared the supremacy of Ŭisang's understanding on many points of Buddhist scripture.

In the year 670, Ŭisang returned to Korea in order to warn King Munmu of Silla that his Kingdom was in danger of attack from Chinese troops under the order of T'ang Emperor Kao-tsung, thus enabling the king to surmount the crisis. Two years later Fa-tsang sent Ŭisang a copy of his selections from *shou-hsuan-shu* along with a letter expressing his deepest friendship, requesting that the manuscript be returned to him with corrections and suggestions for revision. Indeed, a study of Fa-tsang's life and writings reveals that he was influenced as heavily by the Korean Hwaŏm masters Ŭisang and Wŏnhyo as by his own teacher Chih-yen.

In later years, Ŭisang attracted more than three thousand disciples to whom he expounded the principles of Hwaŏm Buddhism. Moreover, Ŭisang ordered the ten cardinal temples in Korea to propogate Buddhism in accordance with the doctrines of the Hwaŏm Sūtra. Finally, Ŭisang's Ocean Seal was placed in the temples throughout Korea in order to instruct monks on the essentials of Hwaŏm doctrine for a thousand years to come. Due to the monumental efforts of First Patriarch Ŭisang as well as his great contemporary Wŏnhyo in the early Unified Silla Dynasty, Hwaŏm became the predominant *kyo* or scriptural study sect of Korean Buddhism, such that traditional Buddhism in Korea is now generally characterized as *t'ong pulgyo* or "Buddhism of total interpenetration." With this biographical account of Ŭisang's life, a brief outline of Ŭisang's autocommentary included in his *Hwaŏm ilsŭng pŏpkye do* would be useful in order to establish the Ocean Seal within its proper context.

As I have included a full translation of Ŭisang's *Hwaŏm ilsŭng pŏpkye do* in the form of an Appendix to this work, I will not elaborate upon its various contents in any detail at this time, but will instead consider the extraordinary design of the seal. Early in his autocommentary Ŭisang articulates the architectonic structure of his 30 verse poem in the Ocean Seal, upon the basis of which I have constructed the below schematization:

Ŭisang's Structural Analysis of the Ocean Seal

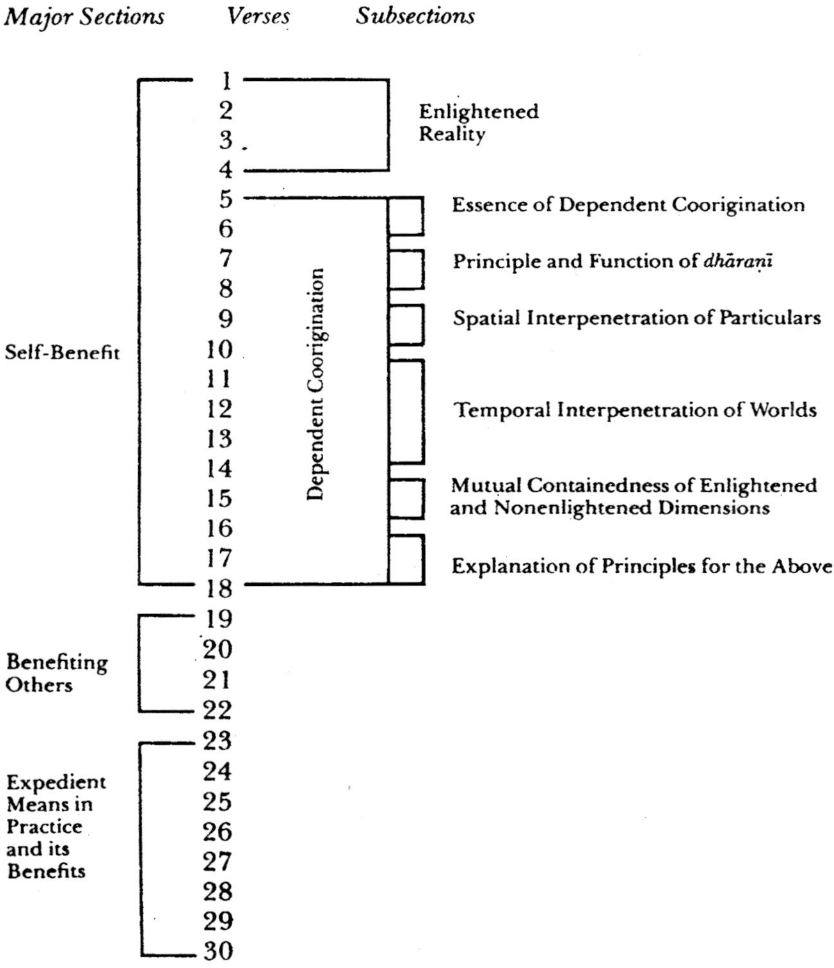

Ŭisang's autocommentary asserts that the structure of his Ocean Seal manifests the famous "Six Marks" *(liu hsiang)* doctrine of Hwaŏm Buddhism, which includes the universality mark and particularity mark, identity mark and difference mark, formation mark and disintegration mark, each pair of contrasts signifying the relation of a whole (i.e., a *Gestalt*) to its various functional parts. The Ocean Seal as a whole designates the universality, identity and formation marks, whereas its many curves, bends and meanderings represent the particularity, difference and disintegration marks. However, since these Six Marks do not attach to self-nature but follow (causal) conditions inexhaustibly, the whole and its constituent parts all interpenetrate without obstruction such that each meandering curve is different and yet identical to the entire seal. In a similar fashion, Ŭisang's Ocean Seal illustrates nearly all of the key doctrinal innovations of Hwaŏm Buddhism.

Yet, what is the mysterious "secret" of Ŭisang's Ocean Seal? At the outset of his autocommentary, Ŭisang instructs the reader as to the correct method of following the meandering *tao* or path of the seal:

> As to the method of reading the poem, you should begin with the character *pŏb* (Skt. *dharma*) at the center [of the seal], going through many curves, bends and meanderings, finally coming [full circle back to the center] to the character *pul* (Skt. *buddha*). Then read following the *tao* (path) of the seal through 210 characters and 54 curves.

Hence in Ŭisang's Ocean Seal or "Diagram of the *dharmadhātu*," both the first and last characters, i.e., dharma and Buddha, are located in the same position at the center of the seal. The autocommentary proceeds:

> Question: For what reason are the characters at the beginning and end put in the center?
> Answer: So to express that the two positions of cause and effect. . . in the dharma-nature school (of Hwaŏm) are both in the Middle Way.

In this way, Ŭisang's Ocean Seal illustrates the key doctrine of Hwaŏm Buddhist metaphysics, namely, that start and finish or cause and effect are both in the same position in the Middle Way, so that they interpenetrate harmoniously together without any obstructions whatsoever. At a deeper level of analysis, the autocommentary clarifies that the Ocean Seal functions to illustrate the fundamental Hwaŏm doctrine of the Fifty-two Stages in the career of Bodhisattva, wherein all Fifty-two Stages (i.e., Ten Faiths, Ten Abodes, Ten Practices, Ten Returnings, Ten Bhūmis, Equal Enlightenment, and Wonderful Enlightenment) all interpenetrate without hindrance such that the first stage of nascent faith contains as its inner contents all the subsequent stages, including the final stage of Wonderful Enlightenment. Hence, the first, last and intermediary stages, or beginning, middle and end (representing past, present and future, respectively) all occupy the same position in the center of the Middle Way. Ultimately, it is this Hwaŏm doctrine whereby a first stage Bodhisattva of newly arisen faith (i.e., the "cause") and a final stage Buddha of Wonderful Enlightenment (i.e., the "effect") fully interpenetrate through unobstructed simultaneous-mutual-containedness which establishes the foundation for the meditative experience of Sudden Enlightenment. In such a manner, then, Ŭisang's ingenius Ocean Seal brilliantly manifests the essentials of the Hwaŏm Buddhist "Round-Sudden" Vehicle of theory and praxis, not only through its doctrinal contents, but also by means of the very construction and design of the seal itself as a concentrically patterned maṇḍala or mystic circle both beginning and ending at the center of the diagram. I have translated Ŭisang's Ocean Seal poem as follows:

Ŭisang's Ocean Seal of Hwaŏm Buddhism

1. Since dharma-nature is round and interpenetrating,
   It is.without any sign of duality.
2. All dharmas are unmoving,
   And originally calm.
3. No name, no form,
   All (distinctions) are abolished.
4. It is known through the wisdom of enlightenment,
   Not by any other level.
5. The true-nature is extremely profound,
   Exceedingly subtle and sublime.
6. It does not attach to self-nature,
   But manifests following (causal) conditions.
7. In One is All,
   In Many is One.
8. One is identical to All,
   Many is identical to One.
9. In one particle of dust,
   Is contained the ten directions.
10. And so it is,
    With all particles of dust.
11. Incalculably long eons,
    Are identical to a single thought-instant.
12. And a single thought-instant,
    Is identical to incalculably long eons.
13. The nine times and the ten times,
    Are mutually identical.
14. Yet are not confused or mixed,

But function separately.
15. The moment one begins to aspire with their heart,
Instantly perfect enlightenment (is attained).
16. *Saṃsāra* and *Nirvāṇa*,
Are always harmonized together.
17. Particular-phenomena (*shih*) and Universal-principle (*li*),
Are completely merged without distinction.
18. This is the world of the Bodhisattva Samantabhadra,
And the Ten Buddhas.
19. In Buddha's Ocean-Seal-Samādhi,
20. Many unimaginable (miracles) are produced,
According to one's wishes.
21. This shower of jewels benefiting all sentient beings,
Fills all of empty space.
22. All sentient beings receive this wealth,
According to their capacities.
23. Therefore, he who practices (contemplation),
Returns to the primordial realm.
24. And without stopping ignorance,
It cannot be obtained.
25. By unconditional expedient means,
One attains complete freedom.
26. Returning home (the primordial realm) you obtain riches,
According to your capacity.
27. By means of *dhāraṇī*,
An inexhaustible treasure,
28. One adorns the *dharmadhātu*,
Like a real palace of jewels.
29. Finally, one reposes in the real world,
The bed of the Middle Way.
30. That which is originally without motion,
Is named Buddha.

海印圖

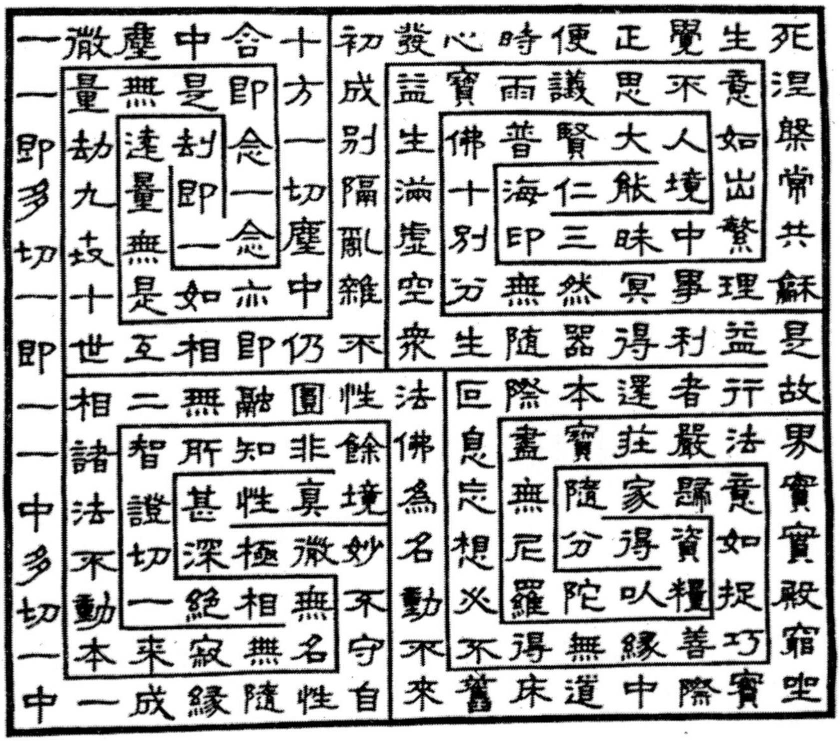
一微塵中含十初發心時便正覺生死
一量無是即方成益寶雨議思不意涅
即劫遠劫念一別生佛普賢大人如槃
多九量即一切隔滿十海仁能境出常
切世無一念塵亂虛別印三昧中繁共
一十是如亦中雜空分無然冥事理龢
即世互相即仍不衆生隨器得利益是
一相二無融圓性法叵際本還者行故
一諸智所知非餘佛息盡寶莊嚴法界
中法證甚性真境為妄無隨家歸意實
多不切深極微妙名想尼分得資如寶
切動一絕相無不動必羅陀以糧捉殿
一本來寂無名守不不得無緣善巧窮
中一成緣隨性自來舊床道中際實坐

Introduction

In his seminal book entitled *The Buddhist Teaching of Totality*, Garma C.C. Chang encapsulates the Hua-yen doctrine of simultaneous interfusion and nonimpeded mutual penetration with the following diagram:[1]

$$\text{mutual penetration} = \begin{cases} \text{simultaneous-mutual-arising} \\ \text{simultaneous-mutual-entering} \\ \text{simultaneous-mutual-containment} \end{cases}$$

Chang goes on to directly equate the doctrine of simultaneous-mutual-penetration illustrated in this diagram with the organic process metaphysics posited by Alfred North Whitehead in the West, asserting: "Hwa Yen philosophy corresponds almost exactly to Alfred North Whitehead's Philosophy of Organism. Here both Hwa Yen and Whitehead stress the mutual-penetrating and mutual-containing aspects of existence in order to disclose an organic and totalistic view of reality."[2] In another book, *Hua-yen Buddhism: The Jewel Net of Indra* by Francis H. Cook, the remarkable proximity of Whitehead's process philosophy to Hua-yen Buddhism is once again noted, for example when the author writes: "Whitehead's statement to the effect that to exist means to exert causal influence is closely paralleled in the Hua-yen vision of a universe where everything . . . functions as a cause for everything else."[3] Moreover, in a text entitled *Creativity and Taoism*, Chang Chung-yuan equates Whitehead's doctrine of creativity not only with the Tao, which he terms "the primordial source of creativity," but also with the Hua-yen Buddhist doctrine of *shih-shih-wu-ai* or non-obstructed complete interfusion, conceiving primordial creativeness in all three cases as signifying the generic notion of unity-in-multiplicity.[4]

It is true enough that Whitehead's metaphysics of process has instituted a major revolution in twentieth-century speculative thought, and that his categoreal scheme provides what is perhaps the most expansive hermeneutical framework yet formulated in Western culture by means of which to interpret East Asiatic thought patterns in general and Hua-yen Buddhism in particular. To begin with, the "ultimate notion of the highest generality at the base of actuality" in Whitehead's categoreal scheme (PR, p. 31), creativity or creative synthesis, is reminiscent of the first principle governing the Hua-yen speculative system, this being summarized in the term, *śūnyatā* or "emptiness" (also translatable as "voidness," "nothingness," "openness," or even "relativity"). Both notions fuse multiplicity into unity, manyness into oneness, and the disjunctive universe into the conjunctive universe at the standpoint of every perspectival locus in nature, so that each event or occasion of reality constitutes a microcosm of the macrocosm. As Francis Cook rightly stated in the above, the philosophical concept of *causation* is the central concern in both the Whiteheadian and Hua-yen Buddhist theoretical frameworks in that each dharma or event functions as a cause or supportive condition for every other event in the universe. In fact, both Whitehead's category of creative synthesis and Hua-yen Buddhist *śūnyatā* represent sophisticated doctrines of universal relativity or dependent origination, in the sense of arising into existence through causation. The argument developed by both systems is that, since each event arises into momentary existence due to its causal relations to every other event in the universe, it includes or contains them all as elements necessary to its own composition; thus a profound social connection, ontological togetherness and cosmic cohesiveness of events is established within each one.

Both Whiteheadian creativity and Hua-yen *śūnyatā* function to seriously undermine the notion of substance, i.e., what Buddhism terms *svabhāva* or independent self-existence. Of special interest with respect to the specific doctrinal innovations contributed by the Hua-yen school is Whitehead's repudiation of substance conceived as simply-localized material in favor of a microcosmic-macrocosmic model of actuality in which the entire spatiotemporal continuum is present in each occasion and each occasion saturates the whole spatiotemporal continuum; so that in a certain sense, everything is everywhere at all times. Or in the more poetic terminology of Hua-yen Buddhism, each dharma departs not from its local position, yet spreads throughout all lands and seas as well as all epochs and millenia, stretching and yet remaining, so that the far is also near and the near is also far, each housing its universe when contracted and pervading its universe when expanded, such that all things are at all places at once.

Thus far the Hua-yen metaphysics of simultaneous intercausation and interpenetration seems virtually identical in structure to

Whitehead's organic process theory of actuality, as suggested by such well-known Buddhologists as mentioned above. However, at this juncture it must be emphasized that the unqualified identification of Whitehead's process metaphysics with the position of Hua-yen Buddhism is seriously misleading, and in fact functions to conceal crucial philosophical problematics. As may be recollected from Priest Ŭisang's Ocean Seal of Hwaŏm Buddhism, all dharmas in the universe are said to interpenetrate (*yung-t'ung*) not only in the spatial sense whereby the "ten directions are immanent in a single particle of dust," but also in the more radical sense of *temporal* interfusion, such that the "incalculably long eons are all identical with a single thought-instant." This is to say that according to the Hua-yen conceptual system, a dharma receives causal influence not only from its predecessors, but from its contemporaries and successors as well, so that all events—past, present and future alike—interpenetrate harmoniously together into a single thought-instant without any obstruction or hindrance whatsoever. However, according to Whiteheadian process theory, past, present and future events do not all "interpenetrate" into a single thought-instant as in Hua-yen Buddhism; but rather, all events *cumulatively* penetrate their successors in a unidirectional flow of causal influence from past-to-present. Or in the more technical terminological apparatus of recent speculative discourse, whereas the Hua-yen theoretical framework establishes a *symmetrical* doctrine of causation in which causal relations are internal at both ends, Whitehead articulates a theory of *asymmetrical* causation in which causal relations are internal at one end and external at the other. Consequently, the very meaning of causation for Whitehead is causation from the past or conditioning by antecedents, such that penetration or immanence between occasions is always cumulative in structure. However, for the Hua-yen position efficient causation flows from past, present and future directions with equivalent force, thus establishing simultaneous interpenetrative harmonization and unhindered mutual containment between all events in the three periods of time.

It may therefore be asserted that in sharp contradistinction to the doctrine of interpenetration, interfusion or mutual immanence between events posited by Hua-yen Buddhism as based upon a wholly symmetrical theory of causal relations, Whitehead's position involves what is termed in this study a metaphysics of "cumulative penetration," "cumulative fusion" or "cumulative immanence," as structured by a strictly asymmetrical theory of causal transmission. Or to restate the distinction between these two theoretical frameworks in more dialectical terms, both Hua-yen and Whitehead argue that actuality is ultimately characterized as a *dialectical penetration* of polar opposites such as unity and multiplicity or subjectivity and objectivity. However, for Hua-yen this means a symmetrical or mutual interpenetration of opposites, i.e., unity-into-multiplicity and multiplicity-into-unity, subjectivity-into-objectivity and objectivity-into-subjectivity, thus establishing a simultaneous-mutual-containment among all events. However, for Whitehead there is only an asymmetrical or one-way dialectical movement of multiplicity-into-unity and objectivity-into-subjectivity; thus a cumulative penetration or cumulative fusion of events within a radically temporal structure is established. This is to say, whereas for Hua-yen, a subject and object simultaneously interpenetrate such that the subject contains the object just as much as the object contains the subject, for Whitehead subject and object are not simultaneous with each other; rather, each newly arising subject contains its multiplicity of antecedent objects, although that multiplicity of antecedent objects does not itself contain the newly arising subject, since the objects emerged into actuality independent of and prior to the subject's existence.

Thus, as opposed to merely elaborating various East-West comparative patterns or cross-cultural and transhistorical parallels, the present work directly addresses a crucial philosophical problem which has been generated by the dialectical tension from the recent encounter of Hua-yen Buddhism with Whiteheadian process theory: namely, the critical problem of interpenetration vs. cumulative penetration, or as it were, simultaneous-mutual-fusion vs. temporally-successive-fusion. More specifically, this work presents itself as a rigorous and sustained critical analysis of Hua-yen Buddhism from the standpoint of Whiteheadian process metaphysics. For instance, I argue that the process theory of cumulative penetration is empirically verified by the prereflective data of experiential immediacy or primordial feeling, which discloses actuality as a radically *temporal* field of causality, a past surging into the present and a present surging into the future, what process theory terms the empirical datum of "felt transitions," or what in modern phenomenological discourse is termed the "protentive-retentive" structure of internal time consciousness.

Aside from the various experiential and empirical arguments elaborated in this study, it is also argued that process theory provides more coherent logical resolutions to certain fundamental metaphysical problems, such as freedom vs. determinism. For example, I argue that the Hua-yen Buddhist speculative theory involves a doctrine of total determinism since each dharma can be exhaustively factored or reductively analyzed into its constituent causes and supportive conditions without remainder. And moreover, since each dharma is an effect which is wholly reducible to its causes or supportive conditions it is completely devoid of *svabhāba*, i.e., substance or unique own-being. However, in Whitehead's process doctrine of actuality, even though each occasion arises into momentary existence through a vast multiplicity of causes and conditions, none can be reductively analyzed or exhaustively factored into its causes without remainder; for what cannot be inherited through causal transmission is the *unity* of all causes in a single new actuality. For this, an "emergent synthesis" or "creative act" is required. Moreover, due to its character of *sui generis* or self-creativity, an occasion is a substance with irreducible selfhood and unique own-being, although it is wholly devoid of substantiality in all the senses disavowed by Hua-yen Buddhism itself, such as simple location, independent existence and permanent endurance. For a Whiteheadian event's free self-constitution is not derived from anything else, and is therefore in an important sense conceivable in itself without making reference to external conditioning factors. It is finally argued that the metaphysics of cumulative penetration expounded by Whitehead and his school accounts for all the ontological togetherness, solidarity and cohesiveness as well as for all the creativeness, novelty and freedom necessary for any balanced descriptive generalization of experiential immediacy.

However, the critique of Hua-yen Buddhism elaborated here is of an especially subtle kind, in that the basic ontological commitments of Hua-yen are essentially affirmed, namely, that in some sense, every event is virtually present or immanent in every other event, such that each one both contains and pervades its entire universe. In consequence of this profound social relatedness and togetherness of events, enlightened perceptivity through causal awareness, universal compassion through sympathetic concernedness, ecstatic bliss or aesthetic-value feeling through dipolar contrast, and final deliverance through transpersonal peace are all intrinsic to the structure of actuality itself, but only in concordance with those strictly asymmetrical infrastructures underscoring the metaphysics of cumulative penetration.

Moreover, the critique of Hua-yen Buddhism from the perspective of process philosophy articulated in the following pages is restricted solely to the order of *physical actuality*, which is radically temporal and thus cumulative or asymmetrical in structure. For in Part Three of this study, entitled "Theology of the Deep Unconscious: A Systematic Reconstruction of Process Theology," Whitehead's revolutionary notion of a dipolar God with both a primordial as well as a consequent nature will be radically retranslated through the Jungian psychological hermeneutic as the collective unconscious. Whitehead stipulates that whereas the primordial nature of God eternally envisages all possibilities, the consequent nature restores all antecedent actualities as imperishable and everlasting data in the divine memory. However, according to Jung, at the empirical level of analysis God is wholly indistinguishable from the unconscious psyche. For this reason, Jung asserts that the Buddhist strategy has always been to reassign those cosmic roles or divine faculties which the West ordinarily attributes to a transcendent God, to the collective unconscious at the depths of the psyche, what in Buddhist depth-psychology is termed the *ālaya vijñāna* or "storehouse consciousness." Thus, in terms of the Jungian psychological hermeneutic, whereas the consequent nature of God corresponds to the unconscious faculty of transpersonal memory constituted by psychically inherited archaic vestiges, the primordial nature corresponds to the unconscious faculty of the archetypal imagination, which is manifested through dreams, spontaneous fantasies and interior visions. Whereas Jung asserts that physical actuality is regulated by the principle of cause-effect or karmic inheritance, the archetypal realm of the collective unconscious is regulated by "synchronicity," the principle of acausal orderedness. I argue in this study that the supreme visionary experience of Hua-yen Buddhism, namely, Ocean-Seal-Samādhi, in fact involves the realization of the primordial nature of God (his atemporal envisagement of all *possibilities* occurring in the archetypal imagination of the collective unconscious) as is empirically verified by the testimony from subjects with retrocognitive and premonitory dreams or inner visions.

Finally, I place this entire scheme within the overall structure of the *trikāya* theory and correlate bardo cosmology expounded by Indo-Tibetan Tantric Buddhism. Third bardo or *nirmāṇakāya* signifies the domain of physical actuality governed by the principle of cause-effect or karmic inheritance and characterized by cumulative penetration; whereas second bardo or *sambhogakāya* signifies the archetypal imagination, the dimension of dreams and inner visions as regulated by synchronicity, the principle of acausal orderedness, and as characterized by simultaneous interpenetrative harmonization in the sense of an atemporal envisagement of all possibilities; and beyond this, there is only first bardo or *dharmakāya*, the clear light of the void, which is itself beyond all characterizations as the formless source of all forms, the indeterminate ground of all finite determinations.

Part I

THE HUA-YEN ROUND-SUDDEN VEHICLE OF NON-OBSTRUCTED INTERPENETRATION

CHAPTER 1

The Syncretic Harmonization Pattern of Hua-yen Dialectical Thought

The Hua-yen (Kor. Hwaŏm; Jap. Kegon) speculative framework, called the "round" (*yüan*) or "all-embracing" doctrine, generally exhibits what may be termed a "syncretic harmonization pattern" of metaphysical thought which functions to unify all fundamental Buddhist teachings, Hīnayāna and Mahāyāna alike, into a single, comprehensive vehicle of theory and praxis. Hua-yen or Flowery Splendour Buddhism was established as an independent sect in China during the Sui T'ang Period (559-900) when Chinese Buddhism was flowering at its apex with such schools as San-lun (Mādhyamika), Fa-hsiang (Yogācāra), Ch'an (meditative practice), T'ien-t'ai (*Lotus Sūtra* sect), Pure Land and Hua-yen (Avataṃsaka-Sūtra sect)—Hua-yen regarding itself as a creative synthesis or syncretic harmonization of all these systems of thought from the perspective of its own doctrinal innovations, namely *li-shih-wu-ai* or the unhindered interpenetration between universal with particular and *shih-shih-wu-ai* or the unhindered interpenetration between particular with particular.[1] In China, this syncretic harmonization pattern characteristic of Hua-yen speculative philosophy culminated in the work of Fa-tsang (643-712), the Third Patriarch and grand systematizer of the Hua-yen sect as well as its true founder in the view of many scholars.

The tendency towards metaphysical syncretism was developed further still in Korea where due to the efforts of Ŭisang and Wŏnhyo during the Unified Silla dynasty, the Hua-yen or Hwaŏm school became so predominant that in general, Korean Buddhist thought is characterized as *t'ong pulgyo* or "Buddhism of total interpenetration." Again, the Korean

Buddhist pattern of speculative thinking has often been characterized as *wŏllyung hoe t'ong* or "syncretic interpenetrative harmonization." Easily, the two greatest syncretists in the tradition of Korean Hwaŏm Buddhism have been Wŏnhyo (617-686) and Chinul (1158-1210). Wŏnhyo, the most prolific and original author in Korea's intellectual history (with over 240 works attributed to him) endeavored to interpenetrate and harmonize all Buddhist sūtras into a single treatise without any hindrance or obstruction. Wŏnhyo's usual strategy for interpenetrating and harmonizing all dialectical contradictions was through the Sinitic *t'i-yung* or "essence-function" formula expounded in the *Ta-ch'eng ch'i-hsin lun* or "The Awakening of Faith in Mahāyāna," one of the most seminal texts in all East Asiatic Buddhism. In Wŏnhyo's work such contradictory categories as *li* (universal-principle) and *shih* (particular-phenomena), *nirvāṇa* and *saṃsāra,* emptiness and form, one and many, subject and object, enlightenment and ignorance, or contemplation and action, were all resolved by respectively analyzing each pair of dialectical opposites into the relation obtaining between essence or *t'i* (representing the noumenal, internal and imperceptible dimensions of reality) and its correlate function or *yung* (representing the phenomenal, external and perceptible aspects). In such a manner then, Wŏnhyo clarified that the *t'i-yung* or essence-function construction (as opposed to the *neng-so* or subject-object construction governing ordinary dualistic thought patterns) is the key to understanding Hwaŏm descriptions of experiential reality. Thus, Wŏnhyo founded his own syncretic harmonization pattern of Hwaŏm metaphysics, calling it *hwajaeng*, the "reconciliation of all disputes."

Characteristic patterns of Wŏnhyo's speculative thought such as *t'ong pulgyo*, *wŏllyung hoet'ong* and *hwajaeng* are reflected in the creative synthesis of Buddhist categories in the Hwaŏm philosophy of Priest Chinul, who is generally regarded as Korea's foremost Master of Sŏn (Chi. Ch'an; Jap. Zen) meditative practice. Chinul, like his precursor Wŏnhyo, diverged from Fa-tsang and orthodox Hua-yen thought in that his primary focus was the syncretic harmonization not of Buddhist theories and concepts alone, but of Hwaŏm *theory* with meditative *praxis*. For this reason, Chinul selected as his basic sources of textual authority both Tsung-mi (780-841), who was not only the Fifth Patriarch of Chinese Hua-yen, but a Patriarch in Shen-hui's Lineage Succession of Ch'an meditative practice Buddhism, and Fa-tsang's lesser known contemporary, Li T'ung-hsüan (635-730), who emphasized the strictly salvific and practicable aspects of the Hua-yen vehicle of Buddhist enlightenment. From Li T'ung-hüan and Tsung-mi, Chinul derived his central problem of harmonizing and systematizing

Sŏn (Chi. Ch'an) or meditative Buddhism with Kyo (Chi. Chiao) or doctrinal study of Buddhism into a single, unified round-sudden vehicle of theory and praxis. Hence, for Chinul, the ultimate meaning of Hwaŏm interpenetration is sudden enlightenment or instantaneous illumination as expounded by the Sŏn school of meditative practice. From Tsung-mi, Chinul derived not only his notions of the syncretic harmonization of Sŏn and Kyo or Ch'an and Chiao, but also such other pragmatic considerations as the doctrinal reconciliation of sudden enlightenment with gradual practice as well as the integration of "other-power" as in *yŏmbul* or Pure Land practice and "self-power" as in Sŏn or Ch'an practice. In general, Chinul adopted Tsung-mi's philosophical principles of *k'an-hui* or comparative investigation and *ho-hui* or syncretic harmonization, an attitude which Tsung-mi stressed as making the intellect wholly flexible, comprehensive, liberal, tolerant, universal and nonsectarian in nature.

Moreover, this syncretic harmonization pattern characteristic of Hua-yen (Jap. Kegon) thought was assimilated by Kūkai (774-835) who endeavored to harmonize the Kegon dialectics of non-obstructive interpenetration and unhindered mutual containment with the Indian Tantra (or Mantra) Vehicle within the unifying context of his Japanese sect of esoteric (*mikkyō*) Shingon Buddhism as based upon the *Mahāvairocana Sūtra.* According to Kūkai's Shingon fusion of Kegon theory and esoteric Tantric praxis, Mahāvairocana Buddha, who is the personification of the Kegon *dharmadhātu*, i.e., the interpenetrative and non-obstructing dharma-field of all-merging suchness, is imitated by the practitioner through *tri-guhya* or the three secrets, namely, *mudrā* (gesture), *mantra* (incantation) and *maṇḍala* (visualization of a non-inherent deity) whereupon the body, speech and mind of the yogin are radically transformed into the paradigmatic Body, Speech and Mind of Mahāvairocana Buddha, such that one is imaginatively reconstituted as a microcosm of the macrocosm. Again, the highly acclaimed Sōtō Zen master Dōgen (1200-1253) incorporated the essential categories and presuppositions of Kegon Buddhism into his own syncretic Zen system of theory and praxis. Dōgen comprehended reality as a discontinuous stream of "dharma-moments," each of which constitutes pure "being-time" (*uji*) itself as the "absolute now" (*nikon*), wherein each absolute now is regarded as the "dharma-position" (*ju-hoi*) or the "total exertion" (*gūjin*) of all existence. Moreover, each absolute now or eternal present of pure being-time is said to contain all worlds of the past, present and future at once so as to establish the complete "simultaneity" (*dōji*) of the three temporal periods within the total exertion of each particular dharma-moment, as directly realized through the radical praxis of *zazen* or "sitting-only," which means precisely to "abide in dharma-position" through upright sitting in *samādhi*. Finally, this syncretic harmonization pattern characterizing Kegon speculative thought has been most recently manifested in the truly innovative theoretical framework of Nishida Kitarō (1870-1945), Japan's foremost contemporary systematic thinker, who endeavored to construct a truly international metaphysics, assimilating the history of Western philosophy into the Kegon infrastructure of his own Buddhist ontology of "absolute nothingness" (*zettai mu*), conceived as the "negative space" or "transparent topos" (*basho*) of "pure experience" (*junsui keiken*), which is itself the "place" (*basho*) of "dependent coorigination" (*engi*) and the "unhindered interfusion of particular with particular" (*ji ji muge*).

The Hua-yen syncretic harmonization pattern of metaphysical thought, not unlike G.W.F. Hegel's speculative synthesis in the West, understands all previous philosophic theories as historical "moments" in its own dialectical unfolding as indicated by Fa-tsang's theory of the Five Doctrines, which represents the Hua-yen *p'an chiao* or doctrinal classification system, in which the various Buddhist schools and sects are all hierarchically ranked according to five progressive stages of theoretical comprehension and experiential insight. This fivefold *p'an chiao* system ultimately signifies the hermeneutical reinterpretation of the concealed or "implicit meaning" (*neyārtha*) of the Buddhist Dharma through its various phases of dialectical evolution into its nonconcealed or "explicit meaning" (*nitārtha*) in the Hua-yen theory of the simultaneous interpenetration of all events within a single thought-instant.

In his extraordinary work entitled *Dialectical Aspects in Buddhist Thought*, Alfonso Verdu develops Tsung-mi's reformulation of Fa-tsang's fivefold *p'an chiao* system in terms of the dialectical stand adoped by each school throughout the history of Buddhist thought on the relationship between unity and multiplicity or subjectivity and objectivity.[2] As Verdu exposits Tsung-mi's five doctrine theory, the dialectical evolution of Buddhist thought is as follows:

First Stage: *Jen-t'ien chiao* (doctrine of man and gods) is the popular form of Buddhist faith which advocates the accumulation of merits to avoid incarnations in hells and to insure rebirth in the higher heavens. Dialectical Stand: The affirmation that both unity and multiplicity or subjectivity (internal identity) and objectivity (external diversity) are mutually opposite and mutually exclusive.

Second Stage: *Hsiao-sheng chiao* (Hīnayāna doctrine) is the theories of Sarvāstivāda scholasticism regarding the plurality of seventy-five dharmas and nirvāna of total extinction. Dialectical Stand: Negation of subjective unity (*anātman* theory) and affirmation of objective multiplicity of dharmas.

Third Stage: *Ta ch'eng fa-hsiang chiao* (doctrine of the dharma characters, i.e., Yogācāra subjective idealism) is the theory of the ontological primacy of subjective consciousness. Dialectical Stand: Affirmation of the unity of subjective consciousness or the transcendental-constitutive ego and negation of the objective multiplicity of real dharmas.

Fourth Stage: *Ta-ch'eng p'o-hsiang chiao* (doctrine of the destruction of all characters or marks) is the negativistic theory of emptiness attributed by Hua-yen to the Middle Way (Mādhyamika) schools. Dialectical Stand: Negation of both the subjective unity of consciousness as well as the objective multiplicity of real dharmas.

Fifth Stage: *I-ch'eng hsien-hsing chiao* (doctrine of the unique vehicle of the manifest Buddha nature) is the Hua-yen (as well as T'ien-t'ai and Ch'an) reinterpretation of emptiness in positive terms as signifying "experiential transparency," i.e., the establishment of *shih-shih-wu-ai yung-t'ung* or the non-obstructive interpenetration of particular with particular, wherein all events are realized as being "in-each-other." Dialectical Stand: Affirmation of both subjectivity and objectivity or unity and multiplicity, but as *nonoppositional*, i.e., as nonimpeded and interpenetrative within the translucent dharma-field of all-merging suchness.

To reiterate, the dialectical interplay between the one and the many and between subjectivity and objectivity was reinterpreted as the evolutionary progression of Buddhist speculative thought through five stages of development, these being: (*i*) Popular Buddhism, the affirmation of both unity and multiplicity as mutually exclusive and impenetrable; (*ii*) Hīnayāna, the negation of unity and the affirmation of multiplicity; (*iii*) Yogācāra, the affirmation of unity and the negation of multiplicity; (*iv*) Mādhyamika, the negation of both unity and multiplicity; and finally (*v*) Hua-yen (also T'ien-t'ai and Ch'an), the affirmation of both unity and multiplicity as mutually non-obstructive and harmoniously interpenetrating.

Verdu further elaborates the dialectical dimensions of Hua-yen and Kegon thought in terms of a threefold dialectical scheme of the Hegelian sort, including the three moments of "thesis-antithesis-synthesis," also termed "position-opposition-composition" or "affirmation-negation-integration." Whereas the first dialectical moment of multiplicity, exteriority and objectification (represented by Hīnayāna) is negated by pure subjectivity, interiority and identity in the second moment (the position of Yogācāra), in the third moment posited by Hua-yen dialectics there is a "negation-of-negation" (what Nishida Kitarō terms "absolute-affirmation-qua-negation-of-negation") wherein the external manifold of objective multiplicity is wholly interpenetrated and mutually fused in one all-merging suchness (Skt.

tathatā; Chi. *chen-ju*), so as to manifest a profound in-each-otherness. Here, suchness ontologically corresponds to the *ālaya vijñāna* or all-embracing storehouse matrix, which in Hua-yen involves the dialectic of twofold permeation (*hsün-hi*) or mutual causality—a dialectical projection of the one out into the many and the return of the many back into the one (as expounded in the *Ta-ch'eng ch'i-hsin lun* or "The Awakening of Faith in Mahāyāna") as opposed to the one-sided permeation of suchness through "causation by mind-only" (*wei-shih yüan ch'i*) as extolled by most Yogācāra sects.[3] In the third dialectical moment of Hua-yen then, the multiplicity of phenomena negated in the second moment by self-absorption into the effulgent radiance of inner consciousness are all *reaffiirmed*, but now they manifest their metaphysical transparency, nonimpededness and interpermeability.

In the first dialectical moment, that of Hīnayāna pluralistic realism (the stage of thesis), a one-sided primacy of the object exists in which unified consciousness is dispersed into sheer multiplicity. This is the stage of mere particularity wherein a myriad of separately existing phenomena erroneously come into appearance. But in the second moment, as represented by the Fa-hsiang Yogācāra sect (the stage of antithesis), the subject (identity) alone is real, whereas the object (difference) is unreal.[4] Thus, in its one-sided subjectivism, the Yogācāra school utterly negates the object (difference) through immersion in the sheer identity of interior consciousness or inward psychic radiance. All objectivity is thereby reduced to a mere content of the one true reality of internal subjectivity. However, in the third dialectical moment as established by Hua-yen dialectics, the subject is a content of the object just as much as the object is a content of the subject, since the very meaning of interpenetration and nonimpededness is that of simultaneous-mutual-containment.

Verdu further explicates the Hua-yen dialectics of interpermeation through the Yogācāra "three-natures" theory as reinterpreted through Hua-yen's own doctrinal innovations. The three natures include *parinispanna* (true universality), *parikalpita* (false concreteness) and *paratantra* (true concreteness). *Paratantra* or true concreteness is the realm of dependent coorigination and intercausality. *Parikalpita* or false concreteness is the world of mere particularity produced by imaginative construction, an illusory world of mutually exclusive phenomena. *Parinispanna* or true universality is the consciousness of interpermeation and mutual containment realized through sudden enlightenment (Chi. *tun-wu*; Jap. *tongo*), a consciousness of the true [nat]ure of *paratantra* or dependent coorigination as suffused by all-[embra]ging suchness. Thus, in *parinispanna*, subject (identity) and object [(diff]erence) interfuse into a totalistic identity-in-difference, establishing *wu-ai* (nonimpededness), *yung t'ung* (interpenetration) and *hsiang-chi* (mutual identification) in the transparent field of all-permeating suchness (*chen-ju*). Verdu diagrammatically illustrates this dialectical interpermeation of opposites through an ingenious use of Tsung-mi's symbolic circles, a modified version of which has been reproduced below.[5]

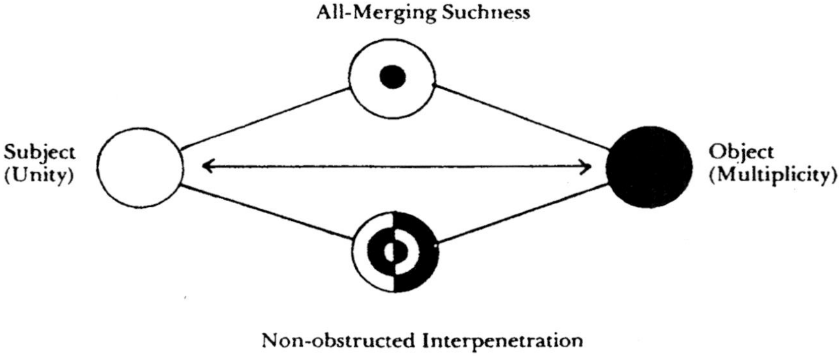

In terms of the basic philosophical problem under consideration in this study, namely, interpenetration vs. cumulative penetration, it is precisely this Hua-yen dialectical interpermeation between subjectivity and objectivity or unity and multiplicity which is the subject for critical analysis from the standpoint of Whiteheadian process metaphysics in Part Two, wherein it is propounded that in fact, it is more logically coherent and empirically valid to argue for a cumulative penetration or cumulative fusion of objectivity-into-subjectivity or multiplicity-into-unity, due to the radically *temporal* structure of experiential immediacy and the stream of consciousness.

CHAPTER 2

Intercausation and Interpenetration

Section I

The dialectical interpenetration of unity and multiplicity or subjectivity and objectivity in Hua-yen Buddhism essentially represents a microcosmic-macrocosmic model of reality wherein each dharma or event becomes a living mirror of the totality, reflecting all other dharmas—past, present and future alike—from its own standpoint in nature, so that the flowery splendor of the one universe is multiplied ad infinitum in a panoramic and kaleidoscopic spectacle of simultaneous-mutual-reflections, not unlike Leibniz's theory of "monads" or perspectival mirrors in the West. For instance, in his *Discourse on Metaphysics*, Leibniz writes:

> Every individual substance [monad] expresses the whole universe in its own manner. . . . Each substance is like an entire world and like a living mirror. . . of the whole world which it portrays, each one in its own fashion. . . . Thus the universe is multiplied in some sort as many times as there are substances. . . . It can indeed be said that every substance. . . expresses, although confusedly, all that happens in the universe, past, present and future.[1]

Indeed, such a microcosmic-macrocosmic universe of simultaneous-mutual-reflections may be expressed in terms of the contemporary "holographic" model, as a three-dimensional multi-colored laser projection, bright and vivid yet wholly transparent, wherein each part is an image of the whole. In Hua-yen Buddhism, this transparent holographic universe of microcosmic-macrocosmic events and simultaneous-mutual-reflections between perspectival mirrors is articulated through a series of similes (*upamā*), perhaps the most famous of which is "Celestial Lord Indra's Net." In the Metaphor of Indra's Net, the *dharmadhātu* (Chi. *fa-chieh*), i.e., the non-obstructed dharma-field of all-merging suchness, a cosmic web of interrelationships or universal matrix of intercausation, is analogous to the vast net covering Celestial Lord Indra's Palace which stretches throughout the entire universe. At each intersection of the latticework is situated a brilliant jewel reflecting all other jewels from its own perspective in the net. Fa-tsang illustrated the mystery of Celestial Lord Indra's Net in his treatise entitled "On the Golden Lion," which is generally regarded as the most systematic as well as the most popular account of Chinese Hua-yen Buddhism. The statue of a golden lion once located in the courtyard of Empress Wu's Royal Palace demonstrates the Hua-yen vision of simultaneous interreflection and infinite realms-embracing-realms. In Fa-tsang's words:

> In each of the lion's eyes, in its ears, limbs, and so forth, down to each and every single hair, there is a golden lion. All the lions embraced by each and every hair simultaneously and instantaneously enter into one single hair. Thus, in each and every hair there are an infinite number of lions. . . . The progression is infinite, like the jewels of Celestial Lord Indra's Net: a realm-embracing-realm ad infinitum is thus established, and is called the realm of Indra's Net.[2]

An old biography reports that on one particular occasion, for the benefit of Empress Wu and her royal assembly, Fa-tsang attempted to demonstrate the mystery of Indra's Net, of Ocean-Seal-Samādhi, of simultaneous-mutual-reflection, of realms-embracing-realms, of many-in-one and one-in-many, and other microcosmic-macrocosmic theories propounded by Hua-yen Buddhism, by means of a hall of mirrors. According to this account, Fa-tsang set a shining golden statue of the Buddha with a flaming torch beside it at the center of a darkened chamber filled with polished mirrors; all assembled beheld the one image of Buddha being multiplied and interreflected ad infinitum, whereupon Fa-tsang explained:

> Your majesty, this is a demonstration of Totality in the dharmadhātu. In each and every mirror within this room you will find the reflections of all the other mirrors with the Buddha's image in them.. . . The principle of interpenetration and (mutual) containment is clearly shown by this demonstration. Right here we see an example of one in all and all in one—the mystery of realm embracing realm ad infinitum is thus revealed.[3]

The *locus classicus* for the Hua-yen Buddhist doctrine of simultaneous-mutual-reflection and the "Mystery of Celestial Lord Indra's Net" is the voluminous Sanskrit text, the *Avataṁsaka Sūtra*. The *sūtra* concerns the acquisition of astounding spiritual powers (*ṛddhibala*) throughout an ascending series of fifty-two states finally culminating in *sāgara-mudrā-samādhi*, wherein all is instantly accomplished "according to your wishes" without obstruction. In sublime poetic verse the sūtra describes an infinitely vast and open crystalline universe composed of iridescent and transparent phenomena all interpenetrated and harmonized together in the non-obstructed *dharmadhātu* of all-merging suchness. Hundreds of thousands of billions of Buddhas are all assembled within a single hair of the *Tathāgata's* head, all performing inconceivable acts, inconceivable vows, and inconceivable miracles while absorbed in unutterable samādhis in indescribable pure lands, raining down their immeasurable compassion like a shower of jewels for the bliss and happiness of all sentient beings, while decorating the *dharmadhātu* with a garland of flowers. In the *Avataṁsaka Sūtra*, each dharma, like a jewel in Celestial Lord Indra's Net, is a reflection (*pratibhāsa*) of all other dharmas located throughout the three ages of time (i.e., past, present and future) whereas each *paramānu* or atomic particle has entrance (*anupraveśu*) into all other particles without hindrance or obstruction (*āvaraṇa*), such that each atom is fully present (*vyāpti*) in every other atom. Moreover, since each atom is a reflection (*pratibhāsa*) of every other atom, and since each dharma is fully present (*vyāpti*) in every other dharma, there is a perfect sameness (*samatā*) between all things in the universe, negatively expressed as *śūnyatā* or emptiness and positively expressed as *amalacitta* or purity.[4] Finally, the fundamental doctrines of the *Avataṁsaka Sūtra*, such as non-obstruction (*anāvaraṇa*), mutual arising (*pratīya-samutpāda*), mutual entering (*anupraveśu*), mutual containment (*vyāpti*), mutual reflection (*pratibhāsa*) and mutual sameness (*samatā*) are all given their most exalted expression in the concluding chapter of the work, the *Gaṇḍavyūha Sūtra*. Here the pilgram Sudhana enters deep into Ocean-Seal-Samādhi and bears witness to the awesome Tower of Maitreya, the supreme abode containing the splendid ornament of all manifestations, whose every stone contains within itself incalculable other towers, all as vast and spacious as the sky itself, each retaining its own structural patterning, yet wholly merged and interfused with all the other towers in perfect harmony with no obstructions whatsoever.

Section II

Hua-yen Buddhism recognizes four distinct levels of *dharmadhātu* corresponding to four ascending stages of theoretical understanding and meditative enlightenment, these being:

1) The *dharmadhātu* of *shih*; the world of mutually exclusive particulars.

2) The *dharmadhātu* of *li*; the all-embracing universal reality.

3) The *dharmadhātu* of *li* and *shih*; the unhindered interfusion of universal with particular.

4) The *dharmadhātu* of *shih* and *shih*; the unhindred interfusion of particular with particular.

The *dharmadhātu* of *li* and *shih* is recognized by T'ien-t'ai (*Lotus Sūtra*) Buddhism in terms of the identity of one mind with all dharmas and the immanence of past-present-future within a single thought-instant, as well as by the syncretic Mahāyāna text, "The Awakening of Faith in Mahāyāna," in terms of the mutual inclusiveness of suchness (*chen-ju*) with arising/ceasing (*sheng-ssu*). However, the *dharmadhātu* of *shih* and *shih* is the specific doctrinal innovation of Hua-yen Buddhism; it is encapsulated by the summary formula *shih-shih-wu-ai-yung-t'ung* or "non-obstructive interpenetration of particular with particular," which according to the Hua-yen *p'an chiao* (doctrinal classification) system constitutes the culminating stage of Buddhist theoretical interpretation and contemplative insight. The well-known Hua-yen Buddhist conceptual models, such as Indra's Net, the Hall of Mirrors, the Golden Lion or the Tower of Maitreya, all illustrate through *upamā* (simile) these last two stages of *dharmadhātu*, namely, the *dharmadhātu* of *li* and *shih* and the *dharmadhātu* of *shih* and *shih*, as well as provide intuitive vision to the various microcosmic-macrocosmic theories formulated by Hua-yen such as all-in-one and one-in-all, mutual penetration and mutual identification, simultaneous-mutual-containment, non-obstructed interfusion, and realms-embracing-realms ad infinitum.

However, besides being supported by the more poetic device of *upamā*, the Hua-yen doctrines of *li-shih-wu-ai* and *shih-shih-wu-ai* are supported by a sophisticated logical framework in terms of the theory of *śūnyatā* or emptiness, which when negatively considered represents a theory of *niḥsvabhāvatā* or non-substantiality and when positively considered represents a theory of *pratītyasamutpāda* or dependent coorigination, in the sense of universal relativity or intercausation. Through Nāgārjuna, the celebrated master of Prasaṅgika-Mādhyamika negative dialectics, the concept of *śūnyatā* or emptiness came to be assigned the specific meaning of *pratītyasamutpāda*, i.e., dependent coorigination or arising into (non-inherent) existence through causation. In his *Fundamentals of the Middle Way* Nāgārjuna asserted: "The 'originating dependently' we call 'emptiness.'"[5] Moreover, Nāgārjuna proclaimed the universal applicability of emptiness to all dharmas whatsoever (including both unconditioned or *asaṁskṛta* as well as conditioned or *saṁskṛta* dharmas), as when he stated: "Since there is no dharma originating independently, no dharma whatever exists which is not empty."[6] Finally, Nāgārjuna explicitly equated emptiness with *niḥsvabhāvatā* or non-substantiality with the statement: "Whatever comes into existence presupposing something else is without self-existence (*svabhāvatā*)."[7] Hence, the meaning of *śūnyatā* as expounded by Nāgārjuna is that all dharmas are empty or void of *svabhāva*; i.e., substantiality and independent self-naturedness, in that they are wholly supported by causes and conditions, which can themselves be reductively factored or exhaustively analyzed into their own causes and conditions, and so on, ad infinitum. Consequently, the doctrine of emptiness was originally of negative purport; since dharmas are supported entirely by external conditions, they are empty of inherent-existence or devoid of intrinsic reality, and therefore, from the *paramārtha* or ultimate level of truth (as opposed to the *samvṛti* or conventional level) the dharmas simply do not arise at all (*anutpāda* or non-origination). Nāgārjuna's understanding of emptiness as *anutpāda* or non-origination is clearly evinced by what is perhaps the most often repeated example of the Prasaṅgika-Mādhyamika fourfold calculus of negations: "Never are any existing things found to originate—from themselves, from something else, from both, or from no cause."[8] In its Mādhyamika context then, emptiness designates the ontological vacuity and unsubstantiality of dharmas, a polemic on the non-origination of events at the *paramārtha* level of truth, utterly depreciating and undermining the basic factors of existence, and utilized soteriologically for the cultivation of spiritual liberation through non-attachment. However, in the Hua-yen hermeneutical framework, the concept of emptiness is radically reinterpreted from what is regarded as its implicit meaning (*neyārtha*) in Mādhyamika dialectical negativism, to its fully explicit meaning (*nitārtha*) in Hua-yen philosophy, where it signifies the profoundly interdependent and interpenetrative character of events, thereby emphasizing the ontological fullness and cosmic togetherness of dharmas as opposed to their utter vacuity. Or in other terms, as opposed to Mādhyamika negativism (*nāstivāda*), the Hua-yen school frames an essentially value-centric cosmology where in *śūnyatā*, comprehended as ontological fullness, total togetherness, or social relatedness implicates the axiological positiveness of reality, such that each dharma becomes charged with intrinsic value precisely because it is a necessary cause for every other dharma in the universe.

In the Prasaṅgika-Mādhyamika dialectical negativism, *svabhāvatā*, conceived as substantiality or self-naturedness, is regarded as an artificial construct which is overlayed, projected or superimposed upon *paramārtha* truth, hence functioning as a concealment or covering (*āvaraṇa*) of reality. Consequently, *niḥsvabhāvatā* or non-substantiality is equated with *anāvaraṇa* or nonconcealment. However, in the hermeneutical framework of Hua-yen, non-substantiality is reinterpreted to mean *anāvaraṇa* in its sense as non-obstructedness. In such a manner then, Hua-yen Buddhism radically retranslates the notion of *śūnyatā* or emptiness into positive metaphysical terms in that *niḥsvabhāvatā* or non-substantiality means non-obstruction and nonimpededness whereas *pratītyasamutpāda* or intercausation means interpenetration and interfusion in the sense of simultaneous-mutual-arising, simultaneous-mutual-entering and simultaneous-mutual-containment. This intricate tissue of interlocked meanings between the Hua-yen categories of emptiness, non-substantiality, nonimpededness, intercausation and interpenetration is illustrated with great perspicacity in Fa-tsang's treatise on the *Hua-yen Sūtra* entitled "Hundred Gates to the Sea of Ideas of the Flowery Splendour Scripture." In this text Fa-tsang asserts that each particle of dust (i.e., each dharma or metaphysical atom) arises through dependent coorigination or the "mystery of coming into existence through causation":

> This little particle of dust arises through causes. This means a dharma. . . this dust and other dharmas depend on and involve each other. . . all dust is formed through causation; this is matter. Matter has no substance; this is Emptiness. . . the theory of all things coming into existence through causation is unfathomable. All things are exhaustively combined as one, and all infinities are embraced to form a totality. . . . The principle of coming into existence through causation is great indeed![9]

By virtue of the mystery of arising into existence through causation, each particle of dust is entirely empty of substance or *svabhāva*; and being devoid of all substantiality, each is said to manifest the character of perfect non-obstructedness or nonimpededness, whereby all interfuse together into a single harmonious totality. In Fa-tsang's words: "Because all facts have no substance they merge together in accordance with principle. And because the dust has no substance, it universally penetrates everything."[10] Lacking any substantiality whatsoever, the large and small thus interpenetrate without the slightest obstruction: "This dust and that mountain, though one is big and the other is small, contain each other. . . . Therefore the large is contained right in the small."[11] Due to the intercausality and non-substantiality characterizing each particle of dust, there is total interpermeation in the spatial sense whereby "an infinite number of lands and seas are always manifested in the dust" such that "one particle of dust universally pervades all lands and seas."[12] Hence, the ten cardinal directions of space are all immanent in a single particle of dust thereby establishing the total non-obstructed mutual fusion of the far and near as well as of the near and far. Fa-tsang writes:

> This dust is near and the world of the ten cardinal directions is far away. But as the dust has no substance, it fully penetrates all the ten cardinal directions. In other words, the ten directions are all those of the dust. Therefore the far is always near. . . . As the ten directions enter into one particle of dust, they are always near although they are far, and as the dust universally pervades all the ten directions, it is always far although it is near. . . . Think of it!"[13]

Moreover, each particle of dust emerging into (noninherent) existence through intercausation, dependent coorigination and conditioned coproduction is considered in two ways: "having power" (as expanded) insofar as it is an active cause for everything else, and "lacking power" (as contracted) insofar as it is a passive effect of everything else, housing all events when contracted and pervading them all when expanded, thereby wholly defying the property which A. N. Whitehead has called "simple location." In Fa-tsang's words:

> The ten directions have no substance and are entirely manifested in the dust through causation—that is "contraction". . . When contracted, all things are manifested in one particle of dust. When expanded, one particle of dust will universally permeate everything.[14]

Finally, Fa-tsang asserts that all particles of dust not only interpenetrate in the spatial sense whereby the ten cardinal directions are immanent in a single atom, but also in the much more radical sense of *temporal* interfusion such that hundreds of thousands of infinitely long periods are immanent in a single thought-instant, thereby establishing the strictly symmetrical structure of internal relations between all events:

> When the dust is perceived, it is a manifestation of the mind at an instant. This manifestation of the mind for an instant is entirely the same as hundreds of thousands of infinitely longer periods. Why?. . . Because an instant has no substance, it penetrates the infinitely long periods, and because the periods have no substance, they are fully contained in a single instant. . . . Therefore in an instant of thought all facts and things in the three ages (past, present and future) are clearly seen.[15]

Section III

The microcosmic-macrocosmic model of reality as articulated in the preceding discussion can be further analyzed in terms of the Sinitic *t'i-yung* or essence-function construction underlying Hua-yen modes of speculative thought (as opposed to the *neng-so* or subject-object construction regulating ordinary dualistic thought patterns). As stated previously, whereas *t'i* or essence denotes the universal, invisible and internal dimensions of reality, *yung* or function denotes its particular, visible and external dimensions. Again, whereas *t'i* designates reality in its static or unmoving aspect, *yung* signifies its dynamic or moving aspect. It is therefore precisely this *t'i-yung* or essence-function construction which underlies Fa-tsang's doctrine of suchness (Skt. *tathatā*; Chi. *chen-ju*) as *sui-yüan pu-pien* or "not moving yet following conditions" so as to be at once both changeless and changing. In Hua-yen Buddhism, the *dharmadhātu* of all-merging suchness (conceived as a cosmic web of interrelations or as a universal matrix of intercausation) is *t'i* (essence) whereas each particular dharma is its *yung* (function). Or again, in terms of the basic Hua-yen formula *li-shih-wu-ai* (the unhindered interfusion of universal and particular), *li* (universal principle) is analyzable as essence (*t'i*) while *shih* (particular events) are analyzable as function (*yung*). Consequently, all particular events (*shih*) are simply a dynamic function (*yung*) of the same underlying essence (*t'i*), this being *li* or universal principle. Each dharma is a contraction or atomization of the same network of causal relations, namely, the *dharmadhātu* (the cosmic web of interconnection and interinclusiveness) such that all are ultimately identical with all others as well as the whole matrix of intercausation. Due to the *t'i-yung* or essence-function structure of reality then, the multiplicity of *shih* or particular events is not only mutually penetrating, but also mutually identical. According to this polemic, since all dharmas are mutually causative, they are mutually penetrating; and because they are mutually penetrating they are mutually identical (*hsiang chi*). Or as developed in the *Avataṁsaka Sūtra*, since all atoms are merely a reflection (*pratibhāsa*) of every other atom, there is ultimately a perfect sameness (*samatā*) among all atoms in the universe, negatively expressed as *śūnyatā* or emptiness and positively expressed as *amalacitta* or purity. Thus, all events are wholly devoid of *svabhāva* or unique selfhood, since everything dissolves into everything else at the ontological level of *śūnyatā*.

The Hua-yen doctrine of *li-shih-wu-ai* is in fact a reinterpretation of the basic theme expounded in the *prajñāpāramitā* literature, namely, *rūpam śūnyatā śūnyataiva rūpam* or form is emptiness and emptiness is form." Each determinate form is *yung* or function whereas emptiness is *t'i* or universal essence. In Hua-yen Buddhism, this theme of the identity of form and emptiness is radically retranslated through its own innovative hermeneutical framework into *li-shih-wu-ai* or the unhindered interpenetration of universal and particular, *li* corresponding to emptiness (Chi. *kung*) and *shih* corresponding to form (Chi. *se*). This Hua-yen restatement of the identity of emptiness and form in terms of the interpenetration of *li* and *shih* was first propounded by Tu-shun, the First Patriarch of Chinese Hua-yen Buddhism, in his essay, *On the Meditation of Dharmadhātu*. At the outset of his text, Tu-shun emphasizes that form is identical only with true emptiness or true voidness, namely, the emptiness of fullness, togetherness and interdependence, as opposed to the negativistic voidness-of-annihilation attributed to Prasaṅgika-Mādhyamika Buddhism. In Tu-shun's words: "Form is not a voidness-of-annihilation, but a true void in its total essence."[16] After developing the total identity of form with emptiness in Part One of his treatise, Tu-shun proceeds to reformulate this theme in terms of the interpenetration of *li* with *shih* in Part Two, wherein he asserts: "All things and events [*shih*] of dependent arising are devoid of selfhood, hence are identical with reality (*li*) through and through."[17] And moreover, Tu-shun makes quite explicit the fact that there is a total interpenetration, and not merely a partial fusion, of *li* with *shih*. Tu-shun writes: "Shih is completely identical, and not partially identical, with Li. Therefore, without causing the slightest damage to itself, an atom can embrace the whole universe."[18]

This mutual penetration and identification of *li* and *shih* is elaborated further as constituting the basis for an even more radical sort of interpenetration, namely, *shih-shih-wu-ai* or the non-obstructive interfusion of particular with particular. Tu-shun writes: "Because shih is identical with the fusing li, it embraces all without obstructions and penetrates into and interfuses with all in a natural and spontaneous manner."[19] Moreover, Tu-shun asserts that although each unsubstantial event (*shih*) fully interfuses with the totality (*li*) as well as every other event (*shih*), there is yet no violation of its own ontological integrity; for it both contains and permeates the whole cosmos while still retaining its unique structural identity and individual pattern: "The shih remains as it is and yet embraces all."[20] Finally, Tu-shun illustrates this mutual penetration and mutual identification of *li* and *shih* through his well-known metaphor (*upamā*) of the Ocean and Waves, whereby due to the indivisibility of the water, each wave or *shih* (corresponding to *yung* or function) envelops the whole ocean or *li* (corresponding to *t'i* or essence) while remaining still a wave, whereas the one ocean enters fully into each wave without being diversified. Tu-shun writes: "The entire

Ocean is embodied in one Wave, yet the Ocean does not shrink. A small wave includes the great Ocean, and yet the wave does not expand. There is no obstruction whatever between them."[21]

Tu-shun clearly argues that the mutual penetration and identification of *li* with *shih* is theoretically grounded in the causal principle of *pratītyasamutpāda* or dependent coorigination. In Part Two of Tu-shun's treatise, entitled "Meditation on the Non-obstruction of Li and Shih," he asserts: "Ten principles are here set forth to elucidate both the fusion and dissolving of Li and Shih."[22] This is followed by the statement: "The above ten principles all consist in dependent arising."[23] Finally, he reformulates his discussion of the unhindered interfusion of *li* and *shih* in terms of dependent coorigination or intercausation in terms of an abstract dialectical analysis of the many and the one. Each *shih* is comprehended as a one arising through complex causal combination out of the many, such that one is all and all is one. In Tu-shun's words: "This truth of the fusing of Li and Shih contains four principles," which are:

> First, one in one.
> Second, all in one.
> Third, one in all.
> Fourth, all in all.[24]

In his treatise entitled "Hundred Gates to the Sea of Ideas of the Flowery Splendour Scripture," Fa-tsang elaborates upon Tu-shun's analysis of intercausation through the dialectic of the one and many in terms of a theory of simultaneous-mutual-establishment. Fa-tsang states:

> The one and the many establish each other. Only when one is completely the many can it be called the one, and only when the many can be completely called the one can it be called the many. There is not a separate one outside the many, for we clearly know that it is one within the many. . . . Only when we understand that dharmas have no nature of their own can we have the wisdom about the one and the many.[25]

Through such correlated theories as the mutual identity of emptiness and form, the unhindered interfusion of *li* and *shih*, and the simultaneous-mutual-establishment of the many and the one through intercausation or dependent coorigination, Hua-yen frames its nondual vision of the universe as structured by the *t'i-yung* or essence-function construction, wherein each dharma is a total togetherness of multiplicity-in-unity, a supreme union of opposites and a microcosm of the macrocosm, an all-embracing unit of reality which both contains and pervades its entire universe while not moving from its local position, stretching and yet remaining, so as to be far although it is near and near although it is far, interpenetrating with all and still remaining precisely as it is. However, with respect to the critical problem under consideration in this study, namely, interpenetration vs. cumulative penetration, what is of special importance here is that Hua-yen Buddhism, like Whiteheadian process theory, understands causation as a process which combines the many into the one at the standpoint of unification provided by each event in nature. Whereas for Hua-yen Buddhism the term "many" refers to a totality, i.e., to future and present events as well as to those of the past, in Whitehead's process metaphysics it refers to past events alone. Again, whereas the philosophy of Hua-yen Buddhism may be encapsulated by the summary formula: "All is one and one is all"—Whitehead's process theory of actuality may be expressed by the formula: "The many become one and are *increased* by one" (PR, p. 21; italics mine). Thus, according to Whiteheadian process thought, the many and one do not interpenetrate or interfuse in a simultaneous manner, since dialectical penetration is always cumulative in structure; it is a radically temporal fusion of manyness-into-oneness or multiplicity-into-unity due to the strictly one-way flow of causal transmission from past-into-present.

CHAPTER 3

Linguistic Analysis and Hua-yen Buddhism on the Simultaneous-Mutual-Establishment of Meanings

Part Two of this study elaborates a metaphysics of cumulative penetration as structured by an asymmetrical theory of causation, in contradistinction to the Hua-yen position of interpenetration as structured by a symmetrical theory of causation. According to the Hua-yen position, dialectical oppositions and polar contrasts like one and many or subject and object arise through simultaneous-mutual-causation or simultaneous-mutual-establishment such as to fully interpenetrate or interfuse in a wholly *symmetrical* manner, which means that the object contains the subject just as much as the subject contains its object. Whereas according to the Whiteheadian process model of actuality, dialectical oppositions arise through *asymmetrical* causation such that there exists only a cumulative penetration of objects-into-subjects, which means that a newly emerging subject contains its antecedent objects but those antecedent objects do not contain that newly emerging subject since they arose independently of its existence as a completed actuality.

However, in the present chapter, I argue that there is another sense in which the fundamental Hua-yen doctrine of symmetrical interdependence is wholly valid, and this is in the sense of the simultaneous-mutual-establishment of *meanings* in the order of *concepts*. Here, Ludwig Wittgenstein's ordinary language philosophy is employed as a contemporary Western hermeneutical framework to demonstrate how words such as "subject" and "object" do not obtain their *meaning* from a correspondence or objective reference to extra-linguistic realities conceived as self-existent or absolute entities, but only through their contextual relation to each other within particular "language games" or linguistic contexts. Thus, practical distinctions such as subjects and objects must derive their meanings from simultaneous-mutual-establishment within particular language games, and in this sense are interdependent or symmetrically related, since the word "subject" is virtually *meaningless* in separation from "object" just as the word "one" is devoid of sense in separation from the word "many."

In his text, *Emptiness: A Study in Religious Meaning*, Fredrick J. Streng has developed an important and edifying interpretation of Nāgārjuna's Prasaṅgika-Mādhyamika Buddhism from the standpoint of Wittgenstein's linguistic analysis or ordinary language philosophy.[1] Wittgenstein developed a theory which denies that words and concepts obtain their meaning by objective reference to extra-linguistic things or by correspondence to absolute entities with self-existence; rather, words acquire their meaning through their "use" within specific "language games," their ordinal location in particular linguistic contexts.

Traditionally, it has been held that words, in particular nouns or substantives, acquired meaning in as much as they named or corresponded to objective referents, i.e., independent, self-existent or *absolute* entities. Wittgenstein asserted that philosophers who presuppose the objective reference theory of meaning are compelled by their own premises to search for those absolute or self-existent entities which they believe must correspond to these words. In Wittgenstein's words: "We feel that we cannot point to anything in reply to them [words] and yet we ought to point to something (we are up against one of the greatest sources of philosophic bewilderment; a substantive makes us look for something that corresponds to it)."[2]

Wittgenstein argues that in most instances, words obtain their meaning through their actual *use* in particular linguistic contexts: "A word has the meaning someone gives to it . . . for a large class of cases—though not all—a word's meaning is its use in language."[3]

Metaphysical categories, regarded as pointing to objective referents, cause puzzlement only because they have been abstracted from the original language game in which they acquired their meaning, so as to be reified as though they actually exist in some extra-linguistic sense, resulting in what Wittgenstein calls the bewitchment of intelligence by language. Wittgenstein thus asserts:

> When philosophers use a word—knowledge, being, object, I, name—and try to grasp the essence of the thing, one must always ask oneself: is the word ever actually used this way in the language-game which is its original home? What we do is bring back words from their metaphysical to their everyday use.[4]

As Streng points out, Wittgenstein's motivation for equating the meaning of words with their use is to shift our attention away from the pursuit of absolute entities and liberate ourselves from the belief that words are names corresponding to self-existent entities. By Streng's interpretation, Nāgārjuna similarly denies that words acquire meaning by referring to something external to the language system. For words are in fact practical distinctions which acquire meaning only through their contextual relation to each other, and are not indicative of ontological status. Nāgārjuna emphasizes that all practical distinctions such as subject and object or seer and seen are interdependent entities wholly relative to each other, and thus neither entity exists independently as such. All such interdependent or relative distinctions obtain their meaning only in contextual relation to each other, being otherwise empty (*śūnya*) of ontological status. Thus, by Streng's interpretation, the theory of emptiness refers to the relativity of meanings within linguistic frames of reference. And it is precisely by exposing this interdependence of all words and meanings that Nāgārjuna endeavors to, as it were, de-construct or de-ontologize all metaphysical absolutes (i.e., self-existent substances), whether these be a plurality of reified ontological ultimates and irreducible elements (*dharmas, dhātus, skandas, āyatanas, svabhāvas,* etc.) or a substantialized monistic principle of some sort (*cittamātra, ālaya, brahman,* etc.). It is on this foundation that the Hua-yen metaphysics of interdependence or mutual causation can be elaborated in terms of the symmetry of meanings.

Fa-tsang's "Treatise on the Five Doctrines" concludes with his famous essay on the "Interpenetration of the Six Characteristics." The six characteristics represent the causal relationship between part and whole, in terms of the interfusion of diversity and wholeness, disintegration and formation and particular and universal, whereby there is a simultaneous-mutual-establishment of the whole and its component parts through mutual causation. This is clearly illustrated by Fa-tsang in terms of his simile of the House and Beams. Fa-tsang writes:

> The beams (and so on) themselves are the house per se. Why? Because all the beams (roof and walls) themselves can establish the house. Apart from beams, and so forth, there would be no house. As soon as the (concept) of beams is established, the (concept) of house is simultaneously established.[5]

What is central to this passage, if Garma C.C. Chang's parenthetical interpolations are valid, is that the *concept* of house (the whole) and the *concept* of beams (the parts) simultaneously and mutually establish each other. The type of reciprocal causality implied here is that of a mutual constitution of meanings, or the relativity of concepts. And it is precisely in this sense of mutual causation as the constitution of meanings that the beams, tiles, walls, roof, floor, and the house itself are mind-only. Moreover, in that all meanings and concepts (such as part-whole, disintegration-formation, or particular-universal) are strictly relative *(śūnya)* to each other, they are entirely without independent self-existence (*svabhāva*). This type of intercausation in the sense of the mutual constitution of meanings is strictly nontemporal; thus the notion of *symmetrical* relatedness entails no inherent contradiction. In terms of the relativity of concepts the notion of a house virtually has no meaning apart from its functional relation to its parts and to the whole, whereas the concept of beams equally has no meaning apart from the house. Fa-tsang therefore asserts: "If there were no tiles (walls or floors) the very name 'beam' would lose its meaning. The very concept of 'beam' depends on tiles and walls."[6]

This atemporal and symmetrical mode of causality in terms of the simultaneous-mutual-establishment of meanings is further clarified in terms of the Counting Series analogy in Second Patriarch Chih-yen's text on the "Ten Mysteries of the One Vehicle of Hua-yen." Since counting is intrinsically a linear, serial and temporally successive operation, it especially elucidates the sense of symmetrical causation implied by the relativity of meanings. Chih-yen writes:

> Because of the very fact that one contains ten, the word "one" is *meaningful.* If there were no "ten," then there would be no "one" (that is to say, if there were only a singular "one" in the whole universe, this so-called "one" would be *meaningless.* The very *meaning* of "one" therefore depends on many.)[7]

To summarize then, the Hua-yen metaphysics of symmetrical interdependence and interpenetration may be valid interpreted from the standpoint of contemporary linguistic analysis or ordinary language philosophy. However, the question posed here is: does the symmetrical constitution and simultaneous-mutual-establishment operating in the order of concepts extend also into the order of spatiotemporal events? For it seems that in the latter case, a strictly *asymmetrical* process of causality is in operation. As the eminent Whiteheadian process philosopher Charles Hartshorne has rightly asserted:

> In general, polar contrasts such as abstract/concrete, universal/particular, object subject, are symmetrical correlates only so long as we think simply of the categories themselves, as concepts, and not of what they may be used

to refer to or to describe. The moment we think of the latter, the symmetrical interdependence is replaced by a radical asymmetry.[8]

Thus, following Hartshorne's insight, it can be argued that dialectical oppositions such as subject/object and one/many may be characterized as symmetrical correlates which are reciprocally constituted through simultaneous-mutual-establishment only at the conceptual level, although this principle of symmetrical interrelationship must not be illicitly extended beyond its proper range of application into the order of spatiotemporal events and physical actualities, wherein causal relationships between polar contrasts are always strictly asymmetrical in structure, in the sense of objectivity-into-subjectivity or manyness-into-oneness.

CHAPTER 4

Interpenetration as Openness, Presence and Nonconcealment: A Phenomenological Interpretation

Preliminary Remarks

In his various writings, especially an extraordinary three-volume set entitled *Kindly Bent to Ease Us*, Herbert V. Guenther has brilliantly developed the phenomenological dimensions of Tibetan Tantric Buddhism based principally on the works of Edmund Husserl, Martin Heidegger and Maurice Merleau-Ponty, wherein the enlightenment experience of "limpid clearness and consummate perspicacity" is described as a radiant and ecstatic "openness" devoid of subject and object or center and periphery.[1] This chapter endeavors to elaborate upon the phenomenological hermeneutic, extending its application to the domain of Hua-yen Buddhism. Hua-yen doctrine is now interpreted as a literal and radically descriptive profile of the open-dimensional *field of perception* as immediately experienced in its primordial presence at the level of originary data evidence which itself lies beneath the multiple strata of "sedimentations" or frozen interpretive patternings that ordinarily conceal the pre-reflective, pre-personal and non-objectified life-world from our gaze. And finally, it is argued that the comprehension of Hua-yen theory as a literal descriptive profile of the ecstatic and radiant "opening" or "clearing" in the perceptual field provides the basis for dramatically reconstituting the panoramic sensorium of experiential immediacy into expanded horizons of aesthetic and imaginative visionary fulfillment at the level of meditative praxis, or what Husserlian phenomenology terms the praxis of creative visioning through "free variation in imagination."

In his treatise entitled "On the Meditation of *Dharmadhātu*," First Patriarch Tu-shun outlines three forms of meditative praxis, these being the contemplative observation of form/voidness, *shih/li* and *shih/shih*—the first two exercises representing the meditation on *li-shih-wu-ai* or the interpenetration of universal and particular and the last exercise representing the meditation on *shih-shih-wu-ai* or the interpenetration of particular and particular.[2] At the outset of his seminal text, Tu-shun emphasizes the indivisibility of form/voidness or form/emptiness (Skt. *rūpam/śūnyata*; Chi. *se/kung*) stating: "Voidness is form. Why? Because True Voidness should on no account be different from form. . . . If Form/Voidness is so, all other dharmas should also be so. Contemplate on this."[3] Tu-shun continues:

> Without abolishing form as such, the Voidness appears.
> The Voidness per se is not different from form. . .
> Therefore when a Bodhisattva observes form, he sees
> Voidness, and when he observes Voidness, he sees form. . .
> Contemplate this and you will understand.[4]

Tu-shun next proceeds to the meditation on *li-shih-wu-ai*, which is a restatement of the form/voidness meditation in terms of Hua-yen doctrinal innovations. Tu-shun writes: "The Shih can hide Li . . . the result is that only the events appear, but the Li does not appear."[5] However, "Shih is not a Shih other than the total Li. For this reason, when a Bodhisattva sees Shih, he also sees Li."[6]

According to the phenomenological hermeneutic, the Bodhisattva's perception of indivisible form/voidness or *shih/li* structures in the Hua-yen Buddhist enlightenment experience is tantamount to the perception of value-laden gestalt (core/horizon) patternings as achieved through phenomenological "seeing" or "creative visioning" by means of free variation in imagination. Moreover, Hua-yen Buddhist *prajñā* (wisdom or non-dual intuitive perception) and *śūnyatā* (emptiness, voidness) correlate with *noetic-noematic* poles, to use technical terminology formulated by Husserl. The concept of *śūnyatā* may be understood as a descriptive profile of "horizons-phenomena" encircling the focal core of the perceptual field at the *noematic* object pole, whereas *prajñā* correlates with the "non-focal" or "decentered" act of perceptual awareness achieved through a radical reversal at the *noetic* or constituting subject pole. Again, in Martin Heidegger's phenomenological terminology, *śūnyatā* signifies the region of openness or the ecstatic and radiant open dimension of the perceptual field corresponding to non-focal *Gelassenheit*, i.e., "letting-be" or "releasement into openness."

The Hua-yen Vehicle of Non-obstructed Interpenetration

The key technical term in Hua-yen Buddhism, as indeed for all Mahāyāna and Tantrayāna Buddhism, is no doubt *śūnyatā* (Tib. *stong-pa-nyid*; Chi. *kung*). which has been most frequently translated/ interpreted by the words "emptiness," "voidness," "nothingness" and alternatively, "relativity," each idea disclosing yet a different shade of meaning and significance, and each (either implicitly or explicitly) presupposing its own theoretical infrastructure. However, Guenther has boldly abandoned all traditional renditions of *śūnyatā*, especially those conveying negative purport, for the revolutionary phenomenological concept of "openness," which emphasizes the experiential positiveness and perceptual expansiveness of the Buddhist term. In Guenther's words: "The technical term shunya(ta) indicates the 'open-dimension of Being.' The customary translations by 'void' or 'emptiness' fail to convey the positive content of the Buddhist idea."[7] As explained in the previous section, the technical concept of *t'ung* meaning interpenetration or interfusion is how Chinese Hua-yen Buddhism radically reinterpreted the notion of *kung* (Skt. *śūnyatā*) as emptiness or voidness. However, the Chinese word *t'ung* also commonly designates "openness" or "opening" in its classical dictionary sense, such as to be in full accord with Guenther's rendition of *kung* (emptiness) as openness or the open-dimension of experiential immediacy. Thus, the following discussion addresses the radical reinterpretration of Hua-yen Buddhist *kung* or emptiness and *t'ung* or interpenetration in terms of their deeper experiential and phenomenological significations as openness, whereupon they both refer to the ecstatic and radiant open dimension of the perceptual field, the horizon of disclosure wherein all determinate forms or particular *shih* shine outwards as nonconcealed presence in their aspect as *li*.

Section I

The term "phenomenological" may be understood through Heidegger's etymological analysis of the word as a composite of two ancient Greek terms, *phainomenon* and *logos*. *Phainomenon* or "that which shows itself" was traced by Heidegger to the archaic Greek verb roots *phy* meaning to emerge, unfold, exfoliate, blossom, open-up or presence-forth, as well as *pha* and *phōs* meaning to shine, glow, radiate, illumine or light up. Whereas *logos* indicates in certain usages "letting something be seen." Thus, "phenomenology" comes to mean: letting-be that which shows itself to shine, glow, radiate or come-to-presence through co-emergent blossoming into unhidden appearance or nonconcealed openness in the horizon of disclosure.[8] As a mode of phenomenological procedure, Hua-yen theory is a literal descriptive profile of the myriad unhidden phenomena (determinate forms or *shih*) glowing and radiating as nonconcealed presences in their aspect as *li* (universal suchness) at the peripheral horizons of the perceptual field, which is precisely the horizon of disclosure termed by phenomenological analysis: the "region of openness."

Phenomenological description centers around a *noetic-noematic* analysis of the perceptual field. The *noematic* (constituted object) pole of the field is characterized in terms of its core/horizon, focus/fringe or foreground/background gestalt patterning, whereas the *noetic* (constituting subject) pole is analyzed in terms of specifiable acts of consciousness such as focusing or attention which "constitute" what is foreground and what is background or what is core and what is horizon in the structure of the *noema*. The technical terms *noetic* and *noematic* (or as nouns, *noesis* and *noema*) are introduced by Husserl to rectify the subject-object bifurcation characteristic of the "natural attitude" wherein subjects are conceived as passive spectators to exterior objects. In contrast, Husserl's *noesis* actively constitutes the structure of the *noema*. Thus, the distinction between the *noesis* or subject pole and *noema* or object pole is precisely the distinction between constitutive acts of consciousness and the constituted entities which correspond to them. In Husserl's words: "A parallelism between noesis and noema does indeed exist. . . . The noematic is the field of units, the noetic that of constituting variety factors."[9]

In the Yogācāra doctrine of "mind-only" (Skt. *cittamātra*; Chi. *wei-shih*), which was appropriated into the Hua-yen syncretic harmonization pattern, this Husserlian distinction between *noesis* and *noema* or constitutive subject and constituted object has long been established in terms of the distinction between *vikalpa/yad-vikalpyate* (Chi. *neng-pien-chi/so-pien-chi*), indicating "discriminative act" and "discriminated entity," respectively. Moroever, according to Hua-yen Buddhist mind-only theory, the form/emptiness (Skt. *rūpam/śūnyatā*; Chi. *se/kung*), *dharma/dharmadhātu* or *shih/li* (particular/universal) structure of the perceptual field is constituted through *vikalpa* or discriminative acts in a manner directly analogous to the way in which the core/horizon structure of the *noema* is "organized" through *noetic* functions in the psyche according to Western phenomenological analysis. And finally, the enlightened perception of indivisible form/emptiness patterns through Buddhist *prajñā*, which in Hua-yen is tantamount to the vision of *li-shih-wu-ai* or the interpenetration of universal and particular, is in fact equivalent to the perception of value-laden gestalt (core/horizon) structures through phenomenological seeing or "creative visioning," which involves a radical *noetic* reversal from foreground to background in Husserlian terms, or the cultivation of non-focal *Gelassenheit* (releasement into openness) as it was subsequently termed by Heidegger.

As indicated above, the *noematic* pole of the perceptual field is characterized by a unified foreground/background or core/horizon gestalt structure with a clear and distinct center and a vague periphery. Husserl writes: "Every experience has its horizon; every experience has its core."[10] Husserl proceeds to describe this experiential datum termed a "horizons-phenomenon" as "an indistinct co-present margin which forms a continuous ring around the field of perception."[11] Husserl's notion of horizons-phenomena is thus intended to correct the natural attitude characterized by a habitual and compulsive (sedimented) perception of mere focal actualities or core-phenomena in isolation from their contextual location within a co-present margin or peripheral background. Husserl writes: "It is obviously true of all experiences that the focal is girt about with a 'zone' of the marginal; the stream of experiences can never consist wholly of focal actualities."[12] It is precisely this notion of a co-present horizon surrounding the focal core of the perceptual field which was subsequently termed the "Region of Openness" in the descriptive phenomenologies of Martin Heidegger and Maurice Merleau-Ponty. For instance, in his famed *Gelassenheit* essay, Heidegger articulates the notion of a horizon as a peripheral phenomena ". . . which encircles the view of a thing—the field of vision . . . we look into the horizon. Therefore the field of vision is something open, but its openness is not due to our looking."[13] In such a manner then, the Husserlian phenomenological datum of a horizons-phenomenon designates the open-dimension of the perceptual field.

According to the phenomenological hermeneutic of Buddhism pioneered by Guenther, the traditional Buddhist form/emptiness (Skt. *rūpam/śūnyatā*) distinction is not simply an abstract metaphysical formula, but is a literal descriptive profile of the core/horizon, foreground/background or center/openness gestalt ratio characterizing the perceptual field of global presence. Thus, whereas "determinate form" (*rūpam*) signifies the foreground or focal core of the perceptual field, "emptiness" or "openness" (*śūnyatā*) signifies its background or peripheral horizon. It is therefore precisely this phenomenological datum of a horizons-phenomenon which Guenther designates by his revolutionary translation/interpretation of *śūnyatā* as openness, conceived as the open-dimension of experiential immediacy. Consequently, the traditional Buddhist dictum concerning the indivisibility of form and emptiness is retranslated by Guenther into the descriptive proposition that "openness is present in and actually presupposed by every determinate form."[14] Guenther proceeds to explicitly describe *śūnyatā* or openness in terms of the phenomenological concept of horizons-phenomena or field-data as follows:

Shunyata [openness] can be explained in a very simple way. When we perceive, we usually attend to the delimited "forms" of objects. But these objects are perceived within a "field." Attention can be directed either to the concrete, limited forms or to the field in which these forms are situated. In the shunyata experience, the attention is on the field rather than on its contents.[15]

This shift of attention or widening of focus from determinate form to its surrounding field or horizon of openness characterizing the *śūnyatā* experience is next related by Guenther to *prajñā* or the enlightened mode of perceptual awareness. Guenther emphasizes that *śūnyatā* as openness is always an objective correlate to an "act" of perception in the mode of *prajñā*: "The perception of shunyata as openness is connected with the development of what is known as prajna . . . Shunyata is the objective pole of prajna, the open quality of things . . . Shunyata is always a reference to perception."[16] Thus, in the more technical terminological apparatus of Husserl, *śūnyatā* and *prajñā* are "intentional correlates," wherein *śūnyatā* represents the *noematic* pole and *prajñā* represents its corresponding *noetic* pole.[17] Through *prajñā* one's attention is dramatically shifted from determinate form (Skt. *rūpam*; Chi. *se*) located at the core of the perceptual field to its co-present horizon at the periphery of the field, such that, in Guenther's words, the object of perception ". . . fades into something which is quite open. This "open-dimension" is the basic meaning of shunyata."[18] This radical shift of attention from core to horizon or from determinate form (*rūpam*) to the dimension of openness (*śūnyatā*) in an act of *prajñā* may thus be comprehended in Husserlian phenomenological terms as a "*noetic* reversal" from foreground to background, such that the foreground is not dominant and the background is not recessive. In a remarkable book entitled *Experimental Phenomenology*, Don Ihde provides a highly illuminating illustration of such a radical and dramatic *noetic* reversal with a phenomenological interpretation of Japanese Zen aesthetics:

A radical shift occurs in a type of traditional Japanese art. In this art some object—a sparrow with a few blades of grass or a simple branch with cherry blossoms—stands out against a blank or pastel background. Our traditional way of viewing would say that the subject matter—what stands out and is dominant in the foreground—is the sparrow or the blossoming branch. The background is merely empty or blank. This is entirely different from the Western tradition in which the background is filled in. Yet the emptiness and openness of a Japanese painting is the subject matter of the painting, the sparrow or branch being set there to make the openness stand out. In this, there is a radical reversal: the foreground is not dominant, the background is not recessive. To understand such a painting calls for a deep reversal in the *noetic* context.[19]

Branch of Cherry Blossoms, Ogata Kenzan, Japanese, Edo period, 1663–1743. Colors and gold on paper, H. 13½". Eugene Fuller Memorial Collection. Courtesy Seattle Art Museum.

This concept of *noetic* reversal from core to horizon is precisely what in Heidegger's descriptive phenomenology is called *Gelassenheit*, i.e., "letting-be" or "releasement." In Heidegger's own words, *Gelassenheit* means: "to release oneself into the openness."[20] In a paper entitled "Phenomenology and the Later Heidegger" Don Ihde has carefully developed Heidegger's concepts of *Gelassenheit* or letting-be and the region *(Gegend)* of openness *(das Öffene)* in terms of Husserl's *noetic/noematic* correlation-apriori, articulating the concept of openness as a literal and radically descriptive phenomenological profile of horizons-phenomena at the *noematic* pole, and *Gelassenheit* as a non-focal mode of perception at the *noetic* pole. Again, Ihde's words are worth citing in full here:

> In Husserlian terms, the *noematic* description must be supplemented by a *noetic* analysis of the "act" which "intends" the world terminus. If now the *noema* is this strange "horizon-phenomenon" of the Openness of Region, what is the *noesis* which correlates with it? Again, *Gelassenheit* seems almost too simple to be true—the *noesis* is characterized by terms which contrast it to any form of direct, central or focal concern . . . horizons-phenomena therefore call for "non-focal" exercises. Thus, Heidegger characterizes the *noesis* as not-willing (*nicht-Willen*), releasement or letting-be (*Gelassenheit*) and waiting (*warten*).[21]

Heidegger derived the technical term *Gelassenheit* from the speculative mysticism of Meister Eckhart, wherein the term assumed the specific meaning of "non-attachment." As such, the non-attached and non-focal mode of perceptual awareness achieved through *Gelassenheit* exhibits an especially close proximity to Buddhist *prajñā*, in which perception of openness (*śūnyatā*) through non-attachment to dharmas is the basis of enlightened experience and liberated vision.

According to the phenomenological hermeneutic being elaborated here then, the Hua-yen Buddhist experience of indivisible form/emptiness or form/openness structures are analogous to the perception of value-laden gestalt (core/openness) patterns as achieved through phenomenological seeing. The Hua-yen Buddhist enlightenment experience of *li-shih-wu-ai* can be phenomenologically analyzed in terms of its *noetic/noematic* intentionality structure so that *prajñā* can be described as a non-focal or decentered act of perceptual awareness resulting from a radical reversal in the *noesis*, i.e., a shift of attention from core to horizon, this being what Heidegger terms *Gelassenheit* or "releasement into openness," and *śūnyatā* is its *noematic* correlate, namely, the region of openness, or the open-dimension of the perceptual field.

This phenomenological analysis may be further elaborated with respect to the specific doctrinal innovations peculiar to Hua-yen Buddhism, wherein the focal core of the perceptual field corresponds to *shih* or determinate particularities and the horizon of openness corresponds to *li* or universal suchness. Again, the focal core of the *noematic* pole corresponds to the finite dharmas whereas the horizon of openness corresponds to the *dharmadhātu* or all-embracing dharma-field. Thus, interpreted as a phenomenological theory of perception, the Hua-yen vision of *li-shih-wu-ai* expresses the indivisibility of core and horizon or the perception of value-laden gestalt (center/openness) structures through *noetic* reversal or non-focal *Gelassenheit.*

The perception of core/horizon gestalt environments through phenomenological *Gelassenheit* as well as the envisionment of what the

Hua-yen Sūtra calls Buddha *kṣetras* (fields), i.e., indivisible form/voidness or *shih/li* patterns through *prajñā*, are both in full concordance with the matter/field or object/space model of reality operant in contemporary relativity and quantum physics. Each material object is itself the most intense and concentrated region of its surrounding electromagnetic field and cannot be separated from that field except by abstraction. Or in terms of the concept of gravitational field as established by Einstein's general theory of relativity, massive bodies generate extensive gravitational fields which in turn manifest as the geometrical curvature of the space surrounding those bodies, such that in the final analysis, matter cannot be separated from the geometry of open space. Thus, at the level of perception one can actually observe the solid surfaces and opaque boundaries defining physical objects become "transparent outlines" which seem to dissipate into the surrounding openness of pure space, as is directly experienced in the Hua-yen enlightenment experience of *li-shih-wu-ai*. This phenomenological interpretation of the Hua-yen enlightenment experience of *li-shih-wu-ai*, comprehended now as a dynamic praxis of multiperspectival field-visioning which envisages the expansive openness or spaciousness accommodating every focal actuality, may be schematically illustrated as in the following diagram.

The Noetic-Noematic Structure of Hua-yen Buddhist Enlightenment: Li-Shih-Wu-Ai as Multiperspectival Field-Vision

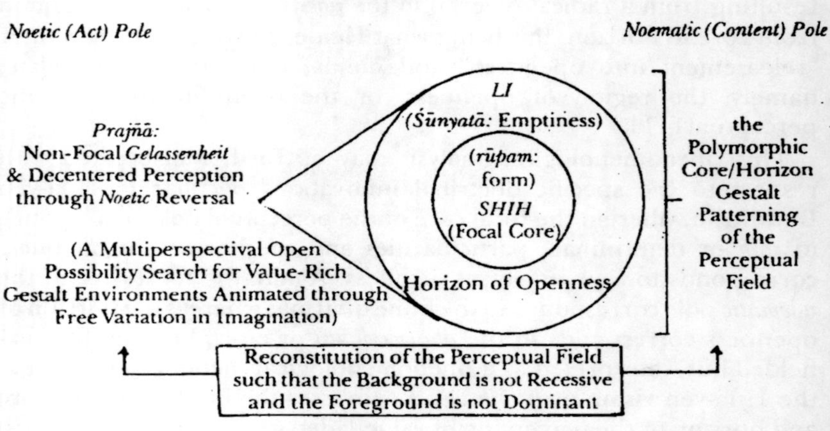

In his great work entitled *Phenomenology of Perception*, Maurice Merleau-Ponty analyzes the perceptual field into two phases:[22] (i) sedimentation (secondary attention) (ii) spontaneity (primary attention). The perceptual field of global presence can be organized either through "secondary attention," i.e., the actualization of already sedimented patternings through the "primal acquisition" of habitual structures, or through "primary attention," i.e., the creative visioning of new gestalt environments or perspectival wholes through imaginative variations. Our secondary attention ordinarily constitutes the foreground as dominant and the background as recessive in a compulsive and habitual style due to sedimentations of interpretation which have become fixated in the *noetic* pole in such a manner as to "freeze" the core/horizon ratio of the perceptual field, resulting in the experience of mere focal figures in abstraction from their co-present margins at the periphery of the field. Thus, Husserlian phenomenology has developed a dynamic experiential praxis of creative visioning termed "fantasy variation" or "free variation in imagination," i.e., what Merleau-Ponty calls "primary attention," which functions to deconstruct sedimented patternings of experience by actively "varying" the *noematic* contents of perception through *noetic* acts of autonomous imagining, whereupon the *noema* now becomes polymorphic, multiperspectival and amorphous, free to assume its full diversity, complexity and richness of topographical possibilities. It is therefore essentially this phenomenological praxis of multiperspectival creative visioning through free variation in imagination, understood as an "open possibility search" for value-rich gestalt variations, that animates the process of *noetic* reversal or non-focal *Gelassenheit* whereby perceptual awareness is "released into openness," which itself involves the radical reconstitution of the core/horizon patterning of the visual field such that the background is not recessive while the foreground is not dominant. Thus, although *Gelassenheit* as non-focal vision is characterized by such *noetic* acts as letting-be, not-willing, waiting, and non-attachment, it is nonetheless the power of imaginative variation which alone enables one to deconstruct sedimented focal-settings such as to dramatically reorganize the panoramic sensorium of the perceptual field into new horizons of aesthetic and creative visionary unfoldment, through the *noetic* constitution of value-rich gestalt environments or global perspectives.

Section II

The present task now becomes that of elucidating the precise manner in which "core" and "horizon" or *shih* and *li* are said to be indivisible, interfused and even identical in our primordial experience of the perceptual field. In his revolutionary conception of "truth" Heidegger posits a clear distinction between conventional truth as "propositional correctness," designating the direct correspondence between mental concepts and physical facts, and primordial truth indicated by the ancient Greek term *aletheia*, comprehended as unhiddenness, non-concealment or openness. At the pre-reflective and non-objectified level of primordial truth as *aletheia*, all phenomena are said to "stand-out" into transparent openness as primordial presence in the horizon of disclosure through *Gelassenheit*, or the letting-be of that which shows itself. In his essay entitled "On the Essence of Truth" Heidegger writes:

> To "let-be"—that is, to let being be as the beings which they are—means to engage oneself with the open region and its openness into which every being comes to stand, bringing that openness, as it were, along with itself. Western thinking in its beginning conceived this open region as *aletheia*, the unconcealed.[23]

Thus, *Gelassenheit* as letting-be (through not-willing), in the sense of ancient Taoist *wu-wei* as non-interference or non-action, means to "let beings be as the beings which they are," by allowing them the freedom to show themselves as unhidden phenomena through exfoliation into overtness and revealment in the open-dimension of Being, which is itself the dimension of primordial truth as *aletheia* or nonconcealment. For this reason, Zen Buddhism often states that in the field of *śūnyatā* or openness, all phenomena are seen "exactly as they are" in their "suchness" *(chen-ju)* so that "willows are green and flowers are red," "mountains are mountains and waters are waters," and true reality is the "cherry blossoms glowing in the morning sun." With respect to the Hua-yen doctrine of *li-shih-wu-ai* the key idea to be assimilated here is that the region of openness is in fact no different from a particular phenomenon situated at the core of the perceptual field, but is simply that phenomenon itself in its manifest nonconcealment or unhiddenness, standing-out into openness in its fullness of presence as primordial truth or *aletheia*. Heidegger comprehends this "standing-out" of phenomena into openness, presence and nonconcealment as constituting their "ecstatic" ontological structure, derived etymologically from the ancient Greek terms *ek-stasis* or *ek-stase*, meaning literally to "stand-outside" one's boundaries. Again, the horizon of openness, presence and nonconcealment is described by Heidegger as the primordial "radiance" of phenomena. For the open-dimension of Being is that "region of dis-closure" wherein all focal configurations at the core of the perceptual field ec-statically shine, glow, radiate, open-up and come-to-presence through coemergent-blossoming into unhidden appearance and nonconcealed openness as primordial truth or *aletheia*. Heidegger therefore describes the region of openness in terms of lighting, brightness, shining, brilliance, radiance or luminescent glow:

> If we think of it [the region of openness] as lighting, this includes not only brilliance, but also the openness wherein everything "comes into shining." . . . The word "light" means lustrous, beaming, brightening. Lighting bestows the shining, opens what shines into an appearance. The open is the realm of unconcealment and is governed by dis-closure.[24]

In terms of the highly specialized vocabulary formulated by Hua-yen Buddhism, it is precisely this character of ecstatic "radiance" or "brilliance" exhibited by *śūnyatā* as openness whereby all particular *shih* may be observed to shine and glow as nonconcealed presence in their aspect as *li*. It is in this context that one can understand an extremely esoteric mode of contemplative practice based specifically on Hua-yen doctrinal innovations articulated by the ascetic Hua-yen master of T'ang China, Li T'ung-hsüan (635-730). In his highly esteemed *Hua-yen ching lun* or "Exposition of the Hua-yen Scripture," Li T'ung-hsüan describes at length various meditations upon the luminous aura or halo of "jewelled colored lights" (*pao se kuang*) radiating like brilliant "lamp-clouds" from the personage of Vairocana Buddha (i.e., the Buddha of "Universally Illuminating Light") as the visible aspect of *dharmadhātu*, based on the elaborate usage of light-imagery and color symbolism depicted in the *Avataṁsaka Sūtra*. Li T'ung-hsüan's meditation on the aura of jewelled colored lights emitted by Buddha in *samādhi* or ecstatic trance subsequently made a major impact on various post-T'ang Hua-yen sects in China, as well as Kōben (1173-1232), an important Kegon master of Japan, and Chinul, the Hwaŏm-Sŏn master of Korea. While expounding the meaning of the title of the famous ninth chapter in the *Avataṁsaka Sūtra* named "Enlightenment as (the Realization of) Light," which comes in the section on the Ten Faiths (chapters 7-12), Li T'ung-hsüan says:

> "Why is it named the chapter of Enlightenment as (the Realization of) Light? Because of the fact that the Buddha radiates light out of the ring on his feet in the midst of Ten Faiths. . . . Upon being illumined by the light one awakens one's faith and begins to practice. Hence, the chapter of Enlightenment as (the Realization of) Light. Practitioners follow every light and see the whole universe, and the mind seeing them are now also inexhaustible and thus becomes identical with the dharma-realm. . . . One who enters the stage of Ten Faiths follows this light of jewelled colored lamp-clouds and sees both one's inner mind and the universe. . . . However, if one fails to see the jewelled colored lights, one cannot accomplish the sea of vows made by Samantabhadra, the miraculous powers of the Tao, and the great functions of all Buddhas will never be achieved."[25]

As continually emphasized by Li T'ung-hsüan in his *Hua-yen ching lun*, the imagery of jewelled colored lights completely permeates the *Avataṁsaka Sūtra* from beginning to end. In the culminating last chapter of the work (i.e., chapter 39) entitled the *Gaṇḍavyūha Sūtra*, the youth Sudhana pilgrimages to fifty-two *kalyāṇamitra* or "good knowing advisors" who roughly correspond to the fifty-two stages of a bodhisattva's career (i.e., ten faiths, ten dwellings, ten conducts, ten transferences, ten stages or *bhūmis*, equal enlightenment and wonderful enlightenment) as outlined within the sūtra itself. All of the fifty-two Buddhas and bodhisattvas met by Sudhana on his journey reveal to him another level of *samādhi* and enlightenment. Each Buddha or bodhisattva is described as abiding in its own heavenly paradise, and each one emanates a luminous halo with its characteristic quality of light and tone of color, conveyed in terms of inexhaustible lamp-clouds of light, waves, beams and rays of light, suns, moons and stars of light, oceans, seas and rivers of light, jewels, crystals, and treasures of light, or palaces, skies and fields *(kṣetras)* of light, all spreading out into infinity so as to pervade the ten realms of the *dharmadhātu* without obstruction (i.e., the ten interfusing realms of hell beings, hungry ghosts, animals, men, gods, asuras, arhats, pratyekabuddhas, bodhisattvas and Buddhas). Indeed, the vision of incalculable Buddhas and bodhisattvas the number of dustmotes radiating auras of precious colored lights which all interpenetrate each other without obstruction may be regarded as the essence of the *samādhi* experience described by Hua-yen Buddhism.

It may be asserted that meditation upon the effulgent halo of jewelled colored lights emitted by Buddhas and bodhisattvas in *samādhi* as described by Li T'ung-hsüan is itself simply a more direct and esoteric approach to the standard Hua-yen contemplation of *li-shih-wu-ai*, wherein each *shih* or particular-phenomenon is seen to shine outwards in its aspects as *li* or universal-principle. It is precisely here where the deep structural proximity between the Hua-yen meditation on *li-shih-wu-ai* and the highly esoteric Tantric praxis of maṇḍala-contemplation through "imaginative visualization" becomes apparent. In the Tantric Vehicle of Buddhism, which has itself fully assimilated the teachings of the *Avataṁsaka Sūtra*, the so-called "secret" *upāya* or skillful means is termed "deity yoga," i.e., the practice of imaginatively envisaging or visualizing various microcosmic-macrocosmic maṇḍala-palaces (mystic circles), each of which enshrines unsubstantial and translucent Buddhas, splendidly adorned with 32 major and 80 minor marks, emanating concentric bands of brilliant multi-colored auras and halos, along with beautiful orbs and satellite orbs of holographic rainbow lights, within the soteriological context of realizing the dream-like emptiness of all inherent-existence. Therefore, Li T'ung-hsüan's meditation upon the jewelled colored auras of light shining like lamp-clouds from the personage of Vairocana Buddha functions only to reveal those more "Tantric" dimensions intrinsic to traditional Hua-yen contemplations of *li-shih-wu-ai*. This may be directly seen in the fundamental Tantric system of practice promulgated by the Shingon sect of Buddhism in Japan founded by Kūkai, (774-835), wherein the yogin utilizes the theophanic imagination of the polytheistic psyche to creatively visualize the sacred *Garbhakosadhātu Maṇḍala* housing Mahāvairocana, the Supreme Buddha of Universally Illuminating Light, such that the body-mind complex of the meditating yogin are realized as identical to the Kegon or Hua-yen *dharmadhātu* of interpenetrative non-obstruction. Finally, from the perspective of the phenomenological framework of interpretation which has been developed in this study, the Tantric praxis of imaginatively visualizing various microcosmic-macrocosmic maṇḍala-palaces enshrining translucent Buddha-images radiating jewelled colored halos and auras of brilliant rainbow lights, consummating ultimately in the Hua-yen vision of *li-shih-wu-ai*, may be comprehended as the holistic perception of value-rich core/horizon gestalt environments achieved through *noetic* reversal and non-focal *Gelassenheit* as animated by the creative visioning exercise of "fantasy variation" or "free variation in imagination."

Through creative visioning, or what is termed imaginative visualization by Tantric Buddhism and free variation in imagination by Western phenomenology, we come to "deconstruct" or "decenter" (to use the phraseology of Jacques Derrida) our deeply sedimented focal-settings which normally freeze the perceptual field into habitual structures, so that the solid surfaces and opaque boundaries ordinarily demarcating physical objects, *without losing their unique particularity*, now become "shining outlines" or "transparent edges" which merge into the spacious dimension of openness, radiance and ecstasy—that open or nonconcealed horizon of disclosure which encircles all unhidden phenomena as what Maurice Merleau-Ponty calls a "halo of Being," conceived as an aura of primordial presence radiating at the level of pre-reflective experience in the form of a "sacral value." This halo of Being as the spacious dimension of openness, radiance and ecstasy, is finally revealed by Merleau-Ponty as that illuminated region of disclosure wherein the entire background of gathered presences becomes "open to my gaze" such that "*every object is a mirror of all others.*" Merleau-Ponty asserts that "it is necessary to put the surroundings in abeyance the better to see the object, and to lose in background what one gains in focal figure."[26] This is equivalent to Tu-shun's assertion cited earlier that "The Shih can hide Li . . . the result is that only the events appear, but Li does not appear." However, through *noetic* reversal or non-focal *Gelassenheit*, what in Hua-yen Buddhism is termed *prajñā*, the recessive background, which is itself the gathered presence of the whole world, now becomes fully open to our gaze, such that each focal object at the core of the perceptual field is experienced as virtually "reflecting" or "mirroring" its entire universe from a "global perspective." In Merleau-Ponty's words:

> To see is to enter a universe of beings which display themselves . . . to look at an object is to inhabit it, and from this habituation to grasp all things in terms of the aspect which they present to it. But in so far as I see those things too, they remain abodes open to my gaze. . . . Thus *every object is the mirror of all others.*[27]

In such a manner then, Merleau-Ponty brings the phenomenological interpretation of Hua-yen Buddhism to its most explicit level of analysis, so that the Realm of Celestial Lord Indra's Net, which comprehends each object as a mirror of all others, is revealed as designating a literal and radically descriptive profile of the "open-dimension" of the perceptual field, wherein each focal actuality stands-out in transparent openness through coemergent-blossoming as nonconcealed presence and unhidden radiance, thus binding foreground/background together into a single, unified, value-laden gestalt pattern of visionary wholeness, as *noetically* constituted or spontaneously organized through the dynamic multiperspectival praxis of free variation in imagination.

Section III

The deep proximity of this phenomenological concept of openness to the non-obstructive *dharmadhātu* or all-permeating *li* in Hua-yen Buddhism becomes still more evident when Heidegger describes the Open as a metaphysical term which signifies, "openness in the sense of a universally prevailing release from all bounds."[28] Heidegger continues by asserting that this metaphysical term, "the Open," means:

> . . . something that does not *block-off*. It does not block-off because it does not set bounds. . . .The Open is the great whole of all that is unbounded. It lets beings . . . draw on one another and draw together without encountering any bounds. Drawing as so drawn, they fuse with the boundless, the infinite. They do not dissolve into void nothingness, but they redeem themselves in the whole of the Open.[29]

Hence, the very meaning of the Open is that which does not *block off*, putting it in perfect consonance with the Hua-yen technical terms *kung* (voidness or openness) and *t'ung* (interpenetration or openness), both of which signify *wu-ai*, non-obstruction or nonimpededness. And finally, Heidegger's concept of the Open as "a universally prevailing release from all bounds" indicates the boundless horizon at the outermost edges of the perceptual field wherein the solid boundaries, opaque surfaces and determinate forms characterizing all physical objects at the focal core are opened-up and made transparent so as to fade-off into the unbounded openness of surrounding space. For this reason, Merleau-Ponty has written that any given focal object contoured by solid boundaries is always located ". . . in an anonymous horizon. . . leaving the object as incomplete and open as it is indeed, in perceptual experience. Through this opening, indeed, the substantiality of the object slips away."[30]

Moreover, this non-obstructive continuum of ecstatic radiance which Heidegger calls "the Open" is wholly divested of any dualistic subject-object bifurcation, which is a basic structural feature of the Hua-yen Buddhist enlightenment experience of *li-shih-wu-ai*. In the ordinary state of perceptual awareness (the natural attitude), the foreground is dominant while the background is recessive; this foreground-background ratio of the *noema* is constituted through specific *noetic* acts of focusing. It may be observed in this sedimented focal mode of perceptivity that the subject-object distinction is fully patent. However, in a non-focal and decentered state of perceptual awareness such as phenomenological *Gelassenheit* or Buddhist *prajñā* there is a non-divided continuum of global presence, a fully open-dimension of experiential immediacy devoid of subject-object, inner-outer or core-periphery distinctions. For as one's focus widens towards the horizon, one's awareness of subject-object or inner-outer diminishes, finally fading away altogether at the outermost horizon of the perceptual field into an undivided continuum of ecstatic openness and radiance. Heidegger therefore writes: "Man is never first and foremost in the hither side of the world as a 'subject.'. . . Rather, before all this man in his essence is ek-sistent in the openness of Being, into the open region, the 'between' within which a relation of subject and object can be."[31]

Our understanding of the ecstatic open-dimension of experiential presence moves towards consummation when openness is at last named the "care" structure of reality and man in his authentic ek-sistence (as standing-out in openness) is termed the "Shepherd of Being." Heidegger writes: "Man is the 'Shepherd of Being.' It is this direction alone that *Being and Time* is thinking when ecstatic existence is experienced as 'care.' "[32] Again, the moral/ethical structure of openness as care is made explicit in Heidegger's thought when he names it through the ancient Greek word *ēthos* from which the term "ethics" is derived: "*Ethos* means abode, dwelling place. The word names the open region in which man dwells."[33] Thus, just as Hua-yen Buddhism emphasizes that a metaphysics of universal interdependence and interpenetration entails an ethics of universal compassion such that *śūnyatā* or openness and *karuṇā* or compassion form an indivisible structure, so too does phenomenology clarify the inseparability of openness and care. The primacy of fields, openings and horizons in perceptual awareness involves the notions of compassionate saving activity, moral responsibility, intersubjective social engagement, being-towards-others, and the rectification of affairs, whereupon man in his authentic existence dwells in openness as the region of care.[34]

In closing, it is of particular interest here to analyze the Hua-yen concept of *yüan* or "roundness" in descriptive phenomenological terms, since the Hua-yen Patriarchs often call their school the "Round Vehicle of Buddhism," thus investing this term with special significance. The basic structural characterization of the non-obstructive *dharmadhātu* or all-pervading reality of *li* is frequently conveyed by the technical Hua-yen term *yüan*, meaning round, spheroid, global or circular. For instance, one may recall the opening stanza of Priest Ŭisang's "Ocean Seal" of Hwaŏm Buddhism: "Dharma-nature is round (*yüan*) and interpenetrating (*yung*) without duality." Ordinarily scholars interpret this term as a generalized metaphysical assertion of total-embrace, wholeness and completion. However, in concordance with the phenomenological hermeneutic being elaborated in this study, the Hua-yen technical term *yüan* or "round" is a literal and radically descriptive profile of the open dimension of the perceptual field. Thus, in his own descriptive analysis of the region of openness, Heidegger repeatedly characterized the Open as a "well-rounded sphere" of global presence wherein all phenomena radiate through coemergent-blossoming into transparent unhiddenness and nonconcealment. Here, Heidegger is articulating the fact that the field of perception is literally a spheroid opening or clearing, an encompassing horizon of global presence. Heidegger writes: "The globe of all beings as a whole is the Open, as the pure forces serried, boundlessly flowing into one another and thus acting toward one another."[35] And finally, referring to the ancient Greek conception of Primordial Being (in the sense of unconcealing presence), *eukuklos sphaire* or the well-rounded sphere, Heidegger asserts:

> This is why Parmenides (Fragment VIII, 42) calls *eon*, the "presence" of what is present, the *eukuklos sphaire*. This "well-rounded sphere" is to be thought of as the Being of beings, in the sense of the unconcealing-lightening-unifying. . . .We must never represent this sphere of Being in

its sphericity as an object. . . .The spherical must be thought by way of the nature of primordial Being in the sense of unconcealing presence.[36]

In the final analysis, such fundamental Hua-yen distinctions as form/voidness, *dharma/dharmadhātu* and *shih/li*, or their phenomenological counterparts, foreground/background, core/horizon and center/openness, may all be comprehended in terms of what Heidegger calls the "ontological difference" between Being/beings, Presence/what is present, Ground/what is grounded, or Nothing/things.[37] All particular beings must be ontologically distinguished from the Ground of Being, which again is the horizon of disclosure wherein all focal actualities ecstatically radiate through coemergent-blossoming as unconcealing presence and transparent openness. What is of special significance here with respect to East-West comparative discourse is Heidegger's explicit identification of Being as unconcealing presence with Nothing, and his equation of the ontological distinction between Being and beings with Nothing and things. Heidegger writes: "The nothing. . . reveals itself as belonging to the Being of beings. Pure Being and Pure Nothing are therefore the same."[38] Thus, the Being of beings which is itself the region of openness wherein all things come to stand in their fullness of unconcealing presence is termed by Heidegger the "place of Nothingness," thereby establishing a yet deeper connection between the phenomenological conception of horizons-phenomena and Hua-yen Buddhist *śūnyatā* (Chi. *kung*) as absolute nothingness. Heidegger's subtle tissue of interconnections between the Being of beings, the region of openness, and the realm of the Nothing is articulated in the following:

> The particular being stands in Being. . . . In the midst of beings as a whole an open place occurs. There is a lighting. . . . This open center is not surrounded by beings; rather, the lighting center itself encircles all that is, as does the *Nothing*, which we scarcely know.[39]

Ultimately, the purport of Heidegger's doctrine concerning the "ontological difference" between Being/beings, Nothing/things, or Presence/what is present, is a claim for the complete inseparability of Noumena and Phenomena, Reality and Appearance or the Absolute and Nature. For no longer does Reality stand behind, beyond or beneath Appearance as a transcendent "Absolute"; rather, Absolute Reality is the natural realm of phenomenal appearances itself as standing-out into openness through coemergent-blossoming in its fullness of Being or unconcealing Presence, thus establishing, in Hua-yen terms, the total indivisibility of form/Voidness, *shih/li, dharma/dharmadhātu* or *saṃsāra/nirvāṇa.*

Section IV

The Hua-yen Buddhist meditative visioning of *li-shih-wu-ai* whereby one comes to directly perceive the Being of beings or the unconcealing Presence of what-is-present, may be comprehended in speculative terms as a theory of *multiperspectival field-vision* as animated by the dynamic praxis of free variation in imagination. Through imaginative variation and *noetic* reversal, sedimented focal-settings are deconstructed; the seemingly solid surfaces and opaque boundaries of physical objects now become shining outlines which diffuse into the translucent openness of surrounding space. This multiperspectival field-visioning involves not only openness to the coemergent primordial presence encircling each actuality as a "halo of Being," to use Merleau-Ponty's phrase, but also openness to value-rich variations and novel topographical possibilities such as to dramatically reconstitute the panoramic sensorium of the perceptual field into ecstatic and radiant core/horizon gestalt environments of aesthetic and imaginative visionary wholeness. Moreover, such multiperspectival field-visioning involves a radical theory of social praxis and intersubjective moral engagement due to the indivisibility of *śūnyatā/karuṇā* or openness and care. Indeed, the Hua-yen Bodhisattva who has awakened such multiperspectival field-vision through radical *noetic* reversals and variations, so as to abide unceasingly in the *dharmadhātu* of *li-shih-wu-ai*, is what in the *Bhagavad Gītā* and ancient Hindu thought was named the *kṣetra-jñānin*, or the "knower of the field (Skt. *kṣetra*) in every field," who with each act saves both self and circumstance through detached social praxis (see footnote 34 of this chapter).

However illuminating the phenomenological mode of discourse might be as an interpretive framework for comprehending Hua-yen Buddhist theory and praxis, there is a major discrepancy between these two schools of thought which must be expressly delineated in order to set the present discussion within the context of the critical problem under consideration; namely, interpenetration vs. cumulative penetration. For whereas the interpenetrating horizons-phenomenon described by Hua-yen Buddhism (i.e., the all-embracing *dharmadhātu* or reality of *li* as the field of *kung* or true nothingness) refers to the gathered presence of an already consummated totality wherein past, present and future events have already been actualized, in Western phenomenology, openness refers to the *radically temporal* structure of ontological presence, as explicitly asserted by Heidegger: "With the word 'time' we no longer mean the succession of a sequence of nows. . . . Time is now the name for the openness which opens-up in the mutual self-extending of futural approach, past and present."[40] This is to say that the horizon of openness encircling the focal core of the perceptual field entails the presence of the actual *past*, as constituted by memory; the future is present only as a fie'd of anticipated possibilities as constituted by the projective imagination. However, the Hua-yen position argues for the total presence of past, present and future events within the open-dimension of Being. In Merleau-Ponty's words: "Each present reasserts the presence of the whole past which it supplants and anticipates that of all that is to come", such that, "the present is not shut up within itself but transcends itself towards a future and a past."[41] Therefore, in the work of Heidegger and Merleau-Ponty, the ecstatic and open character of ontological presence refers explicitly to its *time-bound* structure, whereupon the presence of particular beings is "stretched along ecstatically" throughout the three temporal periods or ecstases—past, present and future—so as to be in this sense "ecstatically open."[42]

Thus, the core/horizon or center/openness structure of the perceptual field requires a strictly temporalized ontological patterning, or as it were, a "synthesis of transition," whereby the primal impression of a now-point is surrounded by both a pastward horizon, constituted through *noetic* "retentions" (immediate memory) of just elapsed phases (perceived as a running off or fading away of phenomena in an ever-diminishing comet-tail of reverberations) and a futural horizon constituted by *noetic* "protentions" or anticipatory expectations (in imagination) of oncoming phases in the temporal stream. In his work, *The Phenomenology of Internal Time Consciousness,* Husserl provides a probing descriptive analysis of the *noetic* protentive-retentive intentionality structure of internal time consciousness and the correlated double-horizon structure of the *noematic* temporal stream as follows:

> In each primal phase which primordially constitutes the immanent content we have retentions of the preceding and protentions of the coming phases of precisely this content. . . . These determinate retentions and protentions have an obscure horizon. . . . Through these retentions and protentions the actual content of the (temporal) stream is joined together.[43]

It is precisely this notion of a protentive-retentive temporal horizon encircling each primal impression of the now-point which was recast by Heidegger and Merleau-Ponty as the "open-dimension of Being." For this reason Merleau-Ponty articulates the region of openness as "the field of presence in its widest sense, with its double horizon of primary past and future, and the infinite openness of those fields of presence that have slid by, or are still possible."[44] In the final analysis then, the Western phenomenological description of experiential presence is more in concordance with the Whiteheadian process theory of cumulative penetration or cumulative presence which recognizes a primacy of radical temporality than with the Hua-yen Buddhist theory of interpenetration or total presence which de-temporalizes actuality.

Western descriptive phenomenology as elaborated by Husserl, Heidegger and Merleau-Ponty ultimately provides empirical testimony for the Whiteheadian process doctrine of cumulative penetration or cumulative presence, a no more condensed summary statement of which can be found than Merleau-Ponty's words cited in the above: "Each present reasserts the presence of the whole past which it supplants and anticipates that of all that is to come." Thus, according to phenomenological analysis, and indeed for process philosophy as well, the present moment contains within itself *the whole of time*; yet, past and future are contained within each present duration in radically divergent manners, since the past is included as a field of actuality or facticity through retentive acts of *memory*, while the future is included as a field of open possibilities through protentive acts of *imagination*, within each radically temporal synthesis of transition.

CHAPTER 5

Interpenetration and Sudden Enlightenment: The Harmonization of Hua-yen Theory and Ch'an Praxis

This chapter seeks to establish the validity of the Hua-yen theory of simultaneous interpenetration within still another specified order of discourse, the order of meditative praxis. For in fact, the central concern of Hua-yen Buddhism is not theoretical in nature, but *soteriological*. Hua-yen Buddhism, being a comprehensive vehicle of religious salvation as opposed to simply a system of philosophy, is concerned not so much to formulate a theory of causation which explains how phenomena arise into appearance through conditioned coproduction as it is to establish a soteriological framework for the achievement of supreme enlightenment. The Hua-yen theory of the unhindered interpenetration of past-present-future into a single thought-instant or the immanence of hundreds of thousands of infinitely long eons in one moment, is highly problematic indeed when understood as a theory of causation. It must instead be comprehended in its proper soteriological context wherein it functions as an *upāya* or expedient means for achieving sudden enlightenment (Chi. *tun-wu;* Kor. *tono;* Jap. *tongo*) as propounded in Ch'an meditative Buddhism. In other words, the doctrine of simultaneous-mutual-penetration among the three ages of past, present and future must be regarded as a remedy for specific afflictions (namely, various modes of attachment and clinging) as opposed to being reified as a final and conclusive interpretive framework for the structure of reality. As an *upāya* or skillful means for the realization of sudden enlightenment, the Hua-yen doctrine of simultaneous interfusion between temporal moments is virtually unassailable and infallible. But as an explanatory theory for the causal process it would seem that the Whiteheadian metaphysics of cumulative penetration represents a significant clarification over the Hua-yen theory of temporal interfusion and simultaneous-mutual-penetration.

The present discourse will focus upon the Hwaŏm/Sŏn or Hua-yen/Ch'an speculative framework postulated by Chinul (1158–1210), who was known as Korean National Preceptor Pojo. His principal endeavor was the syncretic harmonization of Kyo (Chi. Chiao) or scriptural study Buddhism with Sŏn (Chi. Ch'an) or meditative experience Buddhism into a single, comprehensive "round-sudden" vehicle of theory and praxis, wherein the non-obstructive *dharmadhātu* of Hwaŏm metaphysics is equated with the immovable wisdom or universal brightness of one's own True Mind, so that the very meaning of Hwaŏm interpenetration is sudden enlightenment as expounded by the Sŏn school. As stated previously, the characteristic patterns exhibited by Korean Buddhism as established by Wŏnhyo in the Unified Silla Dynasty, such as *t'ong bulgyo* or "Buddhism of total interpenetration," *wŏllyung hoe t'ong* or "syncretic interpenetrative harmonization" and *hwajaeng* or "harmonization of all disputes" were brought to their culminating modality of expression in the creative metaphysical synthesis formulated by Chinul. What is especially interesting in Chinul is that although he was well learned in the thought of Fa-tsang and the entire tradition of orthodox Hua-yen, he instead based his own system of theory and praxis upon a highly unorthodox line of Chinese Hua-yen Buddhism, particularly the thought of Li T'ung-hsüan and Tsung-mi, both of whom emphasized the practicable, salvific and experiential dimensions of Hua-yen Buddhism as opposed to Fa-tsang's more theoretical concerns.

Chinul most explicitly addresses the fusion of Hwaŏm theory and Sŏn practice in his *Wŏndon Sŏngbullon* or "The Round and Sudden Attainment of Enlightenment."[1] Again, in the Introduction to his *Hwaŏmron Chŏryo* or "Synopsis of the Treatise on Hwaŏm," which is a detailed commentary on Li T'ung-hsüan's *Hua-yen ching lun*, Chinul makes a famous statement that Kyo represents the words of Buddha whereas Sŏn represents the mind of Buddha. Thus, the teachings of the sūtras with respect to the Hwaŏm *dharmadhātu* of interpenetrative non-obstruction is perfectly in concordance with the effulgent True Mind of immovable wisdom and universal radiance as realized instantaneously through Sŏn contemplation. While pondering Li T'ung-hsüan's basic idea of awakening faith (*ch'i-hsin*) or arousing *bodhicitta*, Chinul asserts:

> I still was unable to comprehend how ordinary persons today could enter the gate of initial (nascent) faith. Thus I took recourse in Li's *Exposition of the Hua-yen Sūtra*. . . . Subsequently I set down the treatise with great relief

> and stated: "What Buddha spoke with his mouth are his teachings (Kyo) whereas what the patriarchs transmitted directly through the Mind is Sŏn. The Buddha's words and the patriarch's minds cannot be in conflict. Therefore, why do not the votaries of Sŏn and Kyo both enter their common source?. . . Since then I have practiced intensively in order to generate the Mind of Faith."[2]

Prior to Chinul, the Koryŏ Dynasty monk Ŭich'ŏn (1055–1101), known posthumously as Taekak, had already achieved a major synthesis of Sŏn praxis with Hwaŏm and *T'ien-t'ai* (Kor. *Ch'ŏnt'ae*) doctrinal study Buddhism.[3] However, Ŭich'ŏn adopted a predominantly *doctrinal* stand, whereas Chinul conferred a strict primacy to Sŏn meditative practice. For although Chinul regarded Kyo as the words of Buddha and Sŏn as the mind of Buddha, he nonetheless gave priority to Sŏn. In this respect then, Chinul's synthesis of Sŏn with Kyo is a continuation of Wŏnhyo's *t'ong pulgyo* or Buddhism of total interpenetration, which also gave a strict primacy to the meditative, salvific and experiential aspects of Hwaŏm Buddhism.

Chinul derived his basic scheme for the unification of Sŏn (Chi. Ch'an) and Kyo (Chi. Chiao) from Tsung-mi, who was the Fifth Patriarch of Chinese Hua-yen Buddhism as well as a Patriarch in Shen-hui's line of Ch'an Buddhism. Moreover, it was from Tsung-mi that Chinul appropriated his theory of *tono chŏmsu* or sudden enlightenment and gradual practice. This theory is his attempt to reconcile a major doctrinal debate besetting the Ch'an sect regarding sudden vs. gradual or innate vs. acquired concepts of enlightenment, and to establish the radical claim that sudden enlightenment must *precede* all forms of gradual cultivation. Chinul's radical and unorthodox theory of sudden enlightenment and gradual practice is based upon a further distinction which he makes between "initial awakening" and "ultimate illumination," wherein sudden enlightenment is an instantaneous flash of intuitive awakening to the universal brightness of one's own True Mind *(chin shim),* as well as an awakening of faith *(hsin)* in one's primordial identity with Buddha, a sudden awakening that must be followed by gradual cultivation, eventually consummating in the attainment of ultimate illumination or final wisdom. According to Chinul's Hwaŏm/Sŏn system of theory and praxis, one should endeavor to allow one's initial awakening of nascent faith to mature through various modes of gradual cultivation such as *śamatha-vipaśyanā* or *yŏmbul* (Pure Land) recitation. The traditional Ch'an practices of *śamatha-vipaśyanā* (stabilization and insight) and *samādhi-prajñā* (quiescence and wisdom) are understood by Chinul to correspond to the *t'i-yung* (Kor. *ch'e-yong*) or essence-function structure of True Mind, a doctrine which

Chinul appropriated from the Ch'an lineage of Sixth Patriarch Hui-neng and his successor Shen-hui. According to the *t'i-yung* analysis of consciousness, the essence of true mind is its quiescence (*chŏk*) whereas its dynamic function is an active knowing (*chi*), which signifies an "original act of inward illumination." Thus, gradual cultivation practices like *śamatha-vipaśyanā* or stabilization and insight and *samādhi-prajñā* or quiescence and wisdom are not in any way externally imposed, but are simply the essence and function of True Mind itself, operating in concordance with its originally enlightened nature as the innate union of tranquility and intrinsic radiance. Therefore sudden enlightenment *must* precede gradual practice; for analogous to Dōgen's Sōtō Zen in Japan, there must be a complete unity of practice with enlightenment. Ch'an or Sŏn, which is sitting upright in *samādhi* as the true dharma-gate to repose and joy, is not practiced to acquire enlightenment, but rather to dynamically express one's *innate* enlightenment in each eternal now or absolute present.

In his doctrine of gradual cultivation Chinul furthermore attempts to harmonize "self-power" (*charyŏk*) as in Sŏn meditative practice with "other-power" (*t'aryŏk*) in *yŏmbul* or Pure Land practice, arguing that one may efficaciously recite Amitābha Buddha's name and rely upon his primal vow of unconditional compassion as well as long for Pure Land in the Western Paradise, but only in the context of Sŏn meditative praxis, whereupon it is fully understood that in calling Amitābha, one's own name is being recited, and that Amitābha's primal vow of unconditional compassion is simply one's own innate enlightenment or original act of inward illumination, whereas Pure Land is itself identical to the pristine clarity and effulgent radiance of one's own True Mind. Indeed, there has long existed a popular slogan throughout the East Asian tradition of Mahāyāna Buddhism which declares: "Hua-yen for doctrine, Pure Land and Ch'an for practice.' For in fact, one-pointed meditation on *sukhāvatī*, the Pure Land of Ultimate Bliss in the Western Paradise, as well as unceasing repetition of Buddha's name in the form of "*namo Amitābha Buddha, namo Amitābha Buddha. . .*" (i.e., "I bow to the Buddha of Infinite Light"), while maintaining continuous faith in the grace-saving power of Amitābha's primal vow of universal compassion, was itself one of the basic *upāya* or skillful means of meditative practice originally expounded in the *Avataṁsaka Sūtra,* as well as the *Ta-ch'eng ch'i-hsin lun* or "The Awakening of Faith in Mahāyāna." Yet, in order for the other-power (*t'aryŏk*) technique of Pure Land recitation to be effective in the attainment of *mokṣa* (liberation) and *samādhi* (ecstatic trance), it must be practiced both in terms of the self-power (*charyŏk*) context of Ch'an or Sŏn meditation on one's own still and bright True Mind, as well as the Hua-yen or Hwaŏm doctrinal wisdom regarding *li-shih-wu-*

ai or the non-obstructive interfusing of universal-principle with particular-phenomena, as well as *shih-shih-wu-ai* or the non-obstructive interfusing of particular-phenomena with particular-phenomena. Thus, Hua-yen, Ch'an and Pure Land must form an indivisible threefold system combining both theory and praxis as well as self-power and other-power. As stated above, in its Ch'an context, Pure Land practice is altered such that the recitation of *"namo Amitābha Buddha"* is simply calling one's own name, and meditation on Pure Land is seeing into one's own clear and brilliant True Mind, whereas supplicating Amitābha's primal vow of universal compassion is only the realization of one's own "original enlightenment" or "primordial attainment of Buddhahood." However, in its Hua-yen context, Pure Land recitation must be practiced with the wisdom that Amitābha Buddha, i.e., *li* or universal-principle, is completely interfused with and identical to all sentient beings, i.e., *shih* or particular-phenomena, such that the practitioner of Pure Land can adopt the inward attitude: "I am Amitābha Buddha." Since according to the Hua-yen doctrinal formula of *li-shih-wu-ai* all sentient beings throughout space are identical to Amitābha Buddha, they are fully qualified for the attainment of sudden enlightenment and instantaneous rebirth in the Pure Land of Ultimate Bliss. Moreover, due to the Hua-yen doctrine of *chung-chung-wu-chin* or realms-embracing-realms ad infinitum, which is itself a restatement of the Hua-yen formula concerning *shih-shih-wu-ai*, Amitābha's Pure Land as well as hundreds of thousands of millions of other infinitely spacious Buddhalands are all completely interfused and mutually contained within the world of sentient beings, and as such, are easily accessible without any obstruction or hindrance whatsoever. Therefore, Chinul fully advocates the practice of *yŏmbul* or Pure Land recitation, especially to those who are still impeded by various mental obscurations, although once again, only within the context of Ch'an contemplation of True Mind and Hua-yen doctrinal wisdom concerning realms-embracing-realms and unhindered interpenetration between universal-principle and particular-phenomena.

Finally, Chinul's system of gradual cultivation through such methods as the "parallel keeping of quiescence and wakefulness" through *śamatha-vipaśyanā* or the supplication of Amitābha Buddha's Primal Vow of Unconditional Compassion through *yŏmbul* recitation is culminated by the radical Sŏn practice of *hwadu* or *kanhwa* (i.e., *koan* meditation) as extolled by Ta-hui, conceived as the path of "direct cutting" and "inward questioning" (i.e., unbroken reflection upon an inward question like "What is Mind?" which must persist all throughout one's periods of waking, dream and deep sleep), which was regarded by Chinul as the supreme meditative praxis for breaking-apart all dualistic intellectual frameworks in the achievement of True Mind. Indeed, Chinul considers the practice of *hwadu* or "inward questioning" to be so radical, intense and esoteric in its illuminating potency to instantaneously awaken the practitioner to an ultimate realization of True Mind that it cannot be considered a form of "gradual" practice at all, but is rather the "direct cutting" of all attachments and the immediate shift from the sentient being's world of "discrimination" to the Buddha's world of "non-discrimination."

Chinul's Hwaŏm/Sŏn System of Sudden Enlightenment and Gradual Practice: (tono-chŏmsu)

I. Sudden Enlightenment (Initial Insight):
The Awakening of Faith (in one's primordial attainment of Buddhahood)

II. Gradual Practice: The Cultivation of Faith

True Mind (the *dharmadhātu* of Interpenetration)

t'i (Essence) as Tranquility — *yung* (Function) as Immovable Wisdom

(1) *śamatha* (stabilization) — *vipaśyanā* (insight)
samādhi (quiescence) — *prajñā* (wakefulness)

(2) *yŏmbul:* Pure Land Recitation (Supplication of Amitābha Buddha's Primal Vow of Unconditional Compassion).

III. Ultimate Illumination: The Perfection of Faith
(*hwadu* meditation): Direct Cutting and Inward Questioning

As indicated in the chart, the concept of faith (*hsin*) stands at the very heart of Chinul's Hwaŏm/Sŏn system of *tono-chŏmsu* or sudden enlightenment and gradual practice. Sudden enlightenment or initial insight refers to the *awakening* of (nascent) faith, whereas gradual practice as effected by such progressive techniques as *śamatha-vipaśyanā* and *yŏmbul* refers to the *cultivation* of faith, both of these finally culminating in ultimate wisdom through the direct cutting exercise of *hwadu*, which signifies the *perfection* of faith. However, Chinul not only makes the notion of faith central to his system, but also adopts a radical and unorthodox conception of faith which he terms "patriarchal faith" (*tsu hsin*) as opposed to the conventional and orthodox conception of the term which he calls "doctrinal faith" *(chiao hsin)*. In his treatise entitled *Chim shim jik sol* or "A Straight Discourse on True-Mind," Chinul responds to the question, "What is the distinction between 'faith' in the patriarchal and doctrinal schools?" in the following manner:

There are numerous differences. The doctrinal sects advocate faith in the law of cause and effect. . . .Those who rejoice in the result of Buddhahood must have faith that practicing the Six Perfections (of Merit and Wisdom) over three *kalpas* is the basic cause, whereas *Bodhi* and *Nirvāṇa* are its fruition. Correct faith in the Patriarchal Sect is quite different from this, since this sect does not believe in causes and effects. It simply stresses that there exists faith that one's self is originally identical to Buddha, that all persons have perfect self-nature and that the sublime essence of *Nirvāṇa* is fully complete in everyone.[4]

Thus, whereas doctrinal faith signifies the law of cause/effect and the correlate belief that "I can *become* Buddha," the patriarchal faith adopted by Chinul represents the identity and simultaneity of cause/effect as well as the correlate belief that "I am *already* Buddha." Moreover, whereas doctrinal faith is said to be dualistic in structure since it involves an "object" of faith, namely, faith in the *triratna* or "three jewels" (i.e., the Buddha, Dharma and Saṅgha), patriarchal faith is completely non-dual in structure since it requires no external object, but is instead directed inward towards one's own True Mind or One Mind, which is itself identified with the *triratna*. Consequently, in contrast to the *neng-so* or "subject-object" structure characterizing doctrinal faith, patriarchal faith is instead analyzable by the Sinitic *t'i-yung* or essence-function construction, wherein one's own True Mind represents *t'i* or essence and faith represents its dynamic *yung* or function. Hence, in terms of the "round-sudden" (*wŏndon*) or Hwaŏm-Sŏn understanding of Pure Land recitation practice, the faith that one cultivates in Amitābha's primal vow of universal compassion, should not be a doctrinal faith which believes that "I will someday be reborn in Amitābha's Pure Land," but rather one must cultivate an unretrogressive or non-backsliding form of patriarchal faith which believes that "I am *already* reborn in Amitābha's Pure Land."

Chinul appropriated this theory concerning the primacy of faith in Hwaŏm and Sŏn Buddhism and the radical distinction between patriarchal faith and doctrinal faith from the highly unorthodox Chinese Hua-yen master Li T'ung-hsüan, whose *Hua-yen ching lun* was considered by Chinul to be the most profound exegesis of Hua-yen teachings. This emphasis on the central role of faith in Buddhism is a major contribution to Buddhist scholarship discoverable in the works of Li T'ung-hsüan and Chinul. In the Buddhist soteriological system, faith functions as the primary internal dynamic animating the whole salvific process which advances from theory to practice to certification of enlightenment. In the syncretic Buddhist treatise entitled *The Awakening of Faith in* Mahayana the basic theme is how to "arouse the mind of faith" (*ch'i hsin-hsin*) and how to perfect this faith through meditation and practice, so as to realize the "non-backsliding" or "unretrogressive" faith (*pu-t'ui hsin*) of *aniyata rāśi* or the "determined class." This primacy accorded to faith in Buddhist theory, practice and enlightenment is also a major feature of the *Hua-yen Sūtra* itself which proclaims: "Faith is the origin of the Way and the mother of all merit." According to the *Hua-yen Sūtra* a bodhisattva must advance through fifty-two stages of evolution before attaining the Wonderful Enlightenment of a Buddha. The first ten stages of a bodhisattva's career are termed the "ten faiths." However, even with the realization of the very first stage, which is the stage of nascent faith, the fifty-second stage of Wonderful Enlightenment has already been attained, since all fifty-two stages of the path completely interpenetrate without obstruction. This is illustrated by Sudhana's journey in the last chapter of the text on "Entering the Dharma Realm" (the *Gaṇḍavyūha Sūtra*), where the seeker Sudhana pilgrimages to fifty-two teachers, each one revealing to him a different level of *samādhi*, the last teacher also being his first, i.e., Mañjuśrī, the Buddha of supreme wisdom.

This internal structure of the *Hua-yen Sūtra* may be put in the form of a diagram as below:

Complete unobstructed interpenetration of fifty-two stages	Ten Faiths (*shih hsin*) Ten Dwellings (*shih chu*) Ten Conducts (*shih hsing*) Ten Transferences (*shih hui-hsiang*) Ten Grounds or *bhūmis* (*shih ti*) Equal Enlightenment (*teng-chiao*) Wonderful Enlightenment (*miao-chiao*)

Hua-yen scholars often simplify this scheme of fifty-two hierarchically graded stages structuring the *Hua-yen Sūtra* as follows: Faith, Theory, Practice and Enlightenment. However, according to the "round-sudden" perspective of Hua-yen, as soon as we awaken the mind of faith, at that very moment, enlightenment is attained. Thus, all fifty-two stages in the career of a bodhisattva are reduced to a single moment of nascent faith. This attainment of sudden enlightenment through the awakening of correct faith is nevertheless followed by a gradual evolution of the bodhisattva's consciousness. It may be said that with the awakening of faith, one realizes the initial state of *samādhi*, although this trance may be deepened throughout a series of fifty-two phases, finally culminating in perfect Buddhahood. Although all fifty-two stages interfuse without hindrance, still, each stage remains a distinct level with its own intensity of experience and its own criterion for certification. There is thus a perfect non-obstruction of successive gradation (*hsing pu*) and complete interpenetration (*yüan yung*) in the Hua-yen scheme of fifty-two stages.

Chinul's system of *tono-chŏmsu* or "sudden enlightenment and gradual practice" may therefore be said to represent an extraordinary attempt to comprehend the overall internal structure of the *Hua-yen Sūtra*, wherein the first stage is completely interfused with the final stage of Wonderful Enlightenment, yet is still followed by fifty-one stages of progressive development. However, on the basis of Li T'ung-hsüan's teachings, Chinul goes on to demonstrate that *faith* is the key to the Hua-yen scheme of sudden enlightenment and gradual practice, since the first of the fifty-two stages designates the level of nascent faith. Yet, Chinul's point is that if the stage of nascent faith is to be equated with sudden enlightenment, then it must be what he has termed patriarchal faith, which is the resolute conviction that one is *already* identical to Buddha, as opposed to doctrinal faith, which is only a commitment that one has a potentiality to *become* Buddha. This may be seen by contrasting Chinul's position to the more orthodox line of Fa-tsang.

In his study entitled *The Philosophical Foundation of Korean Zen Buddhism: The Integration of Sŏn and Kyo by Chinul*, Jae Ryong Shim develops at length Li T'ung-hsüan's theory of the primacy of faith in Hua-yen and Ch'an Buddhism and its subsequent appropriation by Chinul. Shim demonstrates through copious textual citations that for Fa-tsang as well as for Li, faith is the point of departure for the bodhisattva's career, functioning to sustain the bodhisattva's practice and vows throughout all fifty-two stages of development until at last the non-regressive or non-backsliding level of faith is realized in the final stages of the path, such that enlightenment itself is the perfection of faith.[6] However, Shim carefully distinguishes between Fa-tsang's concept of faith as "a belief in the possibility of attaining Buddhahood through a long period of practical cultivation" and Li's conception of faith as "the resolute conviction that one is already identical to Buddha."[7] Shim therefore writes, that according to Li T'ung-hsüan:

> The usual interpretation of faith as a belief in the possibility of becoming a Buddha through the step by step procedure of faith, understanding, practice and authentication was changed into the new idea that faith is the resolute conviction that one is *already* identified with Buddhahood. This conviction as to each person's primordial attainment of Buddhahood is the basis of the Sŏn doctrine of sudden awakening.[8]

What is of primary concern here is the point stated immediately above: "This conviction as to each person's primordial attainment of Buddhahood is the basis of the Sŏn doctrine of sudden awakening." It is therefore precisely the attainment of nascent faith, conceived as the resolute conviction that one is *already* identical to Buddha, which Chinul came to identify as the experience of sudden enlightenment, understood as a sudden intuitive flash of insight into one's primordial attainment of Buddhahood, whereby one instantaneously realizes the original act of inward illumination which is the very essence *(t'i)* and function *(yung)* of True Mind. It is here that one discovers the deeper reasoning which underlies Chinul's radical and unorthodox claim that sudden enlightenment or nascent faith must necessarily *precede* the process of gradual cultivation; for unless one is firmly established in the resolute conviction that one is already identical to Buddha, all practice will be fundamentally distorted from the very outset, since all efforts will be aimed at becoming a Buddha throughout a succession of time, instead of *instantaneously* realizing the original act of inward illumination or the primordial attainment of Buddhahood intrinsic to the *t'i-yung* structure of True Mind as the innate union of quiescence and immovable wisdom. In the final analysis then, Chinul is concerned with Li's doctrine of the primacy of faith in Hwaŏm Buddhism because it establishes the soteriological basis for one's attainment of sudden enlightenment or instantaneous illumination as propounded by the Sŏn school of meditative praxis.

In his study of Chinul's syncretic harmonization of Sŏn and Kyo, Shim goes on to correlate Fa-tsang's notion of faith as "a belief in the possibility of attaining Buddhahood through a long procedure of practical cultivation" to his theory of the "attainment of Buddhahood through three levels of rebirth" (*san-sheng ch'eng fo*).[9] Hence, despite Fa-tsang's doctrine of the non-obstructed interfusion of all moments of past-present-future into one thought-instant, he still is attached to the conventional framework of chronological time *at the level of practice*, since innumerable *kalpas* of gradual cultivation through the accumulation of merit and wisdom are required for the attainment of Buddhahood. Li T'ung-hsüan therefore regarded this as a major inconsistency infecting Fa-tsang's work. Shim proceeds to correlate Li's own concept of faith as a "resolute conviction that one is *already* identified with Buddha" to his doctrine of the "attainment of Buddhahood in an instant" (*ch'a-na ch'eng-fo*).[10] Hence, Li's notion of faith as an affirmation of one's primordial attainment of Buddhahood is tantamount to a doctrine of original enlightenment and sudden awakening, and as such, is far more in consonance with the basic Hua-yen theory wherein all temporal moments interpenetrate into a single thought-instant. The infinitely long *halpas* required for the attainment of Buddhahood in Fa-tsang's system are now reduced to one moment of nascent faith. Shim therefore writes that in sharp contrast to Fa-tsang and the orthodox line of Hua-yen Buddhism:

> Li T'ung-hsüan eradicated the element of diachronic time from the attainment of Buddhahood. Free from temporal divisions, a practitioner is required to make an instantaneous decision that he himself, just as he is, is Buddha. . . .Here we see the close tie between Li's idea of 'faith'. . . and the unreality of conventional temporal divisions.[11]

Thus, in the unorthodox line of Hua-yen as expounded by Li T'ung-hsüan and Chinul, the usual step-by-step process of attaining enlightenment through gradual cultivation is radically transformed into an instantaneous process of sudden awakening. Both Li and Chinul demonstrated that the very meaning of the Hua-yen doctrine of the "unhindered interpenetration of past, present and future into a single thought-instant" is none other than the realization of *sudden enlightenment* as proposed by the Ch'an School of Buddhism.[12] And this experience of sudden enlightenment is itself no different from the awakening of nascent faith in one's own primordial attainment of Buddhahood, which is precisely the original act of inward illumination constituting both the essence *(t'i)* and function *(yung)* of true mind.

Chinul discovered the philosophical basis for such correlated doctrines as the primacy of faith, the primordial identification of sentient beings with Buddha, and sudden awakening, in Li T'ung-hsüan's radical and unorthodox doctrine of nature origination (Chi. *hsing-chi*; Kor. *sŏnggi*) in contrast to the standard doctrinal formula underlying orthodox Hua-yen, namely, "conditioned origination" or "dependent coorigination" (Chi. *yüan-chi*; Kor. *yŏn'gi*). The term "nature-origination" or *hsing-chi* is the title of an important chapter from the *Hua-yen Sūtra*, and was most likely derived from the Sanskrit term, *tathāgata-gotra-sambhāva*, or, "manifestation of the absolute truth." Shim provides an excellent scholarly synopsis of Chinul's understanding with respect to nature-origination vs. dependent origination which is well worth citing at length here:

> Chinul put his argument against the orthodox emphasis on the doctrine of "conditioned origination" (*yŏn'gi*) this way: while the doctrine of nature-origination does not require any mediating step to identify principle (*śūnyatā*) and phantom-like phenomena (*dharma*), that of "conditioned origination" (*sŏnggi*) must require an intermediary conceptual apparatus of identity and interpenetration in order to bridge the gap between the delusion of sentient beings and the enlightenment of Buddhas. Underlying the theory of "conditioned origination" is a tacit assumption that there

are different substances like numerous jewels of Indra's net, whereas the "nature-origination" denies all relations among numerous events by realizing that the apparently different and numerous phenomenal events are but functions (*yong*) originating from the self-same substance (*ch'e*), the mind-ground. In order to ensure the spontaneous arising of enlightenment from one's own nature or originally pure mind, the Hua-yen doctrine of nature-origination must be given priority over that of conditioned origination which conceived the attainment of Buddhahood as something extrinsic to one's essential nature. What Chinul wants to articulate is the *practical potency* of the doctrine of nature-origination over against that of conditioned origination. Although on the level of theory alone, the two can be construed as being roughly equivalent, the implications for practice are radically different. The concept of nature-origination is capable of merging practice and theory in a way that conditioned origination cannot.[13]

Thus, the concept of nature-origination may be understood as simply a much more radical version of conditioned origination or dependent coproduction. Chinul emphasizes that whereas conditioned origination articulates reality from the perspective of multiple phenomena (*shih*) or dynamic function (*yung*), nature origination articulates reality from the perspective of principle (*li*) or universal essence (*t'i*). Whereas conditioned origination requires an intermediary intellectual framework of interpenetration and mutual fusion to identify principle (*li*) with phenomena (*shih*), the more radical doctrine of nature-origination, instead emphasizes the non-production or non-origination of phenomena and requires no intermediary conceptual apparatus. Following Li T'ung-hsüan then, Chinul argues for the doctrinal supremacy of nature-origination over conditioned origination because the former position implicates a theory of sudden awakening at the level of praxis whereas the latter implies a doctrine of gradual cultivation, since the dialectical oppositions between unity and multiplicity and principle and phenomena must be overcome before one may attain enlightenment. The distinction between Chinul's unorthodox line as opposed to the more conventional and orthodox line of Hua-yen as promulgated by Fa-tsang and the standard Patriarchs may be synoptically schematized on the following page.

The doctrine of nature-origination as extolled by Li and Chinul has tremendous implications for the problem of interpenetration vs. cumulative penetration. Since nature-origination is simply a more radical derivative of dependent coorigination, it certainly does not alleviate the problem when analyzed from the standpoint of the Whiteheadian process critique if regarded solely as a doctrine of causation, or as it were, intercausation. However, the fact is that the primary concern for Chinul, as well as for his precursors Li T'ung-hsüan and Tsung-mi, was

Chinul's "Unorthodox" Line of Hwaŏm/Sŏn	Orthodox Hua-yen Position
1. "Faith" as the resolute conviction that one is *already* identical to Buddha	1. "Faith" in the possibility of becoming a Buddha through gradual practice
2. Emphasis on the sameness of sentient beings with Buddha	2. Emphasis on the theoretical structure of Interpenetration and Non-obstruction
3. Achievement of Buddhahood in one instant of nascent faith (*tono* or Sudden Enlightenment)	3. Attainment of Buddhahood through three *kalpas* of rebirth (Gradual Enlightenment)
4. Nature-Origination (Chi. *hsing chi*; Kor. *Sŏnggi*)	4. Dependent Coorigination (Chi. *yüan chi*; Kor. *yŏn'gi*)
5. The doctrine of interpenetrating temporal moments as *upayā* (skillful means) for realizing Original Enlightenment and Sudden Awakening at the level of salvific praxis	5. The doctrine of interpenetrating temporal moments as an absolutized explanatory theory concerning the ultimate structure of reality

not theoretical in nature, but soteriological, with emphasis being placed on the practicable and experiential dimensions of Hua-yen Buddhism. Consequently, the concept of nature-origination is not intended as a systematic doctrine of intercausality functioning to explain how non-inherent phenomena arise into existence through causes and conditions, but as a practical doctrine pointing directly to original enlightenment and sudden awakening. As Shim asserts: "According to Chinul, the theory of nature-origination was not intended to provide an explanation of the origin of phenomena: the thrust of the doctrine of nature-origination lies in its practical implication in the soteriological concern for spiritual liberation."[14] Therefore, the entire Hua-yen structure of interpenetrating temporal moments and the reduction of all fifty-two stages in a bodhisattva's career to one instant of nascent faith within a framework of nature-origination must ultimately be comprehended as an *upāya* or expedient device for instantly realizing sudden enlightenment. To conclude, the Whiteheadian process critique of Hua-yen Buddhism is directed specifically to the doctrine of dependent coorigination (Skt. *pratītyasamutpāda*; Chi. *yüan-chi*), regarded as the theoretical explanation for the genesis of phenomena through interdependence and intercausation. However, in that the doctrine of nature-origination as emphasized by Li T'ung-hsüan and Chinul functions principally as an *upāya* for igniting sudden enlightenment, it is in no way whatsoever subject to the Whiteheadian critique.

Part II

A WHITEHEADIAN PROCESS CRITIQUE OF HUA-YEN BUDDHISM

Preliminary Remarks

Just as in the East, Hua-yen Buddhism is characterized by its comprehensive syncretic harmonization pattern, so in the West the most syncretic metaphysical scheme has undoubtedly been formulated by Alfred North Whitehead, especially in his cosmological masterpiece, *Process and Reality*. From contemporary physics, for example, Whitehead assimilated the generalized notion of spatiotemporal quantum-fields arising through interacting vector forces, and derived his concept of pulsatory space-time events emerging through prehension or causal vector feeling. Moreover, Whitehead analyzed these spatiotemporal events or quantum-fields not in terms of the traditional two-term (subject-predicate) logic of Aristotelian thought, but through complex multiple-term relations of the new combinatory calculus of mathematical logic. And finally, this entire scientific, mathematical and logical paradigm-shift emergent in the twentieth century was formulated by Whitehead in metaphysical terms, through a massive creative synthesis of the history of Western speculative thought, a synthesis which confers equal validity both to the classical tradition of Western rationalism with its emphasis on intellectual system-building and the construction of internally coherent categoreal schemes, as well as to the romantic tradition with its emphasis on pre-reflective presence, primordial feeling, experiential immediacy, intuitive vision, organic wholeness, creative imagination, and aesthetic-values.

In his various metaphysical works, Whitehead formulated an organic conception of actuality based upon the notion of microcosmic-macrocosmic units of process. This suggests an apparent proximity to the Hua-yen theory of interpenetrative harmonization and non-obstructive mutual containment. Whitehead articulates this microcosmic-macrocosmic model of reality through a succession of bold speculative generalizations such as follows:

> Each actual entity. . . repeats in microcosm what the universe is in macrocosm. (PR, p. 215)
>
> Each actual entity is a throb of experience including the actual world within its scope. (PR, p. 190)
>
> In a sense, every entity pervades the whole world. (PR, p. 28)
>
> Each unit has in its nature a reference to every other member of the community so that each unit is a microcosm representing in itself the entire, all-inclusive universe. (RM, p. 89)
>
> No two actualities can be torn apart: each is all in all. (PR, p. 348)

Moreover, in his famous critique of simple location, Whitehead even proclaims that in some sense, "everything is everywhere at all times":

> . . . My theory involves the entire abandonment of the notion that simple location is the primary way in which things are involved in space-time. In a certain sense, everything is everywhere at all times. For every location involves an aspect of itself in every location. Thus, every spatiotemporal standpoint mirrors the world. (SMW, p. 91)

But Whitehead's massive generalities do not end here. In order to further ensure the ontological cohesiveness, togetherness and solidarity of the cosmos, he postulates an "extensive continuum" as the scheme of potential relatedness atomized by all actual occasions. This extensive continuum at first glance appears similar indeed to the *dharmadhātu* of Hua-yen Buddhism, the cosmic web of interrelations or the matrix of universal intercausation actualized by each dharma. For example, Whitehead writes:

> This extensive continuum is one relational continuum in which all potential objectifications find their niche. It underlies the whole world, past, present and future. . . . Actual entities atomize this extensive continuum. (PR, p. 66 and 67)

Furthermore, each actual occasion both houses and pervades the entire spatiotemporal continuum of extensive relations so as to completely defy the property of simple location, i.e., the notion that an entity occupies only one locus in the spatiotemporal continuum while being wholly absent from all other times and places:

> Every actual entity in its relationship to other actual entities is in this sense somewhere in the continuum, and arises out of the data provided by this standpoint. But in another sense it is *everywhere* throughout the continuum; for its constitution includes the objectification of the actual world and thereby includes the continuum. (PR, p. 67; italics mine)

Consequently, ". . . the continuum is present in each actual entity and each actual entity pervades the continuum" (PR, p. 67). How strikingly similar indeed this passage seems to Fa-tsang's proclamation: "When contracted, all things are manifested in one particle of dust. When expanded one particle of dust will universally permeate everything."[1]

Thus far, Whitehead's speculative framework appears to be a perfect echo of the microcosmic-macrocosmic theory of non-obstructed interpenetration and unhindered mutual fusion formulated by Hua-yen Buddhism. Such a conviction is further strengthened by Whitehead's summary statement of his philosophic position: ". . . Every actual entity is present in every other actual entity. The philosophy of organism is mainly devoted to the task of making clear the notion of 'being present in another entity'" (PR, p. 50). Thus, it is clear that in fact Whitehead does share the deepest ontological commitment of the Hua-yen school, namely, that in some sense, all events are virtually present or immanent in every other event. However, whereas Hua-yen relies mostly upon the device of *upamā* (simile) to articulate its syncretic metaphysics of interpenetrative harmonization (such as its well-known metaphors of the Ocean and Waves, House and Rafters, Indra's Net, Hall of Mirrors, Tower of Maitreya or the Golden Lion), Whitehead instead endeavors to "make clear the notion of 'being present in another entity'" with detailed critical analysis and categoreal precision, to determine in exactly what sense and to what degree, all events are actually "present" in every other event. And as shall be seen, the sense in which each event is present in all others is precisely in the sense of cumulative presence, cumulative immanence or cumulative penetration, as well as the sense of asymmetrical causation, one-way relativity, creative advance, emergent novelty, conformal objectification of the past through reenactive feeling and the negative prehension of incompatible elements incapable of satisfying their categoreal obligations.

The process critique of Hua-yen Buddhist interpenetrative modes of thought begins by an analysis of the two primary notions underlying the asymmetrical infrastructures of Whitehead's categoreal scheme, namely, the Theory of Creativity in Chapter One, and the Theory of Feelings in Chapter Two. The process critique of Hua-yen elaborated in these two chapters will then culminate in an examination of Whitehead's Doctrine of Negative Prehensions in Chapter Three, which represents the most subtle and intricate stratum of analysis in his sustained project of "making clear the notion of 'being present in another entity.'" Finally, Whitehead's process doctrine of actuality is systematized and encapsulated in terms of what is called in this work a "metaphysics of cumulative penetration," as asymmetrically structured by its two underlying pillars, the theory of creativity and the theory of feelings. Here, it shall be argued that all those deepest ontological commitments of Hua-yen Buddhism are provided full theoretic explanation by process doctrine, namely, that all events are present in every other event: and that due to this profound ontological togetherness, cohesiveness and solidarity of events, enlightened perceptivity in the primordial mode of causal feeling, universal compassion through sympathetic concernedness, ecstatic bliss or aesthetic-value feeling through dipolar contrast, and final deliverance through transpersonal peace are all intrinsic to reality itself—but solely in accordance with the asymmetrical infrastructures underlying the metaphysics of cumulative penetration.

CHAPTER 6

Creative Synthesis and Emergent Novelty

An analysis of creativity, the "universal of universals" (PR, p. 21) or the "ultimate notion of the highest generality at the base of actuality," (PR, p. 31) in Whitehead's categoreal scheme, once again reveals profound cross-cultural comparative patterns and East-West structural parallels with Hua-yen Buddhism of the most significant kind. Whitehead's principle of creativity is defined as the ". . . ultimate principle by which the many, which are the universe disjunctively, become the one actual occasion, which is the universe conjunctively" (PR, p. 21). Fa-tsang expounded the dialectical relationship between the many and the one through simultaneous-mutual-establishment as follows: "The one and the many establish each other. Only when the one is completely the many can it be called the one, and only when the many is completely the one can it be called the many."[2] Similarly, in the context of defining his *Category of the Ultimate* (i.e., creativity-many-one) Whitehead states that, "The term 'many' presupposes the term 'one' and the term 'one' presupposes the term 'many'" (PR, p. 21). The first principles governing the Hua-yen Buddhist and Whiteheadian speculative frameworks, these being *śūnyatā* (i.e., universal relativity or dependent coorigination) in the first case and creativity or creative synthesis in the second, both involve theories of universal relativity or arising into existence through causation, i.e., causal processes of fusing manyness into oneness, multiplicity into unity, disjunction into conjunction or the macrocosm into the microcosm, from the standpoint of unification provided by each perspectival event in nature. Moreover, both creativity and *śūnyatā* function to establish a profound ontological togetherness of events within the unity of each occasion. And further still, the ontological and cosmic togetherness of the universe within each event is dipolar; one and many, subject and object, inner and outer, as well as physical and mental are all synthesized into a non-dual union of opposites or state of dipolar fusion. Again, creativity and *śūnyatā* function within the context of their respective theoretical frameworks to seriously undermine the notion of substance or independent self-existence, what Buddhism terms *svabhāva* or "own being." Finally, neither creativity nor *śūnyatā* are reified as having any independent reality of their own but become actual only by virtue of their embodiments in particular momentary events.

However, according to the process theory of creativity, "universal relativity" always means *non-symmetrical* or one-way relativity as opposed to the *symmetrical* relativity propounded by Hua-yen Buddhism, which is so superbly clarified in the works of Charles Hartshorne. Whereas "arising into existence through causation" always means causation from the past in the process framework, in Hua-yen, causation works from past, present and future directions simultaneously. The many unified into a new one by the principle of creativity always signifies an event's historical *antecedents* as opposed to the notion of *śūnyatā* or dependent coorigination wherein the many signify not only a dharma's antecedents but its contemporaries and successors as well. The cosmic togetherness achieved through creative synthesis is not a total togetherness of the sort extolled by Hua-yen but a momentary production of novel togetherness, i.e., an *emergent* togetherness of antecedents into a new unit of actuality. The dipolar fusion characterizing events as a function of creative synthesis is not the simultaneous-mutual-penetration or simultaneous-mutual-fusion of opposites such as subject and object or one and many as is established by *śūnyatā*, but is rather a cumulative penetration or cumulative fusion of manyness-into-oneness or object-into-subject in accordance with the cause-to-effect structure of actuality as posited by the process theory. And finally, the critique of substance which accompanies the process doctrine of creativity is not the complete abandonment of substance required by Buddhist *śūnyatā* in its aspect as *niḥsvabhāvatā* or non-substantiality, but a radical reformulation of substance theory in terms of process categories; for an event is in fact a substance with unique and irreducible selfhood in that it is a self-creative experience constitutive of its own novel and aesthetic unity. However, it is free of substantialization in certain restrictive senses of the term, such as simple location, independent existence and static permanence. Overall, each of the above distinctions between Hua-yen Buddhism and Whiteheadian process theory are special cases of a central critical problem; namely, interpenetration vs. cumulative penetration or simultaneous-mutual-fusion vs. successive fusion.

Whiteheadian creativity functions similarly to dependent coorigination in Hua-yen Buddhism in that both fuse manyness into oneness. However, for Whitehead the many refers to only the *past* world of fully finished historic facts which are unified into a *new* occasion diverse from the many which it unifies. In his classic definition of the theory of creativity, Whitehead writes:

> Creativity is the principle of *novelty*. An actual occasion is a novel entity diverse from any entity in the "many" which it unifies. Thus, "creativity" introduces novelty into the content of the many, which are the universe disjunctively. . . . The ultimate metaphysical principle is the advance from disjunction to conjunction, creating a novel entity other than the entities given in disjunction. (PR, p. 21)

He goes on to say that the ultimate result of an act of creative synthesis (also termed "concrescence") is the "production of novel togetherness" (PR, p. 21). Thus, whereas both Whitehead and Hua-yen grasp co-causation and cosmic togetherness as being at the very heart of actuality, for Whitehead causal origination is a *creative* process resulting in an emergent togetherness or novel togetherness, as opposed to the total togetherness established by *śūnyatā* (universal relativity) and *pratītyasamutpāda* (dependent coorigination). In contrast to the dialectical interpenetration of the many and the one as propounded by Ŭisang in his "Ocean Seal" through such standard Hua-yen doctrinal formulas like "In one is all and in many are one," or "One is identical to all and many are identical to one,"Whitehead instead asserts: "The many become one and are *increased* by one (PR, p. 21). Thus, the multiplicity of events synthesized by a creative act are not simply fused together into a unity; they are also "increased by one." For this reason then, Whitehead describes the metaphysical process of fusing multiplicity into unity as a "creative advance into novelty" (PR, p. 28).

Closely related to Whitehead's category of creativity is his principle of "universal relativity," which states that "every item of the universe, including all the other actual entities, are constituents in the constitution of any one actual entity" (PR, p. 148). Again, the principle of relativity asserts that "every item in the universe is involved in each concrescence" (PR, p. 22). Whitehead's principle of universal relativity is at once reminiscent of the Buddhist concept of *śūnyatā* which was translated as "relativity" and even "universal relativity" by the pioneering Soviet Buddhologist Th. Stcherbatsky, who writes:

> The central conception of Mahāyāna was their relativity (*śūnyatā*). Since we use the term 'relative' to describe the fact that a thing can be identified only

> by mentioning its relations to something else, and becomes meaningless without these relations. . . we safely, for want of a better solution, can translate the word *śūnya* by relative or contingent, and the term *śūnyatā* by relativity or contingency.[3]

Thus, both Whiteheadian creativity and Hua-yen Buddhist *śūnyatā* function to establish the primacy of *relatio* over *substantia* at the metaphysical level of discourse. However, in Hua-yen Buddhism, *śūnyatā* or "universal relativity" designates that each *dharma* is constituted by its internal relations to present and futural events as well as to those of the past, whereas for Whitehead, the principles of creativity and universal relativity signify that each event is internally related only to all prior occasions. While the principle of creativity specifies that only antecedent actualities are included by each new act of synthesis, the principle of relativity, operating as the principle of creativity in reverse, as it were, specifies that each actuality is itself included only in all subsequent acts of synthesis. Therefore, while further defining his principle of relativity Whitehead says: "It belongs to the nature of a 'being' that it is a potential for every 'becoming' " (PR, p. 22). For Whitehead, to be means to be available for inclusion by all future actualities, while in turn including all prior actualities. In other words, to be means to potentially exert causal influence on all subsequent events, while receiving causal influence from all antecedent events. This stands in sharp contrast to Hua-yen Buddhism wherein to be means to be included by, as well as to include, all other actualities, past, present and future alike. Or in causal terms, for Hua-yen Buddhism, to be is to exert causal influence on all events simultaneously, including antecedents and contemporaries in addition to successors, and in turn to receive causal influence from them all as well.

We can now carefully analyze the distinctions between Whiteheadian process metaphysics and Hua-yen Buddhism in terms of the latter tradition's technical categories of "having power" (*yu-li*) vs. "lacking power" (*wu-li*). As explained earlier, in Hua-yen Buddhism each dharma arising into non-inherent existence through dependent co-origination is analyzed under two basic aspects, that of having power (as expanded) in so far as it is an active "cause" (*yin*) for everything else, and that of lacking power (as contracted) in so far as it is a passive "effect" (*kuo*) of everything else, being said to contain all dharmas as contracted and to be contained by them all as expanded. Consequently, each dharma is completely "powerful" as well as completely "powerless." However, in Whitehead's process theory, each actual occasion is powerful only in so far as it exerts causal influence on all subsequent events and is powerless only in so far as it receives causal influence from all antecedent events, and therefore contains all past occasions as powerless and is contained by all future occasions as powerful. Thus, when Whitehead continually asserts that every event both "houses" and "pervades" its entire universe, he means to say that each event houses its entire past universe in its aspect as "lacking power," i.e., as receiving causal influence, and that it pervades its entire future universe in its aspect as "having power," i.e., as exerting causal influence.

As the eminent process philosopher Charles Hartshorne has clarified, whereas both Hua-yen Buddhism and Whitehead propound the universal relativity of all events, for Hua-yen these relations are *symmetrically* structured or internal at both ends, while for the latter these relations are *asymmetrically* structured, or internal at one end and external at the other. Arguing in favor of the process view Hartshorne writes: "One-way relativity (positive in one direction, negative in the other) covers the whole story. Relativity as directional or non-symmetrical is the absolute principle."[4] Thus, according to the principle of one-way or non-symmetrical relativity, while the past is contained in the present, the present is neither contained in the past nor the future in the present, as is the case for the symmetrically structured mode of universal relativity espoused by Hua-yen.

This strictly asymmetrical structure of causal relatedness or universal relativity is carefully and convincingly articulated by Hartshorne in his work, *Creative Synthesis and Philosophic Method* wherein he argues that the "prejudice for symmetry" or the "fallacy of misplaced symmetry" has tacitly structured the history of both Western and Eastern speculative thought since antiquity. Philosophers, says Hartshorne, have assumed that all events are either simply mutually inclusive (e.g. Hua-yen, Bradley, Royce) or mutually exclusive (e.g., Russell, Hume). Both of these alternatives presuppose a symmetrical theory of relatedness, the asymmetrical view being a major innovation emerging in Whiteheadian process metaphysics. Whereas adherents of the theories of mutual inclusiveness and mutual exclusiveness have launched devastating critical arguments against the other, the asymmetrical view of causality has as yet never been refuted. Hartshorne further argues that Nāgārjuna's celebrated critical attack on causal relations in the opening *ślokas* of his *Fundamentals of the Middle Way* also presupposes the prejudice for symmetry.[5] Nāgārjuna considers four alternatives with respect to the notion of causal relations: cause and effect are either identical, different, both identical and different or neither identical nor different. But according to Hartshorne's polemic, all four options enumerated by Nāgārjuna are developed in strictly symmetrical terms. He argues that the concept of asymmetrical relatedness—internal at one end and external at the other—is wholly ignored by Nāgārjuna, and has never been successfully repudiated. Hence, according to Hartshorne, the symmetrical mode of universal relativity in either of its two forms, mutual inclusiveness or mutual exclusiveness, essentially represents an extremist view, whereas the asymmetrical view of universal relativity represents the true middle way extolled by Buddhist systems of thought. Hartshorne proceeds to show that even such eminent process thinkers in the West as Henri Bergson have assumed the symmetrical structure of causal relations arguing for the "interpenetration" of temporal moments, despite the fact that Bergson otherwise elaborates a polemic for the unidirectional and cumulative structure of time. Hartshorne writes:

> Bergson asked, are the moments of duration mutually external or do they "interpenetrate"? The question implies symmetry for either answer. Yet, Bergson believed in a basic asymmetry of time, a closed past and an open future. Unluckily he failed to notice that "interpenetration" implied symmetry. He should have said, "The past penetrates the present," but not the present the past. Penetration is one thing, interpenetration is another.[6]

One might argue here that although in the temporal sense there is only asymmetrical relatedness or what has been termed in this study a doctrine of "cumulative penetration," there can still be a symmetrical relatedness or interpenetration between events in the spatial sense. Yet, Hartshorne forcefully argues that not even spatial relations are symmetrically structured, because relatedness between events is a function of causation, and causation means relation by *inheritance*, which is always temporal, and thus, asymmetrical in structure. "Space," states Hartshorne, is simply the name for "multiple lines of inheritance."[7]

Hartshorne propounds that the doctrine of asymmetrical universal relativity provides for the self-creativity or freedom of decision which is felt in the living immediacy of experience. The symmetrical theory of mutual externality provides ample space for freedom, creativity and novelty, but it does not account for causal continuity or inheritance of order. And the symmetrical theory of mutual inclusiveness accounts for causal connection, but it allows no creative freedom and emergent novelty, in that each event is completely constituted by its causal relations to everything else. However, the option of asymmetrical causation allows for a real dependence and a real independence, since asymmetry implies that relations are closed or determinate at one end while being open or indeterminate at the other, providing space for both causal continuity and creative novelty.

The polemic here is that the Hua-yen Buddhist theory of total non-obstructed interpenetration and unhindered mutual containment with its underlying symmetrical infrastructure has accounted for complete ontological togetherness, cohesiveness and solidarity, but at the expense of all creativeness, novelty and freedom. Each dharma can be exhaustively factored or reductively analyzed into its causal relations and supportive conditions without remainder. By definition, total determinism is entailed by such a view in that each dharma is simply an effect of its manifold of causes: there is no creativity, freedom or novelty. And moreover, since each dharma is merely an effect reducible to its causes, it is wholy devoid of *svabhāva,* i.e., substance or unique selfhood. For there is complete mutual penetration (*hsiang yung*) and mutual identification (*hsiang chi*) between all dharmas in the universe.

Whitehead's doctrines of creative advance and one-way relativity also assert that each event arises into actuality at each moment through a vast multiplicity of causes and conditions. Yet, in contradistinction to the Hua-yen position, no event can be reductively factored into its causal relations or exhaustively analyzed into its antecedent conditions without remainder. For even if all the contents of an event are causally inherited there is still at least one factor which cannot be inherited, namely, the *unity* of them all in a single, unified occasion of experience; for this an *emergent synthesis* is required. This is to say that even if all the elements of an arising event are given for synthesis, even the organizational pattern for synthesis itself, the *act* of synthesis must still be new, i.e., an emergent-spontaneous creation of the present moment. In Whiteheadian process theory then, an occasion's self-creativity is not derived from anything else; in an important sense, therefore, events *may* be conceived *in themselves* without making reference to external conditioning factors. Thus, according to the process view, self-creativity, emergent novelty and spontaneous freedom of decision are all intrinsic to actuality itself. The manifold of antecedent causes at best "condition" an event; but the final element in the process of experiential synthesis is always a spontaneous decision or creative act, a novel response to causal stimuli. Hartshorne's forceful polemic is worth quoting in full here:

> Let me restate the basic argument: the stimuli moulding an experience are many: the five or more senses are operating, memory is relating us, at least unconsciously, to thousands of incidents of the past: but all this multiplicity of influence is to produce a single unitary experience, yours or mine right now, let us say. The effect is one; the causes however, are many, literally hundreds of thousands, billions even, considering the cells in our brain, for example. This vast multitude of factors must flow together to produce a single new entity, the experience of the moment. The many stimuli are given, and certainly they tell us much about the response. But it is a logical impossibility that they should tell us all. An *emergent synthesis* is needed, to

> decide just how each item is to blend in a single complex sensory-emotional-intellectual whole. . . . To experience is a free act or nothing intelligible.[8]

It is furthermore precisely this notion of an event as self-creative experience constitutive of its own novel and aesthetic unity which confers to it a degree of unique selfhood, intrinsic reality and ontological integrity not accorded to the fundamental units of existence in Hua-yen Buddhism. As Whitehead asserts, the concept of an occasion of experience as self-creative satisfies Spinoza's criterion for substance, namely, *causa sui* or self-causation (PR, p. 88). Each occasion of experience emerging into actuality through creative synthesis or self-constitution is a novel entity diverse from its multiplicity of causes, and is in this sense a "substance" with irreducible selfhood. Thus, according to process theory there is no sameness (Skt. *samatā*) or mutual identity (Chi. *hsiang chi*) of all events as in the symmetrical framework of Hua-yen since each occasion is a novel and unique happening with irreducible own-being which transcends all others in a sense just as profound as that manner in which it includes them all in its own composition through novel acts of creative synthesis. Thus, in the final analysis, creative freedom and emergent novelty are a function of the non-symmetrical or *cumulative* structure of actuality. To reiterate Whitehead's summary definition of his Category of the Ultimate or principle of creativity: "'Creativity' is the principle of *novelty*. An actual occasion is a novel entity diverse from any entity in the 'many' which it unifies" (PR, p. 21).

Recently, Nishida Kitarō, the foremost systematic speculative philosopher of Japan, has endeavored to make creative self-determination intrinsic to events while retaining the entire Hua-yen (Jap. Kegon) architectonic framework of unobstructed interfusion as underscored by a wholly symmetrical infrastructure. Nishida elaborates a metaphysics wherein discontinuous moment-events of pure experience devoid of subject-object dualism are each identified with the eternal now or absolute present, understood as "creative points" wherein past, present and future events are all unified in a symmetrical patterning of internal relations through acts of free self-determination. Nishida articulates his notion of microcosmic-qua-macrocosmic events or creative points as follows:

> The world is a creative world filled with life. Our selves are "creative points" of such a world. Leibniz called the monad a "metaphysical point," but I conceive each individual self as a creative point of the historic world. It extends to the eternal future and to the eternal past of the point of self-determination of the absolute present.[9]

One eminent scholar on Nishida Kitarō's thought, Takeuchi Yoshinori, comments on Nishida's notion of the eternal now as below:

> Bergson and more recently an American philosopher, Professor Charles Hartshorne, think that all events of the past are restored in a metaphysical remembrance. It seems that Nishida thought through the problem above more radically: not only events of the past, but also those of the future, are all present in the eternal now.[10]

However, one must ask how anything new can truly emerge into existence, or whether any true creativity is really possible, if all events—past, present and future—are already contained in each moment of experience? In an asymmetrical theory of causality, relations are closed or determinate at one end while being open or indeterminate at the other, allowing for both a real dependence and a real independence, thus providing space for self-creativity and emergent novelty as well as for causal continuity and the inheritance of order. However, in a symmetrical theory of causal relatedness as posited by Nishida, relations are closed or determinate at both ends so that there is virtually no place for creativeness, novelty and freedom in such a framework. Nishida fails to address the critical problem at issue here, but instead ambiguously conjoins the notions of total interrelation and interpenetration with those of creativeness and free self-determination, despite the inherent contradictions which accompany this conjunction. Moreover, one must ask why it is at all necessary to formulate an extreme position of mutual inclusiveness when a doctrine of one-way inclusiveness provides for ontological togetherness and cosmic solidarity through complex multiple causation as well as for creative freedom and emergent novelty through free self-determination.

To conclude, both Whiteheadian creativity and Hua-yen *śūnyatā* comprehend the causal process at the base of actuality in terms of a *dialectical penetration* of dipolar opposites, such as subjectivity and objectivity, unity and multiplicity or oneness and manyness. However, for Hua-yen this dialectical process of dipolar fusion is symmetrical in structure, i.e., subjectivity-into-objectivity and objectivity-into-subjectivity or unity-into-multiplicity and multiplicity-into-unity, in a simultaneous and mutual way; while for Whitehead this process is strictly asymmetrical and cumulative in structure, i.e., objectivity-into-subjectivity or multiplicity-into-unity, within a radically temporal framework. It has been argued throughout this chapter that for Hua-yen, each dharma can be exhaustively analyzed into its field of causal relations, thus resulting in a condition of total determinism and non-substantiality; whereas for Whitehead, no event can be reductively factored into its causal relations without remainder, since what cannot be inherited is the unity of all causes in a new occasion of experience, which requires a creative act of emergent synthesis. As such, self-creativity and emergent novelty become intrinsic to each event without exception. And insofar as an event is a self-creative experience constitutive of its own novel unity, it is a substance with unique selfhood and intrinsic own-being; for since an occasion's character of *sui generis* or self-creativity is not derived from anything else, in a crucial sense it can be conceived *in itself* without reference to external conditions. Therefore, in a theory of interpenetration, the cosmological values of togetherness, solidarity and unification are emphasized at the expense of such equally significant values as creativeness, novelty and freedom. Or in other terms, for Hua-yen the central value at the cosmological level is *universal harmony*. Yet, as Whitehead emphasizes in his book entitled *Adventure of Ideas*, the value of harmony must always be balanced by that of "adventure" (AI, pp. 273–283), which is the primary internal dynamic animating what he terms the "creative advance into novelty." The advantage of a metaphysics of cumulative penetration is thus that it theoretically accounts for all the togetherness, solidarity and unification in addition to all the creativeness, novelty and freedom, as well as all the harmonization and adventure which is demanded for any balanced descriptive generalization of the cosmos.

In the final analysis, the basic discrepancy between Hua-yen Buddhism and Whiteheadian process theory is this: the Hua-yen principle of *śūnyatā* or universal relativity accords a primacy to causal relatedness in terms of a dialectical interpenetration between the many and the one; whereas Whitehead's Category of the Ultimate (creativity-many-one) accords a primacy to the principle of creativity, in terms of a cumulative penetration of manyness-into-oneness, such that the many become one and are *increased* by one. This primacy accorded to creative freedom over causal determination in Whitehead's metaphysics is succinctly expressed by Hartshorne who writes: "The causal drift itself is merely the mass of data formed by acts of freedom already enacted on different levels. . . . Causality is crystallized freedom, freedom is causality in the making."[11] And elsewhere, he writes: "Process is creative synthesis, the many into a new one producing a new many—and so on forever. The synthesis is creative, for how could a plurality dictate its own increase?. . . . The causal conditions for each free act are previous acts of freedom; creativity feeds upon its own products and upon nothing else!"[12] It might finally be suggested here that the Whiteheadian hermeneutic, especially its analysis of creativity, can be used to dramatically revise the traditional interpretation of Hua-yen Buddhist patterns of thought. Through Whitehead's Category of the Ultimate, the

Hua-yen perspective can be radically restructured so that the dialectical process of dipolar fusion between the many and the one is adjusted into a framework of cumulative penetration, whereby the movement of plurality-into-unity and unity-into-plurality becomes a temporal rhythm which is completely animated by the emergent-spontaneity and plenary creativeness at the depths of actuality.

CHAPTER 7

Causality as the Vector Transmission of Feelings

Section I

Having examined at length the doctrine of creative synthesis in Whitehead's categoreal scheme, this discussion focuses on the second pillar of the metaphysics of cumulative penetration, namely, the theory of feelings or prehensions, which calls for a detailed analysis of Whitehead's general doctrine of causal transmission. This analysis is especially indebted to William Christian's text, *An Introduction to Whitehead's Metaphysics*, which clarifies the modes of "social transcendence" in Whitehead's metaphysics so that in important senses events exclude one another from their internal constitutions which counterbalances the various modes of "social immanence" whereby events include each other through the transference of causally efficacious feeling-tones.[1] Christian undertakes the analysis of the various modes of social immanence vs. social transcendence in an effort to determine the "experiential boundaries" of Whitehead's actual occasions with categoreal precision and exactitude. Christian's study especially clarifies the manner in which occasions located in the three temporal periods of past, present and future are immanent or transcendent to any given actuality; it therefore has special relevance in demarcating the distinctions between Hua-yen Buddhism and Whitehead's process metaphysics. Thus, through an analysis of the various modes of social transcendence vs. social immanence in actual occasions we can proceed to examine Whitehead's sustained project of "making clear the notion of 'being present in another entity'." The sense in which events are present or immanent in each other is not in the sense of co-presence or mutual immanence, but in the sense of what has been termed in this work a "cumulative presence" or "cumulative immanence" which occurs through the causal objectification or conformal reproduction of the past in the present through re-enactive feeling-tones. However, before undertaking a detailed analysis of Whitehead's theory of causal process, a brief word is needed concerning his conception of speculative metaphysics in general.

Whitehead conceives of speculative metaphysics as an effort to frame a system of well-defined generic categories or ultimate notions of the highest generality, ". . . in terms of which every element of our experience can be interpreted" (PR, p. 3). A categoreal scheme in Whitehead's sense is a tentative formulation of the ultimate generalities, whose root presuppositions it makes fully explicit so as to make them open to rigorous critical evaluation and empirical verification. A concept becomes a metaphysical category when it is universalized so as to apply to every case of reality without exception, and is derived methodologically through a process of philosophic generalization. Whitehead states: "In this description of philosophic method, the term 'philosophic generalization' has meant 'the utilization of specific notions, applying to a restricted group of facts, for the divinization of the generic notions which apply to all facts" (PR, p. 5). A categoreal scheme of ultimate notions is thus arrived at through the methodological procedure of imaginatively generalizing fundamental concepts drawn from contemporary modes of inquiry, such as quantum and relativity physics (e.g., field theory, energetic quanta, space-time events, vector transmission), the biological sciences (e.g., organism, cell theory, genetic inheritance) or mathematical logic (e.g., multiple-term relations). Such concepts become ultimate notions when they are universally applicable to every fact in nature. However, Whitehead's categoreal scheme of ultimate notions has been methodologically derived also through the descriptive generalization of experiential immediacy as disclosed at the prereflective level of primordial feelings. Whitehead asserts: "The elucidation of immediate experience is the sole justification for any thought. . ." (PR, p. 4). Hence, Whitehead's doctrine of causality as a direct transmission of emotional intensity between occasions of experience is not only modeled after the "vector" transference of energy (i.e., directed flow-patterns of electromagnetic conduction) between vibratory quantum-field events as characterized by contemporary physics or the genetic inheritance of data as conceived in the new biological sciences, but is also based upon the empirical data of what William James has termed "felt transitions" or "transitive feelings" which arise in the immediacy of experience through perceptual awareness in its primordial mode of causal feeling or causal efficacy.

Whitehead's categoreal scheme elaborates two modes of process, nontemporal concrescence and temporal transition, or microprocess and macroprocess (PR, pp. 210–15). These two modes of process are analyzed in terms of genetic and coordinate division, respectively. Concrescence is the process of creative synthesis, an occasion's nontemporal genesis from the past world of pluralistic events into a perspectival subjective unity of immediate feeling. Transition or supersession refers to an occasion's functioning as a causally efficacious object conditioning all subsequent events. Genetic division is the analysis of an occasion in its process of concrescence, tracing its growth throughout various phases of integration as underscored by teleological or final causation. In contrast, coordinate division is the analysis of the fully finished occasion after its concrescence has terminated or "closed up," focusing on its function as an objectively immortal efficient cause which conditions all future occasions through historic routes of transmission or chains of inheritance.[2]

During nontemporal concrescence, an occasion of experience emerges into actuality as a unit-pulsation of emotional intensity through its prehensions or causal feelings of antecedent data (all past events) creatively synthesizing them into an aesthetic pattern of novel togetherness. Whitehead writes:

> Each actual entity is conceived as an act of experience arising out of data. It is a process of "feeling" the many data, so as to absorb them into the unity of one individual "satisfaction." Here "feeling" is the term used for the basic generic operation of passing from the objectivity of the data to the subjectivity of the actual entity in question. (PR, p. 40)

Concrescence or creative synthesis occurs through various phases of growth, commencing with the "conformal" phase where past actualities are merely reproduced in the immediate occasion through simple physical feelings, followed by a "supplemental" phase characterized by an inrush of originative and conceptual feelings, including an "aesthetic" stage (involving valuation and purposive feelings) and in the higher phases of experience, an "intellectual" stage (involving comparative, conscious, propositional, and imaginative feelings). The whole process of experiential syntheses is governed by a subjective aim, conceived as a "lure for feeling" or harmonic value-pattern prescribed by God in his primordial nature as the principle of limitation. Each occasion of experience is thus "dipolar," having both a "physical" pole and a "mental" pole, the physical pole constituting the conformal phases of causal reproduction and the mental pole constituting the supplemental phases of conceptual origination. In the conformal phase, an eternal object or value-pattern in the objective datum is reproduced, re-enacted, or repeated.[3] It is characterized by pure reception, inheritance or reiteration of data such that the past is restored in the present occasion. In the supplemental phase, additional eternal objects ingress or influx to enhance and augment the data. The aesthetic stage of the supplemental phase is characterized by subjective forms (personalizing responses) which are emotional, purposive and valuational, and which determine the relative importance of items in the data in respect to the subjective aim or the governing ideal of the concrescence. The intellectual stage of supplementation characterizes the higher grade of experience, introducing more complex experiential syntheses such as contrasts and comparative feelings whereby conscious awareness emerges. During this phase there arises "transmuted" feelings wherein a multiplicity of data are fused into a single dominating impression (according to an identifying characteristic shared by all members of the nexus of data) as well as "reverted" feelings wherein novel conceptual patterns or combinations of eternal objects are originated. Finally, the whole process of integrating the various feelings consummates in a terminal "satisfaction" whereupon the occasion "closes up" as a single, determinate feeling of the antecedent universe. This satisfaction represents an exhaustion or contentment of the creative urge or principle of unrest by fulfillment of its categoreal demands. Moreover, it achieves an aesthetic-value experience at maximum depth of intensity of feeling because antithetical elements in the initial data are entered as positive content into the final synthesis in the form of patterned contrasts instead of being eliminated as incompatible material. Whitehead writes: "This 'aim at contrast' is the expression of the ultimate creative purpose that each unification shall achieve some maximum depth of intensity of feeling. . ." (PR, p. 249). This achievement of patterned contrast in the satisfaction enjoyed by each unit-pulsation is a *dipolar* synthesis of ideal opposites, being both one and many, subject and object, physical and mental and emotional and conceptual. A simplified diagram of nontemporal concrescence as adumbrated above might appear as on the following page.

Section II

A more focused and detailed consideration of Whitehead's doctrine of causation is called for. This involves a closer analysis of the conformal or reproductive phase of concrescence which deals with the manner in which some entities become present in other entities through causal transmission (the supplemental phases all being originative operations introducing novel content into the entities).

Each occasion of experience arises into existence momentarily as a

Causality as the Vector Transmission of Feelings

The Genetic Analysis of Experiential Synthesis
(Nontemporal Concrescence) in Whitehead's Process Metaphysics

Final Satisfaction

A single, determinate feeling of actuality. The achievement of aesthetic-value feeling and intensity of emotion through patterned contrast. Occasion closes up and superjects into future as an efficient cause conditioning all subsequent events.

↑

Supplemental Phase

Inrush of originative and conceptual feelings. More complex syntheses and integrations.

- Intellectual Phase

  Comparative, propositional, imaginative, judgmental feelings. Achievement of conscious perception.

- Aesthetic Phase

  Emotional, valuational and purposive feelings.

↑

Conformal Phase

Reception. Inheritance. Reenaction. Sympathy. Feeling of feeling. Conformation. Vector transmission. Transference of causal efficacy.

↑

Initial Data: Antecedent Actualities

unit-pulsation of emotional intensity by way of its feelings or prehensions of antecedent data, which were themselves events of emotional intensity. Prehension or feeling is thus the basic mechanism whereby data is absorbed, appropriated, assimilated, included, internalized or objectified into the composition of an emerging experience. Prehension is a metaphysical generalization encompassing three ordinarily disconnected notions, namely, memory, causation, and perception, all three being a feeling of antecedents. To feel (perceive) a prior event is to be causally conditioned by it; both causation and perception are aspects of memory—an awareness of the past. Whitehead writes:

> A pure physical prehension is how an occasion in its immediacy of being absorbs another occasion which has passed into the objective immortality of its not-being. It is how the past lives in the present. It is causation. It is memory. It is perception. . . . (AI, p. 237)

A simple physical feeling is a prehension whose datum is another event. Such physical feelings constitute an act of causal transmission:

> A simple physical feeling is an act of causation. The actual entity which is the initial datum is the 'cause,' the simple physical feeling is the 'effect,' and

the subject entertaining the simple physical feeling is the actual entity 'conditioned' by the effect. . . . Therefore simple physical feelings will also be called 'causal' feelings. (PR, p. 236)

A causal feeling is technically termed a "vector" by Whitehead, indicating the literal transference of a throb of emotional intensity between occasions of experience, or a pattern of energetic transmission between vibratory events. It is this . . ."vector character which transfers the cause into the effect" (PR, p. 237). In his notion of vectors Whitehead makes a direct analogy between the transition of feelings through successive emotional states in the stream of consciousness and the conduction of energetic radiation through electromagnetic fields as conceived in contemporary physical science:

> There is thus an analogy between the transference of energy from particular occasion to particular occasion in physical nature and the transference of affective tone, with its emotional energy, from one occasion to another in any human personality. The object-to-subject structure of human experience is reproduced in physical nature by this vector relation of particular to particular. (AI, p. 188)

This vector transference of emotional intensity from cause-to-effect or from object-to-subject directly underlies the *cumulative* structure or the unidirectional and *asymmetrical* patterning of the temporal process: "This passage of the cause into the effect is the cumulative character of time. The irreversibility of time depends on this character" (PR, p. 237). "Vector" is a technical term borrowed from mathematical physics signifying a magnitude with *direction.* Whitehead believes this property of directedness is fundamental to the causal process whereby energy is transferred between events: "Energy passes from particular occasion to particular occasion. At each point there is a flux, with a quantitative flow and a definite direction" (AI, p. 185). This directional or vector character of causal transmission is its one-way or asymmetrical nature. Moreover, it is this vector character of simple physical feeling that enables one entity to become present in another entity: "Feelings are 'vectors'; for they feel what is *there* and transform it into what is *here*" (PR, p. 87). Not only does the vector transmission of causal efficacy between events transform the there into the here, but also the then into the now, such that the far is made near and the past is made present, which wholly undermines the character of what Whitehead terms "simple location," the notion that an event has only one locus in the spatiotemporal continuum while being completely absent from all other times and places. But the prehensive unification or occasion of experience constitutes its data into a perspectival here-now without losing the vector marks of its origins in the there-then, for a vector is always an act of causal transference from a definite source, with a definite direction and a definite quantity of efficient power.

The vector transference of past into present, cause into effect, or objectivity into subjectivity through simple physical feelings is characterized by Whitehead as a "flow of feeling." "Thus the cause passes on its feeling to be reproduced by the new subject as its own, and yet as inseparable from the cause. There is a flow of feeling" (PR, p. 237). But as Christain emphasizes in his study of Whitehead's thought, such phrases as "flow of feeling" or the "transference of a throb of emotional intensity" must not be taken out of context to imply that the cause is present in the effect in its subjective immediacy. Subjective immediacy is characterized by the feeling of self-creativity or the feeling of the indeterminate becoming fully determinate, at the conclusion of which the emergent occasion closes up, perishes, and superjects over into its role of an *objectively immortal* causal condition to be felt by all future occasions. This is to say that although events are virtually present in other events, they are present only as *objectified* data. In Christian's words, there is no "spilling over of immediacy" between occasions. Thus, Whitehead writes: "Simple physical feelings embody the reproductive character of nature, and also the objective immortality of the past" (PR, p. 238).

The process of causal objectification, then, occurs through *reproduction*. At a more technical level of analysis, Whitehead describes causal prehension in terms of three factors, which he enumerates as "(a) the 'subject' which is prehending, . . . (b) the 'datum' which is prehended; (c) the 'subjective form' which is *how* that subject prehends that datum" (PR, p. 23). The subject therefore reproduces the objective datum by producing a feeling of the datum with a conformal subjective form: "A simple physical feeling enjoys a characteristic which has been variously described as 're-enaction,' 'reproduction' and 'conformation'"(PR, p. 238). Consequently, the flow of feeling or transmission of emotional intensity must be understood as reproduction, re-enaction or repetition of the datum with a conformal subjective form and not a literal transference of the past into the present in its living subjective immediacy. The re-enacted subjective forms of simple physical feelings guarantee the effective transfer of energetic force from past to present, but only as objectified.

Whitehead states that causal feelings are "conformal feelings" (PR, p. 237–38). The subjective form of the present occasion reproduces and conforms to the feeling of the past occasion, "conformance" meaning the ". . . identity of subjective form inherited conformally from one occasion to the other" (AI, p. 186). Or again, "In the conformal feelings the *how* of feeling reproduces what is felt. Some conformation is necessary as a basis of vector transition, whereby the past is synthesized with the present" (PR, p. 164). Whitehead also articulates his concept of causation as the conformation of feeling as follows: "The primitive form of physical experience is emotional—blind emotion—received as felt elsewhere in another occasion and conformally appropriated as a subjective passion" (PR, p. 162). He then proceeds to reformulate his technical notion of conformal appropriation, in the sense of re-enactive subjective form, in the moral-aesthetic terms of sympathy and feeling of feeling. He continues: "In the language appropriate to the higher stages of experience, the primitive element is *sympathy*, that is, feeling the feeling *in* another and feeling conformally *with* another" (PR, p. 162). Finally, Whitehead restates his theory of causal vector transference in terms of inheritance through historic routes of transmission: "The crude aboriginal character of direct perception is inheritance. What is inherited is feeling-tone with evidence of its origin: in other words, vector feeling-tone" (PR, p. 119).

Whitehead's doctrine of causation through simple physical feeling is thus elaborated in such varied terms as the "flow of feeling," "transference of emotional intensity," "conformation," "reception," "derivation," "re-enaction," "sympathy," "feeling of feeling," "vector transmission" and "inheritance of data." As opposed to the notion that causality is a mere "habit of thought" as argued by David Hume, or a "form of thought" as argued by Immanuel Kant, Whitehead argues that causation is a real transference of efficient power from one event to another, in an efficacious actual world. Furthermore, Whitehead argues that such causation can be directly and immediately felt in the primordial mode of perception underlying sensation and cognition, termed "causal efficacy." The importance of this lies, as pointed out by Hume, in the fact that the justification for all inductive inference and scientific prediction stands or falls on the strength of one's doctrine of causation.

In his challenging critique of causality, Hume argues that causal transmission or necessary connection does not present itself as a datum discoverable in the analysis of experience, and therefore is not empirically verifiable. Hume consequently gives causality an associationist's psychological explanation, describing it as a mere "habit of thought," acquired through the repeated observation of constantly conjoined occurrences having a certain sequential order. Whitehead critiques Hume's empiricism after the manner of William James' radical empiricism, which recognizes conjunctive relations, psychic fringes and felt transitions to be directly given empirical data included in the stream of consciousness during states of pure or immediate experience (i.e., experience in the living present anterior to the subject-object distinction). James stated concerning our experience of the stream of consciousness that in addition to the overt "succession of feelings" reported by Hume there are also subtle "feelings of succession" which constitute the connective tissue between discrete moments of sensation, this being what James termed "the feelings of causality at work."[4] Whitehead terms this level of causal feeling "perception in the mode of causal efficacy," and introduces it as the aboriginal stratum of experience underlying "presentational immediacy" (sense perception) and "symbolic reference" (cognition). Whitehead phenomenologically describes these felt transitions arising as pre-reflective experiences in the perceptual mode of causal efficacy in terms of a present state of emotional intensity felt as welling up from the immediate past and surging forth into the immediate future within an ongoing stream of consciousness. For instance, Whitehead writes:

> The former mode [causal efficacy] produces percepta which are vague, not to be controlled, heavy with emotion: it produces the sense of derivation from an immediate past, and of passage to an immediate future; a sense of emotional feeling, belonging to oneself in the past, passing into oneself in the present, . . . towards oneself in the future; a sense of influx of influence from other vaguer presences. . . . This is our general sense of existence, as one item among others, in an efficacious actual world. (PR, p. 178)

In presentational immediacy or sense perception, the dim and vague vector feeling-tones inherited from the past and conformally appropriated as a subjective passion are projected onto a contemporary spatial region, so as to decorate it with clear and distinct sensory qualities, i.e., colors, sounds, scents, flavors, tactile pressures, and precise geometrical configurations. It is the human body, conceived by Whitehead as a complex amplifier, which transforms the vague and dim feeling-tones of causal efficacy into the higher phases of experience in presentational immediacy and symbolic reference (PR, p. 119). Obscure vector feeling-tones from the past are inherited by the bodily organism in dim pulsations, re-enacted and conformally appropriated, and then enhanced, intensified, amplified, and magnified through "transmutations" and novel "reversions" by high-grade living occasions along the bodily routes of causal transmission. However, the discrete, atomistic sensations of presentational immediacy bear within themselves no reference to past or future, and thus do not exhibit necessary connection or causal transference. For it is only the subtle felt transitions in the nonsensory and noncognitive form of perception in the primordial mode of causal efficacy which disclose the past rushing into the present and the present rushing into the future, thus conferring on the present moment what James has termed a "backwardgoing fringe" of causal memory and a "forewardgoing fringe" of anticipatory expectation, or what the phenomenologist Edmund Husserl has termed the "protentional-retentional" structure of internal time consciousness.

Following Hume, Kant explained causality as a "form of thought" (i.e., a universal and necessary a priori condition for knowing built into the formal structure of the understanding for the purpose of providing the ground on which objectivity is based). Whitehead extolls Kant's doctrine that experience is an *act* of constitution, construction or synthesis; yet he repudiates Kant's one-sided subjectivism whereby subjectivity is transformed into objectivity through transcendental-constitutive acts or *noetic* operations of consciousness (namely, the threefold synthesis of apprehension in sensation, reproduction in imagination and recognition in conception, as grounded in the apperceptive unity of self-consciousness). For according to Whitehead's transformation of Kant's doctrine, the order of constructive operations in experience is completely *inverted,* such that it is not subjectivity passing over into objectivity, but objectivity passing over into subjectivity. Whitehead writes: "Thus for Kant the process whereby there is experience is a process from subjectivity to apparent objectivity. The philosophy of organism inverts this analysis, and explains the process as proceeding from objectivity to subjectivity. . . ." (PR, p. 156)

The consequence of Whitehead's transformation of Kantian idealism into a realistic basis is that the objects of experience are not noetically constituted appearances, but are the things themselves, which have been gathered together through creative synthesis into a new subjective unity. For according to Whitehead's "experiential realism," if it may be so called, it is not the perceiver who constitutes objects, but to the contrary, it is the multiplicity of objects which constitute the momentary perceiver. It is true that each act of experience is self-creative; however, self-creative experience does not constitute its own data, but only the novel and aesthetic *unity* of that data in a new moment of reality. Whitehead thus writes: "The process creates itself, but it does not create the objects which it receives as factors in its own nature" (AI, p. 179). Each act of experience is a private unification of public data, a subjective synthesis of objective facts. It is this same kind of transformation of transcendental-idealism into a realistic basis, and dialectical balancing of the interplay between subjectivity and objectivity, which characterizes the critical response of Hua-yen Buddhism to the one-sided subjectivism of Yogācāra metaphysics with its consciousness-only doctrine of "causation by mere ideation."

Section III

It is now possible to understand more fully the manner in which the three temporal periods of past, present and future are said to be either immanent or transcendent to any given occasion of experience. Whitehead's theory of immanence is defined explicitly in terms of the object-to-subject structure of experience:

> *Immanence*. . . is at once the doctrine of the unity of nature. . . . This general principle is the object-to-subject structure of experience. It can be otherwise stated as the vector-structure of nature. Or otherwise, it can be conceived as the doctrine of the immanence of the past energizing the present. (AI, pp. 187–188)

Clearly then, Whitehead's doctrine of immanence is to be construed strictly in the sense of cumulative immanence or one-way penetration, in a directed and non-symmetrical vector transmission of efficacious energy from past-to-present, object-to-subject and cause-to-effect. In his chapter entitled "Past, Present, Future" in *Adventures of Ideas* Whitehead proceeds to analyze the various senses in which the three periods of time are immanent in occasions of experience, arguing that due to the vectorial object-to-subject pattern of experience, contemporary and future occasions must be immanent in much different senses from the immanence of antecedent events:

> The doctrine of the immanence of past occasions. . . has been sufficiently discussed in the previous chapter. . . . But the sense in which the future can be said to be immanent in occasions antecedent to itself, and the sense in which contemporary occasions are immanent in each other, are not so evident in terms of the doctrine of the subject-object structure of experience. (AI, p. 191)

Whitehead commences with an analysis of the immanence of future events in the present, asserting: "Cut away the future, and the present collapses, emptied of its proper content;" (AI, p. 191). Yet, he continues, "The difficulty lies in the explanation of this immanence in terms of the subject-object structure of experience. In the present, the future occasions, as individual realities with their measure of absolute completeness, are non-existent" (AI, p. 192). Thus, Whitehead states conclusively: "In the present there are no individual occasions belonging to the future" (AI, p. 192). The mode in which the future is finally said to have immanence in the present is that of anticipatory feeling. Anticipated occasions are still as yet only hypothetical entities, projected possibilities or even statistical probabilities, and as such are non-existent. As Christian states, anticipatory feelings are only feelings *of* the future, not *in* the future. Consequently, future immanence through anticipatory feeling is immanent only in a weak sense from the standpoint of efficient causation, which comes only from antecedents. Whitehead writes:

> . . . the actual occasions of the past, each functioning in each present occasion, constitutes the causal relationship which is efficient causation. But there are no actual occasions in the future, already constituted. Thus there are no actual occasions in the future to exercise efficient causation in the present. (AI, p. 195)

The analysis of contemporary occasions yields a similar conclusion: contemporary occasions in unison of becoming, not yet definite, still in the process of determining their own definiteness, are as yet unavailable as data for synthesis by an emerging subject. Causal independence thus becomes the very definition of contemporaneity: "It is the definition of contemporary events that they happen in causal independence of each other. . . . two [contemporary] occasions are not in any direct relation to efficient causation" (AI, p. 195). Whitehead regards the causal independence of contemporary occasions as cosmic elbowroom, as it were, allowing the necessary space for freedom of decision, stating: "The causal independence of contemporary occasions is the ground for the freedom within the Universe," (AI, p. 198), so that, "It is not true that whatever happens is immediately a condition laid upon everything else" (AI, p. 198). As Hartshorne has written, if contemporary events were mutually influential and mutually immanent, "in that case a decision here would have had to take account of a decision there that would have had to take account of a decision here taking account of the one there and so on in endless proliferation and confusion."[5] Consequently, Whitehead denies any direct transmission of causal efficacy between contemporary events, although he does assert that there exists a certain indirect immanence of contemporary occasions in each other due to a common overlapping of their causal antecedents as well as of their causal consequences: "The occasions originate from a common past and their objective immortality operates within a common future. Thus indirectly, *via* the immanence of the past and the immanence of the future, the [contemporary] occasions are connected" (AI, p. 195). But again, from the standpoint of efficient causation, contemporaries are mutually immanent only in the weakest and most indirect sense of the term. Yet, what is lost in cosmological solidarity through the mutual exclusion of contemporaries is gained in creative freedom.

According to Whitehead's conception of reality, then, it is only the past universe of fully completed historical fact which is immanent in actual occasions in the strong sense of efficient causation. Yet, even the past is immanent in the present occasion only as *objectified* through the process of causal reproduction or re-enaction, whereby intense feelings of prior occasions are duplicated by a conformal subjective form in the present occasion. There is no sharing or spilling-over of immediacy in the transition of vector feeling from cause-to-effect or from object-to-subject. In Whitehead's doctrine of creative advance, as in Henri Bergson's theory of creative evolution, the past is restored in the present through a kind of cosmic remembrance. However, according to Bergson, the entire past virtually lives in the present as subjectively immediate (the present being conceived as a "duration" which spans the entire current of the *élan vital* or creative impulse, which Bergson regards as a continuum of consciousness or pure memory). This interpretation of Bergson is shared by Stephen Pepper who writes in *Concept and Quality:*

> In Bergson's view. . . the past rolls up snowball fashion into the present and in this way is never lost. . . . As I interpret Bergson's view, the past event literally continues to exist in the interior of the actual present. The literal preservation of the past event in all its qualitative fullness hardly stands up, however, to a detailed scrutiny. Can Bergson mean, for instance, that the battle of Waterloo is being fought today in all its concrete actuality just as it was in 1815?[6]

Hua-yen Buddhism similarly assumes the past to live in the present in its original subjectively immediate form, since all events happen simultaneously in an eternal now. In terms of Pepper's well-known typological classification of world-hypotheses into universalized structural paradigms and their underlying root metaphors, Hua-yen Buddhism would be classified under organicism or the absolutist paradigm, along with Hegel, Bradley and Royce in the West. The general doctrine of time and the ontological status of the past according to the root metaphor of organicism is described by Pepper as follows:

> The organicists proposed a theory of time that met with considerable favor a generation or so ago. . . . Limited experiences go on seemingly in a present time. They appear to come and go and pass away. But for the organicist this is appearance only. In reality no experiences are ever lost, but all have a permanent place in the coherent totality of the Absolute. Thus the past is preserved in its full qualitative richness. . . and the passage of time is provided for as a phenomenal appearance.[7]

Pepper proceeds to discuss the disadvantages of the organicist's world-hypothesis:

> No organicist has been able to account for the transmutation of the passage of time into the changeless 'time' of the Absolute; nor vice versa for the fragmentation of the eternal coherence of the absolute into the limited presents of phenomenal time. For any one impressed with the passage of time, the organicist's treatment detemporalizes time. So, this theory of time does not seem to be adequate.[8]

The Japanese Sōtō Zen Master Dōgen (1200–1253), who appropriated the essential Kegon or Hua-yen metaphysics of temporal interpenetration into his own thought system, also propounded that the past is immanent in the present as subjectively immediate. In his celebrated doctrine of "being-time" (*uji*) Dōgen articulates reality as a discontinuous stream of dharma-moments, each of which constitutes pure being-time (*uji*), itself the absolute now (*nikon*) or eternal present. As in Whiteheadian process theory, Dōgen's doctrine of being-time asserts that time has no independent existence but is an abstraction from the stream of particular dharma-moments or pulsatory events. Each moment-event is itself an eternal here-now, a unique quantum-whole of actuality. It is also of special interest to note that Dōgen's theory of *uji* or being-time bears significant structural resemblances to the Heideggerian thesis as articulated in *Being and Time* that authentic existence (as being-towards-death) in its primordial openness and presence is radically *temporal* in structure, such that being is time and time is being. Yet, for Dōgen, each discontinuous dharma-moment of pure being-time, as the dharma-position (*ju-hoi*) and the total exertion (*gūjin*) of all reality, fully contains all worlds of the past, present and future at once, establishing the absolute *simultaneity* (*dōji*) of the three temporal periods in each eternal now. In his *Shōbōgenzō*, Dōgen writes: "Everything is time, existence, flow, and all existence and all worlds are present in each and every moment."[9] However, at the heart of Dōgen's position is this: although all is time, flow, becoming—*time does not pass!* Dōgen continues:

> It is believed by most that time passes; however, in actual fact, it stays where it is. This idea of passing may be called time, but it is an incorrect one for, since one sees it as passing one cannot understand that it stays just where it is.[10]

Hence, Dōgen says that he is still climbing the mountains and crossing the rivers exactly as he did long ago; for the mountains and rivers are all pure being-time (*uji*) and time does not pass. Consequently, it must be concluded that Whitehead's doctrine of the immanence of the past in the present as causally objectified or conformally reproduced is far less radical than the theory propounded by Kegon and Zen Buddhism, which argues for the survival of the past into the present as subjectively immediate. Even Hartshorne seems to be asserting that past occasions are retained in their full subjective immediacy as preserved everlastingly in the divine memory or consequent nature of God, when he writes:

> Whitehead calls all past events "actual entities" or "actual occasions," and this in spite of his saying that actualities "perish," a metaphor which has sadly misled many (unless something else has sadly misled me). They "perish yet live forevermore" is the final word in *Process and Reality* and to this I adhere whether or not Whitehead did. The perishing, taken anything like literally, is an illusion occasioned by the hiddenness of deity from us. But, as Whitehead at least sometimes explicates the term, it has nothing to do with an internal change from vital actuality to a corpse or skeleton, but is merely the fact that the definite actual subject is now also object for further subjects. . . . This has nothing to do, at least in my theory, with an inner shrinkage or impoverishment.[11]

Whitehead's irreducible rhythmic contrast between subjective immediacy and objective immortality and between creative becoming and perishing seems to be diminished by Hartshorne's interpretation, apparently as a function of the latter's logic of ultimate contrasts whereby one side of a dipolarity is capable of collapse into the more primary side, such as abstraction into concreteness, determinism into creative freedom, objectivity into subjectivity, matter into mind, or being into becoming. For Whitehead, this would mean a diminution of the irreducible dipolar contrast necessary to generate maximum depth of aesthetic-value intensity, which in this case is the rhythmic contrast between creative becoming and accomplished being, which separates subjective immediacy from perishing and objective immortality. It would seem that Bergson, Dōgen, Hua-yen, and Hartshorne are really concerned about preserving the richness and depth of emotion from previouses cases of experience with their claim that events do not perish, or that time does not pass. This concept of the availability of the past in its full vivacity and force of intensity is especially pertinent to the religious praxis of Buddhist Yoga, wherein the powers of "extrasensory perception" (*abhiñña*) attributed to the Buddha in the ancient Pali canons, such as "retrocognition" (*pubbenivāsanussatiñāṇa*) "clairvoyance" (*dibbacakkhu*) or "telepathy" (*cetopariyānāna*) all allow an enlightened one to directly experience past events in their original immediacy. Again, this seems to be a claim for the full availability and recoverability of past events in their wealth of emotional richness. Yet, what Whitehead is more concerned with in his doctrine of perishing is the feeling of indeterminacy becoming determinate; the *decisions* made by occasions as to their determinateness are final and irreversible.[12] To say an occasion has "perished" or that it has lost its "subjective immediacy" in this technical sense then, means it has irrevocably rendered its "decision" as to its final definiteness, although through prehension, the emotional richness and intensity of experience enjoyed by this occasion is indefinitely recoverable and indefinitely repeatable.

In summary, this discussion began as a critical examination of the various senses in which the past, present and future periods of time are immanent or transcendent in any given occasion of actuality in order to determine with categoreal precision and theoretical definiteness its experiential boundaries. It was discovered that the community of actual occasions manifest a profound sense of social immanence through the causal objectification of conformal reproduction of vector feeling-tone whereby efficient power is transferred from past-to-present, from object-to-subject, or from cause-to-effect. Thus, Whitehead's theory of immanence must be understood strictly in the sense of cumulative immanence, one-way penetration or asymmetrical causation. Moreover, each actual occasion transcends all other occasions in three equally profound senses, namely: (1) the exclusion of subjective immediacy in past occasions; (2) the mutual independence of contemporaries in unison of becoming; (3) the external relatedness of future occasions.[13] It is only the past world of completed actualities which are truly immanent in an occasion in the strong sense of efficient causation. Yet, these past events are in the present only in the mode of objective immortality, not as subjectively immediate. However, in the following section, I argue that the immanence of the past as causally objectified vector-feeling undergoes even further qualifications, through the process of "negative prehensions."

Section IV

According to the metaphysics of cumulative penetration then, there does not exist a co-presence, mutual immanence and interpenetration of past, present and future events in a single thought-instant as argued by Hua-yen, but only a cumulative presence, processive immanence and successive penetration whereby the past enters into the present through the vector transference of causally efficacious emotional intensity. Moreover, there is no interpenetration of events even in the spatial sense between various dipolar oppositions such as subject and object and one and many. For as Hartshorne argues, events are related only by causation, and causation means relation through inheritance, which is always temporal and thus asymmetrical in structure. To repeat Hartshorne's words, space means "multiple lines of inheritance." Yet, for Hua-yen Buddhism, the same dipolar opposites interpenetrate through simultaneous-mutual-causation within an all-merging field of suchness. This Hua-yen and Kegon dialectical interpenetration of opposites is directly realized in the non-dual immediacy of the Ch'an or Zen sudden enlightenment experience, such that they are seen to merge together in an undivided continuum of all-fusing suchness, thus establishing *wu-ai* (nonimpededness), *yung t'ung* (interpenetration) and *hsiang chi* (mutual identification).

In twentieth-century Japanese metaphysics, Nishida Kitarō articulates the experience of Zen enlightenment as an event of "immediate experience" or "pure experience" (*junsui keiken*) which he identifies as the "place" *(basho)* of absolute nothingness *(zettai mu)*, a "negative space" or "transparent topos" which functions as the experiential locus for dependent coorigination (*engi*) and the unhindered mutual fusion of particular with particular (*ji ji muge*).[14] However, the Whiteheadian process doctrine comprehends the horizon of experiential immediacy as a transparent space of cumulative fusion or cumulative penetration. For according to process theory, dipolar opposites such as one and many and subject and object cannot be simultaneous with each other, either in the spatial or temporal senses of the term, and therefore cannot interpenetrate or interfuse together in mutual transparency. Rather, causal transmission always involves the directed and asymmetrical vector transference of efficacious emotional intensity from an antecedent object (or multiplicity of objects) into a new subject. Thus, the non-dual immediacy of experience as felt in its primordial presence indeed discloses a dipolar fusion of opposites, but only a cumulative fusion or cumulative penetration of object-into-subject and multiplicity-into-unity in strict concordance with the radically temporal cause-to-effect structure underscoring the vector transmission of reproductive feelings from past-into-present.

Whitehead considers there to be scientific empirical evidence that there exists some lapse of time before we perceive events due to the finite velocity of luminal transmission. Perception as causal feeling is thus always of the *past* such that "memory" is the basic paradigm for awareness. Consequently, in each act of experience, the perceiving subject is analyzable as the "effect" and the perceived object as the "causal condition" of the effect. Moreover, at the phenomenological level of originary data evidence, which is the pre-reflective, pre-objectified and non-thematic field of primordial presence, each temporally thick span or duration is felt as having a tripartite structure of past-present-future with both rearward and forewardgoing horizons, thus constituting the protentive-retentive structure of internal time consciousness. Or in process vocabulary, perceptual awareness in the primordial mode of causal efficacy directly reveals a "past rushing into the present" and a "present surging into the future," what James terms the data of "felt transitions" or the "feeling-of-causality-at-work," which provides empirical testimony for the strictly asymmetrical and cumulative structure of temporal actuality. As such, the accurate descriptive generalization of experiential immediacy must elucidate the dialectical relation between dipolar opposites by articulating in an explicit manner the strictly processive fusion of object-into-subject and manyness-into-oneness in accordance with the asymmetrical perimeters structuring the metaphysics of cumulative penetration.

Whitehead himself sometimes employs the phrase "mutual immanence" in his writings to characterize ultimate matters of fact, such as when he writes: "The togetherness of things involves some doctrine of mutual immanence. In some sense. . . each happening is a factor in the nature of every other happening" (MT, p. 226). However, as has been clearly evinced in previous segments of this work, Whitehead defines his theory of immanence strictly in terms of the object-to-subject structure of experience, such that it represents what has been termed here a doctrine of "cumulative immanence" or "cumulative presence." According to the metaphysics of cumulative penetration as developed by Whitehead, Hartshorne and the rest of the process tradition of speculative thought, mutual immanence, interpenetration or interaction only occurs between historical routes, careers or sequences of events, and never between two simultaneous happenings. Two serially ordered societies of events, say A and B, interact only in the sense that A affects B one moment, then B affects A in the next, whereas A once again affects B, and so on, throughout an historic sequence of reciprocal causation and mutual influence. But such interaction occurs only in an *alternating*, and never in a simultaneous mode of exchange, and again, only between event-sequences, not singular actualities.

Another consideration here is that if the Hua-yen doctrine of simultaneous-mutual-causation and unhindered interpenetration is applied uncritically to the level of physical actuality, then one of the most profound and central doctrines of Buddhism—Hīnayāna, Mahāyāna and Vajrayāna alike—becomes wholly invalidated; namely the inexorable law of karma (from the Sanskrit verb-root *kṛ* meaning "to act") representing the principle of cause and effect whereby each thought, word or deed incurs a consequence of commensurate proportion and degree. According to the doctrine of karma, the stream of *saṃsāra* is perpetuated by one's subconscious accumulation of causally inherited *vāsanās* or habit-energies. All acts plant seeds *(bijas)* in the soil of *ālaya vijñāna* or storehouse consciousness and inevitably come to fruition either later in one's life or in some future rebirth during the process of transmigration. It is the law of karma which directly underlies the Buddhist doctrine of the two perfections, which refers to the gradual accumulation of merit and wisdom throughout a succession of rebirths in an effort to realize Buddhahood and supreme enlightenment. The doctrine of karma is clearly cumulative in structure and becomes meaningless unless causality means "conditioning by antecedents." Otherwise, what use is the Bodhisattva's vows of compassion or his efforts to accumulate merit and wisdom? In fact the Whiteheadian doctrine of prehensions may be interpreted as providing strong explanation for the Buddhist doctrine of karma, comprehended as the "causal inheritance" of antecedent data through historic routes of transmission. However, in the final analysis, it is not at all evident how the Hua-yen principle of simultaneous-mutual-causation is in any way compatible with a doctrine of karmic inheritance, at least insofar as physical actuality is concerned, which is always asymmetrical and radically temporal in character.

Section V

At the deeper levels of radical reflection, we must comprehend Whitehead's theory of feelings in terms of a doctrine of *"embodiment."* For the multiplicity of causal feelings entering into the constitution of an occasion of experience are precisely *physical* feelings, so that each occasion literally embodies or incarnates its whole actual world at every instant as a corporeal situation. This is to say, that each occasion of immediate experience is a unified cluster of physical feelings or causal prehensions of the whole antecedent universe, such that our true "body" is the entire actual world. For this reason, Whitehead writes:

> Notice the peculiarly intimate association with immediate experience which Descartes claims for his body, an association beyond the mere sense-perception of the contemporary world—"these hands and feet are mine". . . . But in principle, it would be equally true to say, "The actual world is mine" (PR, p. 77).

In East Asian Hua-yen Buddhism, and indeed, for Tantric Buddhism as well, the compassionate Bodhisattva or Buddha realizes the whole *dharmadhātu* to be his true body. That is to say, at each moment, an Enlightened One physically embodies the whole *dharmadhātu* as a corporeal totality, through the supreme mysteries of *śūnyatā* or universal relativity, *pratītyasamutpāda* or dependent coorigination, *anātman* or no-self, as well as *karuṇā* or sympathetic compassion. Thus, analogous to Whiteheadian process theory, Hua-yen Buddhism propounds that through causation we come to physically embody the whole actual world at every instant, although once again, in terms of our problematic of cumulative penetration vs. interpenetration, process theory argues only for an ongoing embodiment of the whole *antecedent* universe, in contrast to Hua-yen Buddhism which espouses an ongoing embodiment of the entire *dharmadhātu,* understood as a corporeal totality of past, present and future alike.

Whitehead's doctrine of prehensions, which asserts that each occasion of experience is a complex physical feeling of the whole antecedent universe, is raised to a new degree of clarification through the phenomenological doctrines of operative motor intentionality, physical embodiment, and the body-as-lived framed by Maurice Merleau-Ponty in the West. As has been pointed out by other scholars, Whitehead's concept of prehension, whereby a subject physically prehends its objects through sympathetic feeling, is analogous in significant respect to Merleau-Ponty's doctrine of embodiment whereby a subject physically sympathizes with its objects through operative motor intentionality, which is the physical intentionality of our body-as-lived. Thus, an act of physical prehension or sympathetic feeling is a "molecule of intentionality," whereas intentionality expresses the *dipolar* structure intrinsic to every act of prehension.[15]

In his *Phenomenology of Perception,* Merleau-Ponty states that beneath act or thetic intentionality at the levels of reflection and judgment functions a more primordial dimension of operative motor intentionality at the non-reflective and preobjectified levels of perception, which itself makes the former possible.[16] In contrast to thetic intentionality whereby a subject "posits" its *noematic* contents through objectifying acts of *noetic* constitution, which is the basic mode of intentionality developed by Kant and Husserl, operative motor intentionality or the primordial physical intentionality of the body-as-lived is described by Merleau-Ponty as meaning "to-be-at" *(être à)* its contents by "opening out onto" its whole perceptual field. Elsewhere, he develops operative motor intentionality as establishing a primordial "contact," "alliance," or "communion" with its field of objects. Again, he describes the operative motor intentionality of our lived body as a primitive *sympathy* with the world, whereby all focal objects situated at the core of the perceptual field are seen to radiate into unconcealed openness so as to be encircled by a luminous "halo of Being," i.e., a glowing aura of global presence which enshrines each object like a sacral value. Hence, Merleau-Ponty writes:

> If qualities radiate around them a certain mode of existence, if they have the power to cast a spell and what we just now called a sacramental value, this is because the sentient subject does not posit them as objects, but enters into a sympathetic relation with them, makes them his own and finds in them his momentary law.[17]

Whereas the intentionality of act developed by Husserlian constitutive phenomenology is a form of transcendental idealism, Merleau-Ponty's notion of operative motor intentionality stands in profound agreement with Whitehead's doctrine of physical prehensions, wherein the subject does not "posit" its objects through *noetic* constitution, but instead establishes a primordial contact with them through sympathetic feeling at the pre-reflective levels of perception. According to Merleau-Ponty, whereas thetic or act intentionality posits our body as a localized object which is "in" space, operative motor intentionality is the spontaneous motility of the lived body, which is itself said to *inhabit* or "combine" with space, thereby physically embodying the whole perceptual field as a "corporeal situation" or a global sensorium of intersensory synaesthesia.[18] Thus, operative intentionality embodies a primordial spatiality of *situation*, not a spatiality of localized position.[19] Moreover, intentionality of act posits time as an objectified now-point, thereby "shrinking" the temporal perspective into an impoverished present, while operative motor intentionality physically embodies the whole temporal stream so as to be ecstatically opened out upon or distended throughout all three dimensions of past, present and futuricity in a "synthesis of transition."

The more experiential and practicable dimensions of Merleau-Ponty's phenomenological theory of perception become especially manifest through his contrast between primary vs. secondary attention.[20] Our secondary attention, which is a function of thetic or act intentionality, designates the habitual reenactment of sedimented focal-settings through primal acquisition. However, our primary attention, which is itself a function of operative motor intentionality, deconstructs all sedimented focal-settings through imaginary variations, resulting in an ongoing embodiment of value-rich focus/horizon gestalt situations of foreground/background global perspectives. Hence, analogous to the Hua-yen Buddhist praxis of embodying microcosmic-macrocosmic *shih/li* structures or the Tantric Buddhist praxis of embodying form/emptiness maṇḍala patternings, Merleau-Ponty propounds the ongoing physical embodiment of focus/horizon gestalt situations or global perspectives through the operative motor intentionality of primary attention. However, the physical embodiment of the whole spatiotemporal field of perception at each moment as a corporeal situation or global sensorium through the operative intentionality of our lived body is strictly *cumulative* in structure, as it is for

Whitehead's process metaphysics, since to repeat Merleau-Ponty's words, "each present reasserts the presence of the whole past which it supplants, and anticipates that of all that is to come."[21] Yet, as is discussed in the final chapters of this work, the cumulative structure of the body-as-lived as an ongoing embodiment of new spatiotemporal gestalt situations defines only the "physical body" at the level of *nirmāṇakāya,* although beyond this, there is still the "body of imagination" at the level of *sambhogakāya,* as well as the "body of clear light" at the level of *dharmakāya.* It is therefore necessary for us to adopt the Mahāyāna Buddhist *trikāya* or "triple body" theory of reality in order to finally complete our doctrine of ongoing embodiment.

CHAPTER 8

Negative Prehensions

Whitehead asserts that the philosophy of organism is mainly devoted to the task of elucidating the concept of interfusion: "The task of philosophy is the understanding of the interfusion of modes of existence" (MT, p. 71). Yet, he explicitly repudiates the notion of *total* interfusion when he writes: "[Actuality] is the outcome of limitation . . . The mere fusion of all that there is would be the nonentity of indefiniteness" (SMW, p. 94). Previously in the discussion it has been demonstrated that Whitehead's metaphysics of creative process maintains the causal independence of contemporaries and the external relatedness of futural events, allowing only for a strong sense of immanence (i.e., in the sense of causal efficacy) with respect to fully constituted antecedent actualities. But even these antecedent actualities are appropriated into the present only under strong qualifications not imposed by the Hua-yen theory of totality, since they are in fact appropriated as causally objectified through re-enactive conformal feelings, which entails the perishing of subjective immediacy; thus, the past survives into the present only in the mode of "objective immortality." However, Whitehead's theory of process places the causally objectified or conformally reproduced occasions under still further qualifications through the doctrine of "negative prehensions" whereby certain aspects of each actual entity as well as numerous eternal objects are prevented from making positive contribution to the emerging novel occasions of the present. For an occasion in the process of emerging into determinate actuality must satisfy all of its categoreal obligations and conditions before it can complete the creative, novel and aesthetic synthesis of feelings in which it is immersed. Any available elements conflicting with those categoreal conditions, as well as with the overall subjective aim or initial value-pattern governing the synthesis, is necessarily excluded from positive contribution, i.e., negatively prehended.

Whitehead stipulates that there are in fact two species of prehensions: "(a) 'positive prehensions' which are termed 'feelings,' and (b) 'negative prehensions,' which are said to 'eliminate from feeling'" (PR, p. 23). Thus, whereas positive prehensions are causal or conformal feelings functioning to objectify data into the new occasion, negative prehensions function conversely to eliminate from feeling, or again, to "hold its datum as inoperative" (PR, p. 23). Whitehead does not maintain that whole actual occasions are negatively prehended by an arising occasion: "All the actual entities are positively prehended, but only a selection of the eternal objects" (PR, p. 219). A selection of eternal objects are dismissed into negative prehension, as indicated above, as well as certain *aspects* of each actual occasion. This is demonstrated by the analysis of a prehension into five distinct factors: "(i) the 'subject' which feels, (ii) the 'initial data' which are to be felt, (iii) the 'elimination' in virtue of negative prehensions, (iv) the 'objective datum' which is felt, (v) the 'subjective form' which is *how* that subject feels that objective datum" (PR, p. 221).

Negative prehensions occur in concordance with the principle of intensive relevance and the category of conceptual valuation. Whitehead writes: "The data for any one pulsation of actuality consist of the full content of the antecedent universe as it exists in relevance to that pulsation" (MT, p. 89). Moreover, each pulsation of actuality is said to be "a process of composition, of gradation and of elimination" (MT, p. 89). Each unit-pulsation of process is a creative unification of data producing subjective forms or emotional responses involving valuational feelings that hierarchically grade the data into its respective orders of relevance to that unit, irrelevant data being eliminated from feeling or held as inoperative. According to the principle of intensive relevance, any item in the universe, whether actual fact or ideal form, "has its own gradation of relevance, as prehended in the constitution of any one actual entity," as located on a graduated scale from strong relevance to lesser or minimal relevance, ending at the extreme limit of "zero of relevance involved in the negative prehension" (PR, p. 148). This gradation of relevance is determined with respect to the governing ideal or subjective aim of an occasion, which is an aesthetic-value pattern or harmonic mode of togetherness prescribed by the primordial nature of God, functioning as a "lure for feeling" eliciting maximum depth of emotional intensity in that occasion: "Each temporal entity. . . derives from God its basic conceptual aim. . . . This subjective aim, in its successive modifications, remains the unifying factor governing the successive phases. . ." (PR, p. 224). All data is valuated up or down in accordance with its relevance to the subjective aim governing concrescence, all items relegated to zero relevance being excluded.

Furthermore, all data must satisfy categoreal demands to avoid elimination through negative prehension: "The negative prehensions are determined by the categoreal conditions governing feelings, by the subjective form, and by the initial data" (PR, p. 221). These categoreal conditions are imposed by Whitehead's nine categoreal obligations, those especially important here being the category of subjective unity (CO i), the category of subjective harmony (CO vii), the category of objective identity (CO ii), the category of objective diversity (CO iii) and the category of conceptual valuation (CO iv). Regarding the first categoreal condition, Whitehead states that: "The limitation, whereby the actual entities [are] felt" is ". . . imposed by the Categoreal Condition of Subjective Unity, requiring a harmonious compatability in the feelings of each incomplete phase" (PR, p. 237). Whereas the category of subjective unity requires a harmonious compatability in the feelings of the initial data, its correlate principle, the category of subjective harmony requires a harmonious compatability in the subjective forms or emotional responses which is *how* an occasion feels and valuates that initial data. All elements not fulfilling these two categoreal demands are necessarily eliminated from feeling or rendered inoperative. The category of objective identity stipulates that no datum can be felt twice: "There can be no duplication of any element in the objective datum of the 'satisfaction' of an actual entity. . ." (PR, p. 26). The category of objective diversity asserts that: "There can be no 'coalescence' of diverse elements. . ." such that any two elements entering into the synthesis exhibiting an "identity of function" must also undergo elimination through negative prehension (PR, p. 26). The category of conceptual valuation asserts that all data is to be valuated and graded up or down according to its relevance to the subjective aim governing the synthesis as well as its ability to comply with the other categoreal conditions. All data of zero relevance is omitted from positive contribution to the synthesis. However, the category of subjective intensity (CO viii) discourages all such eliminations. It aims at maximum depth of emotional intensity, which is accomplished by entering a massive diversity of mutually inhibitory feelings as an aesthetic pattern of mutually adjusted harmonic contrasts, thus avoiding dismissal of those elements through negative prehension. In Whitehead's words: ". . . the heightening of intensity arises from order such that the multiplicity of components in a nexus can enter explicit feeling as *contrasts*, and are not dismissed into negative prehensions as *incompatabilities*" (PR, p. 83).

Negative prehensions also function to dismiss irrelevant eternal objects. Eternal objects or ideal forms are the determinants of process which confer finitude, limitation, structure and definiteness to actuality and function as the modes of togetherness whereby a multiplicity of diverse data can be patterned into harmonic contrasts during the concrescence of an event. Only some eternal objects are accepted as relevant to an occasion in its process of becoming, these being selected through its decisions, all others being dismissed by negative prehension. An occasion's gradation of eternal objects and their order of relevance for influx into it, is determined by the occasion's subjective aim which has been derived from God in his primordial nature. In Whitehead's words:

> In this sense God is the principle of concretion. . . he is that actual entity from which each temporal concrescence receives that initial aim from which its self-causation starts. That aim determines the initial gradations of relevance of eternal objects for conceptual feeling. . . . (PR, p. 244)

The doctrine of negative prehensions is an ingenious conceptual mechanism functioning to provide for the gradation, selection and elimination of data, including both actual fact and ideal form, in the achievement of determinate actuality. Ultimately, these concepts—selection, elimination, and definiteness—lie at the very heart of Whitehead's axiologically centered cosmology, which equates aesthetic-value with determinate actuality. Whitehead writes: "Value is the outcome of limitation. The definite finite entity is the selected mode which is the shaping of attainment. . . ." (SMW, p. 94). And it is in this context that Whitehead asserts: "The mere fusion of all that there is would be the nonentity of indefiniteness."

It is precisely at this point, concerning the negative prehension of eternal objects (what was termed *li* or eternal thought-patterns in Chinese neo-Confucianism, a school which severely criticized Buddhism for its neglect of *li*), that it is difficult to see how Hua-yen Buddhism can withstand the force of the Whiteheadian process critique. In previous sections of this work Hua-yen Buddhism is criticized for its categoreal deficiency with respect to such notions as creativity, novelty and freedom. Moreover, it was argued that the Hua-yen doctrine of symmetrically patterned causation violates the very meaning of efficient causation as conditioning by antecedents, thus rendering meaningless the fundamental Buddhist doctrine of karma which is essentially cumulative in structure. Now the question which emerges for critical analysis is: How can Hua-yen consistently argue that each dharma "fuses with all that is," to use Whitehead's phrase, while still maintaining a single structural pattern or determinate form, without some mechanism accounting for the gradation, selection and elimination of eternal objects, as is provided by Whitehead's theory of negative prehensions? Remember Ŭisang's proclamation in his "Ocean Seal":

"In one is all and in all is one. . . . In one particle of dust is contained the ten directions. . . . The incalculable long eons are identical to a single thought-instant. . . .Yet (all these interpenetrating worlds) are not confused or mixed, but function separately (*jeng pu tsa luan ke pieh cheng*)." And reiterating Tu-shun's assertion: "The shih remains as it is and yet embraces all!"

One might argue here that Whitehead's doctrine of negative prehensions, while allowing for the possibility of determinate form through the exclusion of alternative structural patterns, nevertheless stands in direct contradiction to his doctrine that each actuality includes every other item in its universe, both actual and ideal. Yet such an objection involves a misinterpretation of Whitehead's theory of negative prehension. Whitehead writes:

> An actual entity has a perfectly definite bond with each item in the universe. This determinate bond is its prehension of that item. A negative prehension is the definite exclusion of that item from positive contribution to the subject's own real internal constitution. This doctrine involves the position that a negative prehension expresses a bond." (PR, p. 41).

Hence, even a negative prehension requires a bond or determinate relation to that item it has eliminated from feeling. And as Whitehead explicitly stipulates, an entity includes or contains the entire actual world precisely in the sense that it bears a determinate relation to every item within that world: ". . . each actual entity includes the universe, by reason of its determinate attitude towards every element in the universe" (PR, p. 45). Moreover, although the negative prehension functions to exclude certain materials from contribution to synthesis, still, ". . . the negative prehension of an entity is a positive fact with its emotional subjective form. . ." (PR, pp. 41-42). Thus, the inrush of valuational feelings springing from the subjective form or emotional response of the negative prehension, whether it be aversion, disinterest or sheer antipathy, is itself a positive fact contributing to the occasion: "Elimination is a positive fact, so that the background of discarded data adds a tone of feeling to the whole pulsation" (MT, p. 87).

In synopsis then, each prehension of an actual occasion may be factored into five components: (i) the "subject" which feels, (ii) the "initial data" to be felt, (iii) the "objectified data" which have been felt, (iv) the "subjective form" or emotive response, which is "how" the subject feels its objectified datum, and (v) the "eliminations" resulting from negative prehensions (PR, p. 221). Thus, each prehension of an antecedent actuality involves some elimination of incompatible elements. All data are graded in orders of relevance with respect to the subjective aim as well as the categoreal conditions governing the integration of feelings, being graded up or down on a graduated scale from strong relevance to the zero relevance of negative prehensions. All negatively prehended data, incompatible for synthesis into the selected pattern of togetherness by virtue of antithetical elements incapable of satisfying their categoreal demands (as imposed by the categories of subjective unity, subjective harmony, objective identity, objective diversity, and conceptual valuation) are subsequently "eliminated from feeling," "held inoperative," "excluded from positive contribution," "relegated to zero relevance," or "replaced by negative prehensions." Through the decisions made by occasions of experience, there is a selection of eternal objects or organizational patterns whereby definiteness of structure is conferred to actuality, the remaining multiplicity of alternative eternal objects being dismissed into negative prehensions. Gradation, selection, limitation and elimination represent the achievement of intrinsic value in each ultimate matter of fact as a determinate actuality. Furthermore, all negative prehensions have their own subjective forms, such that the discarded data adds a tone of feeling to each unit-pulsation of actuality, thus constituting a positive fact. Finally, each prehension, whether of the positive or negative species, represents a determinate bond; and it is by virtue of these definite bonds to very item in the universe that an occasion is said to include or pervade its universe, thereby establishing the solidarity and cohesiveness of the cosmos.

Whitehead's doctrine of negative prehensions appears to have no counterpart in the Hua-yen School of Buddhism. In consequence, this school is here charged with having no adequate conceptual apparatus by which to argue both for the retention of a single determinate form by each dharma, and for the total "fusion of all that is." For if an actuality is to possess definiteness of structural pattern, or uniqueness and singularity of form, there must be some mechanism in the Hua-yen system for the gradation, selection and elimination of alternative patterns; but then one cannot argue for the total fusion of all that is. Whitehead's theory of negative prehensions therefore stands as a brilliant effort to account for the precise manner in which some data is included and some excluded from the creative process of experiential synthesis, thereby presenting a scheme adequate enough to interpret the exactitude and uniqueness of each moment of experience, each one having its own novel intensity of emotional tone and qualitative immediacy. To conclude then, the doctrine of negative prehensions belongs to the most subtle and intricate stratum of analysis in Whitehead's sustained project of "making clear the notion of 'being present in another entity.'"

CHAPTER 9

A Process Theory of Substance

Section I

The theme to be propounded in this section is that Whitehead's occasion of experience is in fact a substance with unique own-being and irreducible selfhood to the extent that it is sui generis or self-constitutive of its own novel and aesthetic determinateness, but devoid of substantiality in all those restrictive senses of the term disavowed by Hua-yen Buddhism, such as simple location, static endurance and independent self-existence. This is to say, that just as Buddhism provides the most relentless critique of the notion of *svabhāva* or independent self-naturedness in the East, it is Whitehead who provides the most thoroughgoing and sustained criticism of the concept of substance which has yet been elaborated in the Western world. However, whereas the Buddhist doctrine of *śūnyatā* or emptiness entails the total abolition and abandonment of the category of substance, Whitehead's doctrine of creativity functions to radically *reformulate* substance theory in terms of reconstructive process categories. However, prior to analyzing the ontological status of Whitehead's actual occasions, an examination of creativity is required.

One of the most intriguing features of the Whiteheadian/Buddhist dialogue is that the category of creativity resists any sort of reification or substantialization; it is in consonance with one of the deepest ontological commitments of Mahāyāna Buddhism, that even emptiness is itself empty, i.e., empty of any independent self-existence or absolute status. For creativity, as the "universal of universals characterizing ultimate matter of fact," (PR, p. 21), is only the most generic trait common to all occasions of experience and has no separate existence apart from them. Whitehead writes:

In all philosophic theory there is an ultimate which is actual in virtue of its accidents. It is only then capable of characterization through its accidental embodiments, and apart from these accidents is devoid of actuality. In the philosophy of organism this ultimate is termed 'creativity.'. . . (PR, p. 7)

This is to say that creativity does not independently exist over and against the momentary events themselves as some kind of ultimate or absolute reality, but is the notion of abstract "synthesis" as conditioned by efficient causation from the past. Buddhist *śūnyatā* is similarly devoid of any independent actuality apart from its embodiments in particular dharmas. This is the basic purport of the famous declaration of the *Heart Sūtra: rūpam śūnyatā śūnyatāiva rūpam* or "form is emptiness and emptiness is form." In his highly acclaimed treatise, "A Commentary on the Heart Sūtra," Fa-tsang criticizes those negativistic or nihilistic Mādhyamika sects which, in his own words, "regard Voidness as that which negates or destroys forms and accepts Voidness as annihilation."[1] At the other extreme, he criticizes those clinging to the eternalistic view which "regards Voidness as different from form *(rūpam)* and thinks that Voidness exists outside form."[2] It is this second aberration which functions to reify *śūnyatā* as an independent reality abiding in separation from concrete particular facts. In Fa-tsang's words, one who reifies *śūnyatā* "considers Voidness as a 'thing' and regards it in some manner as existing. To dispel this (notion), the sūtra points out that Voidness is form per se and excludes the idea of taking Voidness as an existing Voidness."[3]

Thus, in order to show the total indivisibility between form and emptiness (or voidness) Fa-tsang asserts: "Emptiness does not have any mark of its own. It is through forms that Emptiness is revealed."[4] In words at once reminiscent of this statement, Whitehead writes: "Creativity is without a character of its own. . . It cannot be characterized, because all characters are more special than itself. But creativity is always found under conditions, and described as conditioned" (PR, p. 31).

Therefore, just as in Hua-yen Buddhism "Emptiness does not have any mark of its own" but is only revealed in and through particular forms or dharmas, for Whitehead, "creativity is without a character of its own," but is only found as conditioned by particular occasions of experience. What is of special interest here is that both Whitehead and Hua-yen Buddhism endeavor to correct the intellect's propensity toward abstraction by directing it toward the concrete particularities of this world. Hua-yen Buddhism's key doctrine of *li-shih-wu-ai*, the unhindered interfusion between universal and particular, represents a fundamental restatement of the Mahāyāna doctrine of the indivisibility of emptiness and form. Through the doctrine of *li-shih-wu-ai* Hua-yen counters those Mahāyāna Buddhist sects which aggrandize the universal-principle (*li*) over and above the realm of phenomena (*shih*) by exalting particularity as the concrete locus in and through which universality manifests itself. Thus, as it functions within the context of Hua-yen Buddhism, the principle of *śūnyatā* maintains that nothing is more real than anything else—behind, beneath or beyond the interdependence of everything that is, including such notions as Buddha *(tathāgata)*, enlightenment *(nirvāṇa)* or emptiness *(śūnyatā)* itself. In Whitehead's categoreal scheme, this is given expression by the "ontological principle" which states that: "whatever things there are in any sense of 'existence,' are derived by abstraction from actual occasions," (PR, p. 73), such that, "There is no going behind actual entities to find anything more real," (PR, p. 18), including either God or creativity. In this manner, Whitehead endeavors to surmount all conceptual models of transcendence that dichotomize appearance and reality which characterize most speculative ontologies in the West. His conception of creativity does not stand over against the world of particulars as a transcendent principle with independent existence or preeminent status. Rather the concrete flux of creative, novel and aesthetic occasions of experience arising in the stream of process constitute reality itself: "Thus nature is a structure of evolving processes. The reality is the process" (SMW, p. 72). In the final analysis then, creativity is only an abstraction from actual occasions and is not reified or absolutized as existing independently from particular cases of reality but instead is simply the "universal of universals" or that "ultimate notion of the highest generality characterizing ultimate matter of fact"; it is that notion of pure activity or abstract synthesis as conditioned by the objective immortality and efficient causation of the past.

Section II

In his critique of the Western substance tradition, Whitehead aims his polemics largely against the Aristotelian substance-attribute theory and its restatement in the dualistic Cartesian metaphysics. Yet, as has been stated, Whitehead does not abandon substance entirely, but seeks to radically reformulate the concept of substance in terms of reconstructive process categories. For in fact, Whitehead defines the creative process by what is essentially Aristotle's notion of substance or *ousia*, "the actualization of potentiality" (AI, p. 179). And his theory of actual occasions shares a deep alliance with Aristotelian substance theory in several other significant respects. But at the same time, Whitehead specifically repudiates the following aspects of substance, all of which are defined in the metaphysics of Aristotle:

(i) The substance-quality/subject-predicate (two-term) mode of analysis.
(ii) Substance as independent self-existence.
(iii) Substance as "always a subject and never a predicate," i.e., as "neither asserted of a subject nor present in a subject."
(iv) Substance as a permanent or enduring subject of change.

Whitehead furthermore proceeds to criticize two additional characteristics of substance, although here his polemic is aimed more specifically at the scientific materialism of the eighteenth century:

(v) Substance as simple location.
(vi) Substance as vacuous actuality.

The following analysis develops Whitehead's critique of these six aspects of substance in further detail.

(i) Whitehead argues that, "All modern philosophy hinges round the difficulty of describing the world in terms of subject and predicate, substance and quality. . . . The result always does violence to [our] immediate experience" (PR, pp. 49-50). The Aristotelian notion of substance-quality or thing-attribute implies the idea of passive matter (*hylē*) as structured by an indwelling substantial form (*morphē*). This notion of structured matter or of a substance with an inherent attribute is in turn dependent upon a subject-predicate "two-term" mode of logic which analyzes nature solely in terms of the relation of a subject to its indwelling substantial predicate. Whitehead endeavors to replace this substance-attribute metaphysics and correlate subject-predicate logic with an organic concept of nature structured by a complex relational or combinatory calculus in consonance with the developments of contemporary logic. Thus, Whitehead criticizes "the obstinate refusal of philosophers to take seriously the ultimate fact of multiple relations," explaining that "By multiple relations I mean a relation in any concrete instance of its occurrence necessarily involves more than two relata" (CN, p. 150). He continues: "Some schools of philosophy, under the influence of the Aristotelian logic and Aristotelian philosophy, endeavor to get on without admitting any relations at all except that of substance and attribute" (CN, p. 192). Whitehead regards the two-term subject-predicate/substance-attribute mode of thought as wholly antiquated in light of the contemporary logic of multiple-term relations within a system pioneered by Whitehead himself along with Bertrand Russell in their monumental work on mathematical logic, *Principia Mathematica*.

At the empirical level of analysis, Whitehead agrees with David

Hume that immediate experience provides no datum of a Lockean underlying substance which supports the qualities of nature; rather, there is only experience of a rapid sequence of immediately felt qualitative events possessing no underlying substantial identity. The Yogācāra school of "consciousness-only", which was absorbed into the syncretic harmonization pattern of Hua-yen metaphysics, developed parallel empirical arguments against the substance-attribute distinction. For example, in his work, *The Yogācāra Theory of Knowledge,* C. L. Tripathy states:

> The Yogācāra does not accept the existence of real substance. . . . Further, the Yogācāra states that substance and qualities are not different but identical. There is no cognition of a substance without the cognition of its qualities. If they were different their perception would have to take place separately.[5]

Thus, Tripathy continues:

> When one sees an object, e.g., a blue lotus, we simply see the blue lotus and not the blue and lotus separately. In the same way, when we perceive one lump of sugar, we never perceive an object called sugar as distinct and apart from the qualities of whiteness and sweetness.[6]

In Yogācāra Buddhism, this idea that the qualities of experience (e.g., colors, flavors, scents, sounds) are invariably perceived together with their objects (i.e., the substances to which they are thought to inhere) is technically termed *sahopalambhaniyama,* which asserts that for two things to be established as different they must first be perceived apart, or else they must be identified as one. Arguing along similar lines, Whitehead elaborates a metaphysics of qualitative immediacy, analogous to the speculative schemes of such American process philosophers as Charles Peirce and John Dewey, in which nature is analyzed as a flux of novel and aesthetic qualitative events devoid of underlying substance which are immediately and primordially felt at the prereflective levels of experience. Qualities such as sound, color and scent do not statically exist through the simplified two-term relation of inherence between subjects and predicates, but "ingress" or influx into events in complex *multiple-term* relations. To illustrate his theory of qualitative immediacy, Whitehead considers the "ingression of blue into the events of nature" (CN, p. 152), for example, in our aesthetically immediate and primordially felt sense-awareness of a blue lake. The subject-predicate/substance-quality mode of logical analysis compels one to factor his panoramic experience of a blue lake into two-term relations such that the predicate blue inheres in its underlying physical substance as the function of a single variable, namely, the water in the lake. However according to the philosophy of organism, our sense-awareness of blue in its concrete aesthetic immediacy is a qualitative event with momentary and dependent status in which the blue color ingresses in a complex multi-term relation as the function of a multiplicity of variables, including the state of the water, atmospheric temperature, degree of sunlight, the sensory apparatus of the observer, and a multiplicity of other factors conditioning the event. In Whitehead's words: "The sense-awareness of the blue situated in a certain event which I call the situation is exhibited as the sense-awareness of a relation between the blue, the percipient event of the observer, the situation and intervening events." (CN, p. 152)

By means of his theory of qualitative immediacy and its correlate doctrine of multiple-term relations, Whitehead endeavors to surmount the philosophical problem which he terms the "bifurcation of nature into two systems of reality" (CN, p. 152), these being the subjective reality of secondary qualities (flavor, scent, color, sound, tactile pressure) and the objective reality of primary qualities (extension, motion, configuration). According to the substance-quality/subject-predicate mode of analysis, qualities necessarily inhere in a simple two-term relation in some underlying substance, either an exterior physical substance or an inner mental substance. In other words, qualities are simply-located either exclusively in the subject or the object. According to the modern subjectivist bias introduced by Descartes, sensory qualities such as warmth, hardness, loudness, fragrance or blueness inhere only in one's mental substance, whereas the objective world of extended material substance is that of electrical waves, atoms and molecules. In consequence of this bifurcation of nature into an interior subjective world of secondary qualities and an exterior objective world of primary qualities, there emerges the axiological problem that nature is divested of the panorama of aesthetic qualities which give actuality its intrinsic value, as well as the epistemological problem that experience becomes an appearance (phenomenon) standing over against the things-in-themselves (noumena). In Whitehead's words:

> The bodies are perceived as with qualities which in reality do not belong to them, qualities which in fact are purely the offspring of the mind. Thus, nature gets credit which should in truth be reserved for ourselves: the rose for its scent: the nightingale for his song: the sun for his radiance. . . . Nature is a dull affair, soundless, scentless, colourless: merely the hurrying of material, endlessly, meaninglessly." (SMW, p. 54)

However, in critical response to the two-term subject-predicate/

substance-quality mode of analysis, which bifurcates nature into two systems of reality, Whitehead's metaphysics involves a doctrine of "pervasive quality," to use a term central to John Dewey's process thought. According to this doctrine, the qualities discoverable in the primordial presence of experiential immediacy as they are directly felt at the pre-reflective level of awareness permeate or saturate the entire occasion of experience as its aesthetic and pervasive quality. This is what binds together the social relations of an occasion of experience and unifies it into a single, unique whole of awareness. Thus, the immediately felt qualities of experience cannot be predicated exclusively either of the physical substance of external objects or of the mental substance of interior subjects, but pervade the entire occasion of experience which includes both subject and object in its scope. In the case of the panoramic experience of the blue lake, the quality of blueness as it is aboriginally felt at the pre-reflective level of awareness is not simple-located in either the water (physical substance) or the observer's mind (mental substance); rather, it ingresses momentarily as a complex multiple-term relation such as to saturate or permeate the whole undivided continuum of experience as its aesthetic and pervasive quality, thus being located in both subject and object at once so that inner and outer are one. It is in such a manner that Whitehead's metaphysics endeavors to eliminate those epistemological and axiological problems besetting the substance-attribute/subject-predicate mode of analysis with its underlying logical scaffolding of two-term relations, and its bifurcation of nature. The distinction between the process metaphysics of qualitative immediacy and the traditional substance-quality mode of speculative analysis is contrasted in the chart below:

Qualitative-Immediacy	*Substance-Quality*
Felt (Pre-intellectual) Quality	Intellectual Quality
Multiple-term Relatedness	Two-term Relatedness
Momentary Ingression	Static Inherence
Pervasive Quality	Simply-Located Quality

(*ii*) and (*iii*). The next two characteristics of substance criticized by Whitehead, independent self-existence and the inability to be a predicate may both be considered together since they are fundamentally interlocked. In the following passage, Whitehead explicitly repudiates both of these two characteristics ordinarily ascribed to a substance with attributes, asserting that his philosophy of organism involves a complete denial of ". . . the Cartesian doctrine, of. . . 'an existent thing which requires nothing but itself in order to exist.' It is also inconsistent with Aristotle's phrase, 'neither asserted of a subject nor present in a subject'" (PR, p. 59). The very essence of the first principles governing both the Whiteheadian and Hua-yen Buddhist categoreal schemes, creativity and emptiness respectively, is that each unit-event emerges into momentary actuality by virtue of its universal relativity, i.e., by virtue of its causal relations and social connections to all events, so as to include them within its real internal constitution. Whitehead therefore formulates his principle of universal relativity as follows: "The principle of universal relativity directly traverses Aristotle's dictum, 'A substance is not present in a subject.' On the contrary, according to this principle an actual entity *is* present in other actual entities" (PR, p. 50). Consequently, the final meaning contained in the principle of universal relativity is that ". . . every item of the universe, including all other actual entities, is a constituent in the constitution of any one actual entity" (PR, p. 148). Thus, due to universal relativity each event is virtually present in every other event, although once again, for process theory this always means one-way relativity and cumulative presence as distinguished from the symmetrical relativity and total presence posited by Hua-yen Buddhism.

(*iv*). The next basic point of contention with the notion of a substance with attributes is its character as an enduring subject of change, i.e., as a permanent and static entity which remains numerically the same throughout a succession of attributes. Whitehead states: "The simple notion of an enduring substance sustaining persistent qualities. . . expresses a useful abstract for many purposes of life. . . . But in metaphysics the concept is sheer error" (PR, p. 79). He abandons the notion of a permanent substance in favor of the concept of atomic occasions of experience or momentary process-events, conceived as unit-pulsations of emotional intensity. Indeed, so fleeting and transitory is an occasion of experience that it nearly fulfills the radical Mādhyamika criterion of *niḥsvabhāvatā* or non-substantiality as *anutpāda* or non-origination, since the being of an event is its becoming, which perishes immediately upon attainment of completion, such that "It never really is" (PR, p. 84). Moreover, due to Whitehead's atomic or epochal theory of time, which is the equivalent of the general Buddhist doctrine of momentariness (*kṣanika*) or impermanence (*anitya*), events neither change nor do they move; they simply emerge into actuality (outside of time) through genetic self-constitution and perish. There is no "continuity of becoming," says Whitehead, but only a "becoming of continuity" (PR, p. 35), such that entire lapses of time and change arise into being instantaneously in quantum leaps. There is no literal motion or change occurring in a single event, but only different events along historic routes of events pulsating into existence with different spatiotemporal perspectives. Motion is therefore only the measurement of accomplished change between successive quanta of process. Consequently, Nāgārjuna's brilliant dialectical critique of motion and change in his "Fundamentals of the Middle Way" which demonstrates that continuous motion is logically impossible is wholly inapplicable to Whitehead's theory of process as is Zeno's critique of motion and change in the West.[7]

Whitehead's doctrine that occasions of experience neither change nor endure but only become and perish may be contrasted to Leibniz's theory of monads, which is the major Western historical precursor of Whitehead's theory of microcosmic-macrocosmic events. Leibniz endeavors to abandon the notion of material substance for the idea of spiritual monads, conceived as "metaphysical points" or perspectival expressions of the universe, each one a microcosm of the macrocosm. Yet, Leibniz still maintains a theory of substance since the monad or microcosmic universe is a permanent subject undergoing adventures of change. Each monad is described as a living mirror of the universe reflecting all other monads and the whole world from its own standpoint in nature. The successive states of its reflections occur according to a permanent law, i.e., an indwelling Aristotelian substantial form. In his *Monadology* Leibniz therefore writes that each monad ". . . has perceptions and its individuality consists in the *permanent law* which forms the succession of its perceptions, hence it is not necessary to receive influence from without."[8] Thus, it is clear that the Leibnizian microcosmic-macrocosmic monad is an enduring subject structured by an inherent Aristotelian substantial predicate or permanent law, standing by itself as a wholly independent entity, receiving no causal influence from other monads. Whitehead therefore sharply contrasts his own doctrine of microcosmic-macrocosmic events to Leibniz's theory of monads as follows:

> This is a theory of monads; but it differs from Leibniz's in that his monads change. In the organic theory, they merely *become*. Each monadic creature is a mode of the process of 'feeling' the world, of housing the world in one unit of complex feeling. . . . (PR, p. 80)

In Whitehead's metaphysics the concept of physical endurance is reformulated in terms of the notion of the "repetition of form" throughout an event-sequence. Continuity of order is established not by enduring subjects but through the "massive inheritance" of eternal objects or organizational patterns characterizing the data through historic routes of causal transmission. In Whitehead's words, physical endurance is ". . . the process of continuously inheriting a certain identity of character transmitted throughout a historic route of events" (SMW, p. 136). Or again: "In the philosophy of organism it is not 'substance' which is permanent, but 'form.' Forms suffer changing relations; actual occasions 'perpetually perish' subjectively. . ." (PR, p. 29).

Consequently, according to the process doctrine of actuality, the notion of a permanent substance with attributes is derived only by prescinding abstract patterns or eternal forms which have been causally inherited throughout an historic route of actual occasions, thereby erroneously suggesting an abiding physical material remaining numerically identical throughout successive changes. Thus, the notion of a permanent physical substance is an instance of what Whitehead has termed the "fallacy of misplaced concreteness," which is defined as: "the accidental error of mistaking the abstract for the concrete" (SMW, p. 51). Similarly, in the Yogācāra Buddhist school of consciousness-only, the concept of an enduring substance with attributes is called *vikalpa*, i.e., an imaginative construct or false discrimination arrived at through acts of mental abstraction from instantaneous moments of sensation. For example, in his text entitled *Buddhist Logic,* Th. Stcherbatsky describes the empirical basis for the Yogācāra Buddhist theory of *kṣanika* or momentariness in a manner at once consonant with Whitehead's radically empirical methodology: "Since all external objects are reducible to sense data, and the corresponding sensations are always confined to a single moment, it becomes clear that all objects, as far as they affect us, are momentary existences."[9] He proceeds to assert that according to Yogācāra Buddhism, the notion of an enduring substance with inherent attributes is *vikalpa,* i.e., an imaginative construction or erroneous inference not warranted by empirical testimony:

> The duration of the object beyond the moment of sensation cannot be warranted beyond the sensation itself, it is an extension of sensation, a construction of the imagination. The latter constructs the "image" of the object, stimulated by sensation; but sensation alone, pure sensation, points to an instantaneous object.[10]

Hence in the final analysis, both process theory and Buddhism regard the idea of permanent substances with attributes as mental constructs derived through *abstraction* from successive momentary events of sentient experience, what Whitehead has termed "the fallacy of misplaced concreteness."

(*v*) From the standpoint of Hua-yen Buddhism, Whitehead's abandonment of "simple location" forms the most radical and interesting part of his critique of the substance-attribute conception. For whereas all Buddhist schools are sharply critical of the substance-attribute notion in general, along with its correlate notions of independent self-existence and physical endurance, the denial of simple location is directly associated with the specific doctrinal innovation of the Hua-yen school, namely, *shih-shih-wu-ai* or the unhindered interpenetration of phenomena with phenomena. Of course, Whitehead's denial of simple location is directly connected with his criticism of Aristotle's dictum that "A substance cannot be present in another subject." For at the very heart of his denial of simple location is the notion that events *are* virtually present or immanent in the real internal constitution of every other event, so that each one both houses and pervades its entire universe, whereupon in the senses specified by process theory, "everything is everywhere at all times."

According to Whitehead's analysis, simple location is not merely a basic property of material substance, but its defining characteristic. Whitehead writes: "What I mean by matter, or material, is anything which has this property of *simple location*" (SMW, p. 49). Furthermore, he states that if one is to formulate an accurate descriptive generalization of ultimate matter of fact, ". . . we should first criticise. . . the concept of *simple location*" (SMW, p. 58). In his sustained critique of the substance-attribute mode of thought, he states: "The difficulty really arises from the unquestioned acceptance of the notion of simple location as fundamental for space and time and from the acceptance of the notion of independent individual substance as fundamental for a real entity" (SMW, p. 156). Whitehead gives his classic definition of simple location as follows:

> To say that a bit of matter has *simple location* means that, in expressing its spatio-temporal relations, it is adequate to state that it is. . . in a definite region of space, and throughout a definite finite duration of time, apart from any essential reference. . . of that bit of matter to other regions of space and to other durations of time." (SMW, p. 58)

In contradistinction to the notion of simply-localized material substances, Whitehead's philosophy of organism posits microcosmic-macrocosmic occasions of experience as the fundamental ontological units at the base of actuality. According to it, ". . . every location involves an aspect of itself in every other location," so that ". . . every spatio-temporal standpoint mirrors the world" (SMW, p. 91). Thus, Whitehead completely repudiates simple location: ". . . my theory involves the entire abandonment of the notion that simple location is the primary way in which things are involved in space-time. In a certain sense, everything is everywhere at all times" (SMW, p. 91). Indeed, Whitehead's proposition that "in a certain sense, everything is everywhere at all times" may be regarded as one of the most powerful and far-reaching metaphysical generalizations in Western speculative thought. It also places his metaphysics into fundamental alliance with some of the deepest presuppositions of Hua-yen Buddhism. However, once again it must be recollected that the specified senses in which "everything is everywhere at all times" are precisely those of cumulative immanence, asymmetrical causation, one-way relativity, creative advance, emergent novelty, conformal objectification of the past through re-enactive feelings and the negative prehension of incompatible data incapable of satisfying categoreal obligations—*not* in the sense of total non-obstructed interpenetration as posited by the Hua-yen doctrine of *shih-shih-wu-ai.*

It is not that an occasion of experience has no definite spatio-temporal location; it is only that it is not *simply* located. To repeat Whitehead's words:

> Every actual entity in its relationship to other actual entities is in this sense somewhere in the continuum, and arises out of the data provided by this standpoint. But in another sense it is *everywhere* throughout the continuum; for its constitution includes the objectifications of the actual world and thereby includes the continuum. . . . Thus the continuum is present in each actual entity, and each actual entity pervades the continuum. (PR, p. 67; italics mine)

Whitehead's abandonment of simple location as formulated above almost perfectly echos First Patriarch Tu-shun's principle of the non-obstruction of the universal whole and the local spot as expressed in his famous Hua-yen treatise, "On the Meditation of Dharmadhātu," written almost 1500 years ago:

> A shih (event) departs not from its position and yet extends into all atoms. Again. . . an atom stretches in all the ten directions, yet it is far and also near, stretching and also remaining; there is no hindrance and no obstruction whatsoever.[11]

Whitehead's abandonment of simple location acquires special importance by virtue of its capacity to provide speculative interpretation of contemporary developments in the physical sciences. In his book, *The Structure of Scientific Revolutions,* Thomas Kuhn suggests that major revolutions in scientific thought are structured by radical changes in conceptual paradigms or models.[12] Whitehead's revolutionary cosmological scheme may be regarded as a systematic speculative reconstruction based on the radical paradigm-shift from the simple location model of reality underlying the Newtonian world-view to the field model of reality underlying contemporary quantum and relativity physics. In his *Optiks,* Newton declared: "It seems to me that God, in the beginning, formed matter in solid, massy, impenetrable particles."[13] According to the Newtonian cosmology, reality consists of simply-located material particles swirving in rational configurations governed strictly by mechanical laws and efficient causes. However, with the epoch-making work of Faraday and Maxwell in the area of classical electrodynamics, the notion of an electrical field was introduced into the physical sciences. In 1844, in a paper entitled "A Speculation Touching Electric Conduction to the Nature of Matter," Faraday endeavored to describe physical reality in terms of interpenetrating and all-pervasive electrical charges with central regions of intensity: "Matter is not merely mutually penetrable, but each atom extends, so to say, throughout the whole solar system, yet always retains its center of force."[14]

According to classical electrodynamics as developed by Faraday and Maxwell, an electric field is the condition of the region surrounding a charged entity generating a force affecting any other charged entities within that region. Magnetic fields are produced by charges in motion, i.e., by electrical currents, and produce magnetic forces which are felt by other moving charges. In the relativistic formulation of classical electrodynamics, the notions of charges and currents and electrical and magnetic fields are combined into a single electromagnetic field, since all motion becomes relative to a velocity frame of reference, such that every charge can also manifest as a current or any electrical field can manifest as a magnetic field. According to the science of electrodynamics, it is this electromagnetic field which is the fundamental physical reality; a particle of matter or substance exhibiting simple location represents a minute region in the electromagnetic field within which the field strength assumes especially high values, i.e., it represents the most intense or concentrated region of the entire field. Commenting on Faraday's experimental work in the field of classical electrodynamics, Whitehead writes:

> As long ago as 1847 Faraday in a paper in the Philosophic Magazine remarked that his theory of tubes of force implies that in a sense an electrical charge is everywhere. The modification of the electromagnetic field at every point of space and at each instant owing to the past history of each electron is another way of stating the same fact. (CN, p. 146)

This radical paradigm-shift from simple location to field theory in contemporary physics may be observed in terms of another major force in the macroscopic universe, namely, the force of gravity. According to the concept of the gravitational field established by Einstein's general theory of relativity, matter and open space are inseparable. Each massive physical body such as a stellar or planetary mass generates a gravitational field which in turn manifests itself as the geometrical curvature of the space surrounding that body. Consequently, matter cannot be separated from its gravitational field, and this gravitational field cannot be separated from the geometry of space. Matter and space are thus wholly indivisible, if not simply identical. This inseparability of matter and space at once confers strong scientific validation on the Hua-yen doctrine of the indivisibility of form/voidness or *shih/li*. Each particular *shih* becomes inseparable from the expanse of open space (*li*) which encircles it. At the level of enlightened perception (*prajñā*) one may therefore actually observe the solid boundaries and opaque surfaces of material objects become "transparent outlines" which dissolve into the surrounding openness of pure space, as is directly experienced through the Hua-yen meditative praxis of *li-shih-wu-ai*.

Einstein expresses this concept of the inseparability of material objects from their surrounding electromagnetic and gravitational fields in his work *The Evolution of Physics* when he writes:

> From the relativity theory we know that matter represents vast stores of energy and that energy represents matter. We cannot, in this way, distinguish qualitatively between matter and field. . . . Matter is where the concentration of energy is great, field where the concentration of energy is small. . . . There is no sense in regarding matter and field as two qualities quite different from each other. We cannot imagine a definite surface separating distinctly field and matter.[15]

Thus, the matter/field or object/space model emerging in recent physics is a restatement in contemporary Western scientific terms of the form/voidness or *shih/li* model of reality articulated by the Hua-yen school of Mahāyāna Buddhism in the ancient East.

It is therefore partly scientific evidence for the existence of electromagnetic and gravitational fields that led Whitehead to abandon the premise of simple location in favor of the idea of universally diffused events which permeate the whole spatiotemporal continuum from the standpoint of their own perspectival locus in nature. However, it must also be recognized that Whitehead does not regard the notion of simple location as merely erroneous; for it functions pragmatically as a useful and even necessary concept for common-sense. But at the level of metaphysical discourse, the concept of simple location represents another species of the fallacy of misplaced concreteness, or the error of mistaking abstract mental constructs for concrete actuality itself. In Whitehead's words: "I hold that by a process of constructive abstraction we can arrive at abstractions which are the simply-located bits of material. . . . Accordingly, the real error is an example of what I have termed: The Fallacy of Misplaced Concreteness" (SMW, p. 58). And finally, "... substance and quality, as well as simple location, are the most natural ideas for the human mind"; but, from the speculative level of discourse these notions are only "... simplified editions of immediate matters of fact... they are in truth only to be justified as being elaborate logical constructions of a high degree of abstraction" (SMW, p. 52).

(*vi*) Another species of the fallacy of misplaced concreteness is the concept of vacuous actuality or the notion of, "vacuous material existence with passive endurance, with primary individual attributes, and with accidental adventures" (PR, p. 309). Whitehead defines the notion of vacuous actuality as a material substance "devoid of subjective immediacy" (PR, p. 29); "devoid of self-enjoyment" (AI, p. 219); or "void of subjective experience" (PR, p. 167). This notion of vacuous actuality or lifeless substance therefore stands in direct opposition to a fundamental notion underlying the philosophy of organism, namely, the "reformed subjectivist principle," which propounds the ontological primacy of subjective experience ("reformed" because it is balanced by the objectivity of its data). According to the reformed subjectivist principle, all metaphysical generalization must be derived by analogy from human subjective experiences since, "... those substances which are the subjects enjoying conscious experiences provide the primary data for philosophy, namely, themselves as in the enjoyment of such experience" (PR, p. 159). Consequently, "... the whole universe consists of elements disclosed in the analysis of the experiences of subjects" (PR, p. 166), such that "... apart from the experiences of subjects there is nothing, nothing, nothing, bare nothingness" (PR, p. 167). Hence, the reformed subjectivist principle makes explicit those idealistic and panpsychic dimensions of Whitehead's process metaphysics, by articulating reality as consisting solely in creative acts of experience, which emerge into actuality as a creative synthesis of all previous cases of experience in a universe of pure experience: "The final facts are all alike, actual entities; and these actual entities are drops of experience, complex and interdependent" (PR, p. 18).

At the heart of Whitehead's cosmology is his doctrine of experiential togetherness, wherein the entire antecedent universe exists "experientially together" at each standpoint in nature as a complex unity of feelings. Thus Whitehead can write that each occasion of experience "... is a mode of the process of 'feeling' the world, of housing the world in one unit of complex feeling. . . ." (PR, p. 80), such that, "Each actual entity is a throb of experience including the actual world within its scope" (PR, p. 190). This doctrine therefore asserts that all events are "experientially together" in the unity of every other event, and that there is absolutely no mode of togetherness apart from such togetherness in experience. In Whitehead's words:

> Again the term "together" is one of the most misused terms in philosophy . . . . No things are "together" except in experience; and no things *are*, in any sense of "are," except as components in experience or as immediacies of process which are occasions in self-creation. (AI, p. 236)

It is clear that by his doctrine of experiential togetherness Whitehead fully rejects any "vacuous" mode of actuality, conceived as existing apart from or outside of subjectively immediate experience. Whitehead's theory is itself derived from F. H. Bradley's doctrine of experiential togetherness. The latter equates reality with sentient feeling or immediate experience such that nothing exists outside of the psychical. Bradley writes: "Sentient experience, in short, is reality, and what is not this is not real. We may say, in other words, that there is no being or fact outside of what is continuously called psychical existence."[16]

In Yogācāra Buddhism, the very meaning of its central doctrine of consciousness-only *(vijñaptimātratā)* is the total rejection of substance or matter existing externally to sentient experience. This is explicitly expressed by Hsüan-tsang for example, when he defines consciousness-only as follows: "The word 'only' is employed merely to deny what ordinary people take to be real matter definitely separated from the various consciousnesses."[17] The theory of experiential togetherness developed by Whitehead and Bradley exhibits a significant resemblance to the Yogācāra idea of *sahopalambhaniyama* which asserts that since the external object or matter is invariably perceived together with the experience of it, its independence is untenable.[18] For to establish the difference between two things it is first necessary to perceive them apart. Thus to assert the independence of the external object it must first be perceived separately from experience, or known when *ex-hypothesi* it cannot be known. This invariable "togetherness" *(sahaja)* of the external object with sentient experience thus leads to the total identification of reality with experience in the Yogācāra idealism. The Yogācāra principle of *sahopalambhaniyama* is almost exactly reverberated in Bradley's famous idealistic experiment:

> Find any piece of existence, take up anything that anyone could possibly call a fact, or could in any sense assert to have being, and then judge if it does not consist in sentient experience. Try to discover any sense in which you can still continue to speak of it, when all perception and feeling have been removed; or point out any fragment of its matter, any aspect of its being, which is not derived and is not still relative to this source. When the experiment is made strictly, I can myself conceive of nothing else than the experienced. Anything in no sense felt or perceived, becomes to me quite unmeaning. . . . I am driven to the conclusion that for me experience is the same as reality.[19]

Whitehead adopts Bradley's theory of experiential togetherness with its equation of reality with experience, although with important reformations. For as Whitehead states at the outset of *Process and Reality* in the context of expressing his relation to Bradley, the philosophy of organism involves ". . . a transformation of some main doctrines of Absolute Idealism onto a realistic basis" (PR, p. xiii). Thus, while propounding the explicit ontological primacy of subjective experience, the concept of experience itself is defined in terms of a philosophical realism by Whitehead as meaning "the self-enjoyment of being one among many, and of being one arising out of the composition of many" (PR, p. 145). Consequently, Whitehead's subjectivist principle and doctrine of experiential togetherness are both reformed in terms of the objectivistic and realistic status of the data involved. It may also be asserted that while Hua-yen Buddhism adopts the consciousness-only theory of the Yogācāra school, it performs a similar transformation of certain doctrines of Absolute Idealism onto a realistic basis, whereupon each "one" is constituted by the inseparable togetherness of the "many."

Finally, one should not overlook the fact that the explicit identification of experience with reality in both process metaphysics and Hua-yen Buddhism becomes combined in the syncretic thought system of Nishida Kitarō, the celebrated founder of the Kyoto school in Japan. In his text, *A Study of Good (Zen no kenkyū)* Nishida identifies true reality with momentary events of pure or immediate experience, which he conceives, following the process thought of William James, as pristine reality existing anterior to the subject-object bifurcation.[20] David Dilworth, a leading interpreter of Nishida's thought, has written that Nishida continuously reformulated and deepened his notion of experiential immediacy throughout his career until "it culminated in a generalized Buddhist notion of 'pure experience' (*junsui keiken*) now interpreted in terms of the key concept of 'absolute nothingness' (*zettai mu*) as the topos or 'place' (*basho*) of the immediacy of experience."[21] Dilworth articulates Nishida's concept of pure experience or *junsui keiken* as "a topos of transparent immediacy" or as a "negative, experiential space."[22] Nishida then proceeds to incorporate the basic theoretical infrastructure of Hua-yen or Kegon Buddhism, whereupon absolute nothingness (*zettai mu*) conceived as the "negative space" or "transparent topos" of experiential immediacy, becomes the "place" (*basho*) of dependent coorigination (*engi*) and unhindered interfusion of phenomena with phenomena (*jiji muge*) within a field of interresonating co-presences.[23] Of course, from the standpoint of Whiteheadian process theory, Nishida's probing phenomenological profile of immediate or pure experience would have to be recast in wholly asymmetrical terms. Pure experience would then become in fact the place (*basho*) or topos of cumulative fusion or successive penetration in the negative space of transparent immediacy.[24]

Section III

Whitehead's metaphysics does not entirely abandon the concept of substance, then, as does the Hua-yen Buddhist doctrine of *niḥsvabhāvatā* or non-substantiality, but seeks to radically reformulate substance theory in terms of reconstructive process categories. What must now be opened up for critical discussion is whether or not Whitehead has in fact reified or substantialized his actual occasions beyond justification. In his text *Metaphysics of Natural Complexes*, Justus Buchler has elaborated a brilliant critique of Whitehead's ontological primacy of events. Whitehead states that events or actual occasions are the irreducible and ultimate ontological elements which are somehow "more real" than the other categories of existence.[25] However, Buchler is closer to certain Mādhyamika Buddhist ontological commitments and argues that no category of existence can be conferred ontological primacy, centrality or ultimacy in any way whatsoever. Buchler thus seeks to undermine the ontological primacy accorded to events, arguing that they have been absolutized, substantialized or hypostatized beyond justification. As David Dilworth points out, Buchler's critique of Whitehead's theory of the ontological primacy of events is especially interesting in view of the fact that it repeats an analogous historical pattern which occurred in Buddhism, when the Mādhyamika school elaborated a critical analysis of the dharmas or irreducible elements which were accorded ontological primacy by the Hīnayāna school.[26]

In his "Fundamentals of the Middle Way," Nāgārjuna not only equated *śūnyatā* or emptiness with *pratītyasamutpāda* or dependent co-origination but also with *niḥsvabhāvatā*, i.e., non-substantiality or non-selfnaturedness. Nāgārjuna asserts: "Anything which comes into existence presupposing something else is without self-existence (*svabhāva*)."[27] With his Prasaṅgika-Mādhyamika calculus of negations and logic of critical deconstruction, Nāgārjuna endeavored to demonstrate the relative and interdependent status, the emptiness and the utter non-substantiality of all reified entities by analytically factoring them into a multiplicity of causes and supportive conditions, all of which are themselves dependent, empty and unsubstantial, being capable of reduction into their own causes, and so on, ad infinitum. In such a manner, to use Dilworth's phrases, Nāgārjuna relentlessly "de-ontologized," "de-substantialized" and "de-absolutized" all reified concepts without exception.

The radical and uncompromising position of *niḥsvabhāvatā* adopted by Nāgārjuna can perhaps best be comprehended when considered in its historical context with respect to Hīnayāna Buddhism. Early Hīnayāna Buddhism applied the formula of dependent coorigination with great tenacity to the conception of a separate, independently existing ego or self (*ātman*), factoring it into a multiplicity of dharmas. However, these dharmas were the ultimate moments, irreducible elements or ontological absolutes of existence. Thus, the Mādhyamika school of Nāgārjuna charged the Hīnayāna theorists with having constructed a pluralistic realism wherein only the reality of the self (*ātman*) is negated, while the dharmas themselves are wholly reified as having some sort of absolute, irreducible and independent existence of their own. At the other extreme, the Mādhyamika school charged the Yogācarā Buddhists with having constructed a monistic idealism wherein such notions as consciousness (*vijñāna*), one mine (*ekacitta*) and the storehouse (*ālaya*) are all hypostatized as the ontological ultimates. Nāgārjuna and his successors in the Prasaṅgika-Mādhyamika tradition such as Candrakīrti and Śantideva argue that the Hīnayāna and Yogācarā sects developed an erroneous conception of the nature of conventional or pragmatic (*saṁvṛti*) truth in relation to ultimate (*paramārtha*) truth. The Hīnayāna and Yogācarā schools both go astray by conferring absolute validity on concepts having their place only on the level of pragmatic truth. The Hīnayāna concept of ultimate moments (dharmas) and the Yogācarā concept of consciousness-only (*vijñaptimātratāta*) are only *upāya* or expedient means, having merely provisional (*neyārtha*) status, which from the *paramārtha* level of truth are purely fictitious, i.e., mentally constructed (*vikalpa*) and artificial (*kṛtrima*) fabrications. Finally, "with a single blo" (as Mādhyamika dialecticians are fond of proclaiming), Nāgārjuna critically undermined all dharmas without exception through his statement: "Since there are no dharmas whatever originating independently, no dharma whatever exists which is not empty."[28] Thus, on the *paramārtha* level of truth there are no ontological ultimates, absolutes or finalities of any kind—no one, no many, no things, no emptiness; nothing is "more real" behind, beneath or beyond the interdependence of everything that is.

In an analogous manner, Justus Buchler challenges the ontological primacy accorded events in Whitehead's process realism. He rejects Whitehead's notion that events are somehow more real than other categories of existence while concurrently elaborating his own alternative framework based on what he terms "multi-ordinality" and "ontological parity." According to Buchler's theory, anything discriminated by the mind in any way is a "natural complex" and every natural complex or "disciminandum" is fully "real" within its own "ordinal location" or ontological context. Due to the multi-ordinal nature of reality, no complex is more real than any other. There exists a full "ontological parity" or equality of existential status between all discriminanda without exception. Dreams, hallucinations, mirages, fantasies, myths, being, becoming, time, space, subjects, objects, mind, matter, ideas, events, substances, processes—all have equivalent reality and ontological integrity in the respective orders in which they are located; for each natural complex is a discriminadum and possesses the being which allowed it to be discriminated, and therefore cannot be consigned to non-being without suffering patent contradiction.

Buchler seeks to expose and critically analyze a tacit presupposition or suppressed premise which has been structuring all Western speculative discourse since its inception in Greek antiquity, namely, the principle of ontological primacy or ontological priority. Governed by the principle of ontological primacy, philosophers have ranked entities hierarchically into "degrees" of being or "levels" of existence or "gradations" of reality such that some discriminanda are arbitrarily assigned as being "more real" or "most real" while all else is designated as "less real" or "unreal." While some philosophers in the West have assigned ontological primacy to a plurality of ultimate elements, such as forms (Plato), substances (Aristotle), monads (Leibniz) or events (Whitehead), others have assigned priority to a single, monistic absolute, such as the One (Parmenides), Mind (Hegel), or the Felt Totality (Bradley). Buchler has endeavored to undermine this entire tradition of ontological primacy from its very foundations, seeking to, as it were, wholly de-ontologize, de-absolutize and de-substantialize all discriminanda which have been accorded ultimate ontological status, whether this be a multiplicity of irreducible elements or a single totalistic absolute. Like the Mādhyamika Buddhists, Buchler recognizes that the mind can reify or substantialize any discriminandum whatsoever into an "absolute", i.e., something independent, self-existing, irreducible, and simple or non-relative. However, again analogously to the Mādhyamika system, Buchler seeks to divest all absolutized discriminanda of their ontological primacy by ramifying or factoring them ad infinitum into inexhaustible complexity.

Applying his critical deconstructive apparatus to Whitehead's categoreal scheme, Buchler discovers two incompatible trends, designated Trend I and Trend II.[29] Trend I seeks to delineate certain kinds of ontological distinctions and to interconnect them into a coherent system: Trend II seeks to rank them hierarchically into degrees of reality or degrees of experiential concreteness. It turns out that process-events or actual entities are accorded ontological primacy over all other discriminanda, including both their ingredient components (such as qualities, relations, eternal objects) as well as societies or nexūs, which the events themselves go to constitute. In his work, *Metaphysics of Natural Complexes* Buchler writes:

> It turns out, then, in Whitehead, that the atomic actualities are always components in an order or nexus of actualities. Yet somehow the former kinds of components, considered as realities, are less real, less "ultimate," than the latter kind of components. Atomic actuality is more real than its components, while an order (society) of such actualities is less real than its components. Both that which goes to constitute an atom and that which an atom goes to constitute are less real than the atom.[30]

Buchler proceeds to de-absolutize, de-ontologize and de-substantialize Whitehead's irreducible events or metaphysical atoms; that is to say, he proceeds to divest them of their alleged ontological primacy by means of what is essentially a Mādhyamika critical strategy of exposing the interdependence and relativity of the various discriminanda. The events, the components of events and the societies of events are virtually meaningless apart from each other, so that all have equal ontological status. Buchler continues: "All this, curiously, in spite of the fact that atoms are as inconceivable without their components as the components are without them; and in spite of the fact that these atoms are as inconceivable apart from an order as these orders are apart from them."[31]

Buchler especially criticizes the ontological primacy of actual entities over eternal objects. He inquires as to "why pure possibilities (eternal objects) should be secondary and actual entities primary, when it is repeatedly stated that neither of these two kinds of being is conceivable apart from the other."[32] Here Buchler is questioning the whole nature of the Aristotelian distinction between "primary" and "secondary" being. Primary being is always *ousia* for Aristotle, the particular independent substances, whereas secondary being is all other discriminanda, such as relations, qualities and forms, which have being only in the derivative sense of being components in substance. Whitehead's ontological principle, which he also calls the "Aristotelian principle," retains this distinction between primary and secondary being. All discriminanda such as prehensions, eternal objects, and the other categories of existence have their being only insofar as they are components in events or actual entities which are the "primary", "concrete", and "really real" modes of existence. Thus, in this sense Whitehead's actual entities are in fundamental agreement with Aristotle's doctrine of primary substance.

In rebuttal to Whitehead's Aristotelian doctrine concerning the ontological primacy of actualities and their division into primary and secondary (or concrete and abstract) modes of being, Buchler argues that the components or "traits" of events are in fact "sub-altern" complexes located in their own orders, such as to be on an ontological parity with the events themselves; these traits are in turn constituted by their own sub-altern complexes and so on, ad infinitum. Nature is thus characterized by its inexhaustible complexity and multi-ordinality, with no ontological simples or irreducible elements, and with no absolute termini of analysis. Buchler writes: "The classic difficulty lies in the. . . suggestion that what traits belong to, as contrasted with the traits themselves, is 'primary' in its being. From this bog we begin to emerge when we conceive every trait as a natural complex."[33]

In a rejoinder to Buchler's acutely argued critique of Whitehead's event ontology, Ivor Leclerc stresses the Aristotelian aspects of Whitehead's thought whereby there are many senses of "being," although events have being in a primary sense, as opposed to the way other discriminanda exist, just as for Aristotle, *ousia* "is" in a primary mode in relation to the way in which other things "are." The manner in which events are primary, just as the manner in which *ousia* is primary for Aristotle, is that only events "act" or have "agency." As Whitehead states: "The Aristotelian doctrine, that all agency is confined to actuality, is accepted" (AI, p. 197). An event is a creative *act* of synthesis and unification and only events possess agency of this sort. In Leclerc's words:

> The respect in which and the ground upon which Whitehead, with complete consistency, accords priority to actual entities, is that it is only actual entities which are agents. . . . all other entities being "agents" or "efficacious" only either as factors in actual entities, i.e., as contributory to the "act" of all entities (e.g., eternal objects, prehensions, subjective forms, propositions) or as derivative from actual entities (e.g., nexūs, societies). This is "ontological" priority because "act" is fundamental to "being."[34]

Charles Hartshorne, in his own rejoinder to Buchler's critique, emphasizes that Buchler has not adequately grasped the radical *asymmetrical* structure of temporal process, as opposed to the symmetrical structure of conceptual relations. Repeating Hartshorne's words:

> In general, polar contrasts, such as abstract/concrete, universal/particular, object/subject, are symmetrical correlates only so long as we think simply of the categories themselves, as concepts, and not of what they may be used to refer to or describe. The moment we think of the latter, the symmetrical interdependence is replaced by a radical asymmetry.[35]

Whitehead understands events to be actual, concrete and particular in relation to eternal objects which are possible, abstract and universal, attributing an ontological primacy to the former triad over the latter. Buchler's polemic is that such polar opposites are symmetrical in structure, such that neither can be accorded ontological primacy over the other. Hartshorne's response is that Buchler has only demonstrated that the dipolar contrast of abstract/concrete is ultimate; but always the concrete includes the abstract, the particular the universal and the actual the possible. Thus, the abstract/concrete distinction is wholly *asymmetrical* in structure. This ontological primacy of the concrete over the abstract and events over eternal objects may be considered an illustration of Hartshorne's logic of ultimate contrasts whereby one side of a dipolar contrast is always reducible to the other, such as the object into the subject, the many into the one, matter into mind or in this case, the abstract into the concrete.[36]

Thus, in a summary statement of his rejoinder to Buchler's critique of the ontological primacy of events, Hartshorne writes:

> We are told (by Buchler) that if eternal objects are not comprehensible apart from actualities, neither are actualities apart from eternal objects. But this is only to say that the contrast abstract/concrete is ultimate; nevertheless, the concrete entities include the abstract ones, not vice versa. Thus, it is the concrete which enjoys this contrast.[37]

In rebuttal to Buchler, then, Hartshorne argues that it is precisely the *asymmetrical* structure of temporal process as opposed to the symmetrical structure of conceptual meanings that justifies the ontological primacy accorded events in Whitehead's thought. Leclerc, complementing Hartshorne's argument, asserts that physical events are primary in that they are the locus of agency. Moreover, Robert C. Neville has developed the polemic that although Buchler's multiordinal ontology is a brilliant description of Whitehead's "coordinate" level of analysis, it entirely neglects the "genetic" level that depends on an actual occasion subjectively coming into being through creative synthesis; it is here that the primacy of occasions over their components is established.[38] Further still, Neville argues that it is misleading to assert that actual occasions are "more real" than their components or that components are "less real" than actual occasions; rather, actual occasions are real only as a unified synthesis of their components and components are real only as necessarily contained within the unity of actual occasions.

However, Buchler would counter that Whitehead's categories are simply not *generic* enough to encompass all discriminanda without exception. This is the case with any categoreal scheme based on the premise of ontological primacy. Reality is characterized by multi-ordinality and ontological parity. What Hartshorne in fact proves by his distinction between physical asymmetry and conceptual symmetry is that there are different orders of being, each as valid as all the others. Whitehead and his followers claim that reality is to be equated with physical processes, happenings, events and agency. But Buchler replies that "such a conception is not intolerable but only narrow; for not all complexes are happenings."[39] Asymmetry is the structural invariant of certain orders, but not for others such as the order of conceptual meanings. Stephen Ross has a forceful statement on this dialectical tension between Whitehead's process theory and Buchler's multi-ordinal ontology, asserting that both, "achieved not a minor metaphysical world-view, flawed in a central respect, but a monumental conception of the world. The future of metaphysical understanding will flow from the dialectical tensions generated between them, especially on the subject of ontological priority."[40] The present work adopts a modified version of the Buchlerian multi-ordinal framework in order to achieve the most generic levels of speculative discourse. Thus, this work assumes an irreducible plurality of ordinal locations, the order of physical events being structured by the cause-effect principle of asymmetry; whereas other domains, such as the order of concepts, as well as the orders of imagination and dreams (as argued in the final chapter of this study) are regulated by the acausal principle of symmetry or synchronicity. Thus, metaphysical confusion arises in part from the illicit extension of principles beyond their proper range of application into orders where they do not in fact obtain.

CHAPTER 10

Metaphysics of Cumulative Penetration

This chapter provides a synoptic encapsulation of the process doctrine of actuality as reformulated in terms of a metaphysics of cumulative penetration which is then systematically applied to the fields of epistemology, ethics, axiology and soteriology. The thesis propounded here is that process theory shares the deepest ontological commitments of Hua-yen Buddhism, namely, that every event is in some sense virtually present or immanent in every other event such that each occasion both contains and pervades its universe: and moreover, in consequence of this profound togetherness, cohesiveness and solidarity of events, enlightened perceptivity *(prajñā)*, compassion *(karuṇā)*, aesthetic-value immediacy or ecstatic bliss (*mahāsukha*) and deliverance through final peace (*nirvāṇa*) are all intrinsic to the structure of actuality itself. However, as I argue throughout the text, this ontological togetherness of events does not implicate a theory of interpenetration among events as propounded by Hua-yen Buddhism, but a doctrine of cumulative penetration, in concordance with the strictly asymmetrical infrastructure underlying the process model of actuality. According to the metaphysics of cumulative penetration, past, present and future occasions do not simply interpenetrate into a single thought-instant as in Hua-yen Buddhism; rather, they *cumulatively* penetrate their successors through the pulsatory transition of vector feeling-tones. The two pillars of the metaphysics of cumulative penetration are the doctrine of creativity and the theory of feelings. The principle of creativity correlates with the ultimate category of Hua-yen Buddhism, namely *śūnyatā,* in that both represent a doctrine of universal relativity in the sense of "arising into existence through causation." However for Whitehead, universal relativity always means asymmetrical relativity as opposed to the symmetrical mode of universal relativity posited by Hua-yen. Again, both *śūnyatā* and creativity function within their respective speculative frameworks to fuse manyness into oneness, multiplicity into unity, disjunction into conjunction or the macrocosm into the microcosm at the standpoint of unification provided by each event in nature. Yet, for process theory, the "many" makes reference only to the past world of completed actualities, not to past, present and future events alike as in Hua-yen Buddhism. Moreover, both creativity and *śūnyatā* establish the "togetherness" of all events within each event. For as Whitehead's principle of experiential togetherness asserts, the whole universe abides "experientially together" as an aesthetic and harmonized unity of feelings at the standpoint of each event in nature. Yet, this experiential togetherness produced through an act of creative synthesis is not the total togetherness of past-present-future as established by *śūnyatā,* but only the momentary production of novel togetherness.

According to the doctrine of *śūnyatā,* each unit-event can be reductively analyzed or exhaustively factored into its causal relations and supportive conditions without remainder. Implicit in this doctrine is a theory of total determinism, since each event is an effect which is wholly reducible to its causes. Therefore, it is *niḥsvabhāva,* non-substantial, with no unique selfhood or intrinsic own-being. However, process theory argues that what cannot be inherited is the *unity* of all causes in a single, unified occasion of experience, and for this an *emergent synthesis* is required. Even if all the components of an occasion are given for synthesis, even the pattern for synthesis itself, the act of synthesis must still be new, an emergent-spontaneous creation of the present. Thus, creative self-determination, emergent novelty and freedom of decision are all intrinsic to actuality itself as experiential synthesis. And further still, insofar as each occasion of experience satisfies the criterion of *sui generis,* i.e., self-creativity or free self-constitution, it is in fact a substance with intrinsic reality, transcendent with respect to all other occasions and diverse from that data which it unifies, the multitude of antecedent occasions given in disjunction. An occasion's character of *sui generis* or self-creativity is not derived from anything else; in a crucial sense, then, occasions may indeed by conceived in themselves without making reference to external causes and conditions. It is therefore precisely this notion of self-creative experience constitutive of its own novel and aesthetic unity which confers on each occasion a degree of unique selfhood and irreducible own-being not accorded to the fundamental units of existence in the Hua-yen doctrine of *niḥsvabhāvatā* or total non-substantiality. Thus, it may finally be asserted that the metaphysics of cumulative penetration accounts for as much cosmic togetherness, cohesiveness and solidarity as well as all the creativeness, novelty and freedom necessary for any balanced descriptive generalization of experiential immediacy.

The theory of feelings, the second pillar of the metaphysics of cumulative. penetration, argues that the very meaning of efficient causation is "conditioning by antecedents". Each moment-event emerges into actuality as a unit-pulsation of emotional intensity through its causal vector feelings or prehensions of every other event in its universe, finally harmonizing the whole multiplicity of feelings together into an aesthetic and novel occasion of experience through an emergent-spontaneous act of creative synthesis. Prehension or feeling is a metaphysical generalization encompassing three ordinarily disconnected notions, namely, memory-causation-perception, all three being conceived as a feeling of antecedents. To feel (perceive) a prior event is to be causally conditioned by it, and both causation and perception are aspects of "memory"—an awareness of the past. Thus, each unit-pulsation of emotional intensity restores its antecedent universe through remembrance. A prehension or causal feeling is termed a "vector" by Whitehead, indicating the literal transference of a throb of causally efficacious emotional intensity between occasions of experience after the analogy of directed flow-patterns of electromagnetic conduction or energetic transmission between vibrating field-events in contemporary physical science. This vector character transfers the cause into the effect, the object into the subject and the past into the present thus conferring on actuality its strictly asymmetrical and cumulative character. To repeat Whitehead's words, it is this ". . . vector character which transfers the cause into the effect. . . . This passage of the cause into the effect is the cumulative character of time." (PR, p. 237). Feelings are vectors in that they transform there into here, and then into now, such that far becomes near and past becomes present, thereby wholly undermining the character of what Whitehead terms "simple location," the notion that an occasion occupies only one locus in the spatiotemporal continuum while being entirely absent from all other times and places. Thus, it is through the vector transmission of emotional intensity that occasions are made present or immanent in other occasions. But prehension does not establish a total presence or mutual immanence among all occasions, only a cumulative presence or successive immanence.

According to the metaphysics of cumulative penetration, there cannot be a mutual immanence between dipolar opposites such as one and many or subject and object as posited by Hua-yen: the object is present in the subject but not the subject in the object. For subject and object are not simultaneous with each other. Perception or feeling is always of the *past* such that memory is the basic paradigm for awareness. The perceiving subject is the effect and the perceived object the causal condition of the effect. Thus, each act of creative synthesis involves the gathering together of a vast multiplicity of antecedent objects into an emerging subject in the immediate occasion. There is a *cumulative* penetration of objects-into-subject and multiplicity-into-unity. Consequently, it is only the *past* world of completed actualities that is present in an immediate occasion in the strong sense of efficient causation or vector transmission of emotional intensity. However, the past is present not in its living subjective immediacy, but only as an objectified presence which occurs through the process of conformal reproduction or causal re-enaction. Finally, its objectified presence is subjected to further qualifications in that all incompatible data incapable of satisfying categoreal demands is "eliminated from feeling," "held inoperative" or "replaced by negative prehensions." To conclude then, according to the process model of actuality, every event is "present" in every other event in the cosmos such that in some sense, "everything is everywhere at all times." Yet the specified sense in which this fact obtains is not in the sense of "total presence" as asserted by Hua-yen Buddhism, but precisely in the sense of "cumulative presence," as well as in the senses of creative advance, emergent novelty, one-way relatively, conformal objectification and negative prehension, in full accordance with the asymmetrical infrastructures underlying the metaphysics of cumulative penetration.

(i) Enlightened Perceptivity in the Primordial Mode of Causal Feeling and Imaginative Synthesis

In Buddhist epistemology, *prajñā* (non-dual wisdom) or "enlightened perceptivity" is the immediate experience of the emptiness or universal relativity (*śūnyatā*) of all determinate forms (*rūpam*). Thus, *prajñā* is a direct perception of the field of causal relatedness (*śūnyatā*) of which each dharma is a particular function. As was developed earlier, *prajñā* and *śūnyatā* may be comprehended as *noetic-noematic* correlates, whereby *prajñā* is the *noetic* or constitutive subject pole and *śūnyatā* is its correlate *noematic* or constituted object pole. Moreover, it was described how the *noematic* side of the perceptual field is characterized by a core/horizon, foreground/background or focus/fringe gestalt patterning which is itself directly organized by such *noetic* constitutive acts as focusing or attention. Whereas ordinary perception fixates exclusively on the focal core of the perceptual field, *prajñā* or enlightened perceptivity involves a radical *noetic* reversal whereby attention is shifted from foreground to background, i.e., from determinate form (*rūpam*) to the surrounding field of emptiness, nothingness and voidness, or as it were: the "horizon of openness." This entire phenomenological theory of perception may be itself entirely reformulated in purely Whiteheadian process terminology.

Whitehead has also analyzed the essential structure of the perceptual field in terms of the foreground/background or focus/fringe distinction: "In the background there is triviality, vagueness, and massive uniformity; in the foreground discrimination and contrasts. . ." (PR, p. 112). In Whitehead's theory of perception, he states that anterior to the levels of clear and distinct sense data (presentational immediacy) and cognitive interpretation (symbolic reference) arises a more primordial stratum of perception in the mode of "causal efficacy" or "causal feeling." It can be asserted that causal feeling is precisely the perception of the background or penumbral fringe of causal relations encircling the clear and distinct data of sense perception located at the focal core of the experiential field. In the technical terminology of phenomenological discourse, Whitehead's primordial perception in the mode of causal efficacy involves a radical "*noetic* reversal" or shift of attention from the foreground of clear and distinct sense data to the felt background of causal relations. This primordial mode of perception or feeling in Whitehead's system of thought may thus be said to function analogously to what is termed the perception of *śūnyatā* through *prajñā* in Buddhist epistemological discourse. Yet, upon deeper analysis, the Hua-yen Buddhist field of *śūnyatā* or universal relativity is in fact more consonant with the felt background described by the British Absolute Idealist F.H. Bradley than as described by Whitehead himself. Bradley elaborates his description of the felt background of experiential immediacy which accompanies all objects located at the focal core of the perceptual field as follows:

> In immediate experience there is no distinction between my awareness and that of which it is aware. There is an immediate feeling, a knowing and being in one with which knowledge begins; and though this [immediate experience] is in a manner transcended, it nevertheless remains throughout as the present foundation of my known world. . . everything which comes in the form of an object or relation implies still the *felt background* against which the object comes. . . immediate experience is not a stage which may have been there at some time but has now ceased to exist. . . . Every distinction still rests on an *immediate background* of which I am aware.[1]

However, for Bradley this felt background of experiential immediacy designates an Absolute Reality, what he calls the "felt totality," comprehended as an undivided whole of sentient feeling devoid of subject and object or center and periphery. Through their infinite internal relations to everything else, all relata of the past, present and future dissolve into their immediate backgrounds so as to ultimately become transmuted into a single, all-embracing felt totality. Bradley's felt background of immediate experience is therefore in this respect analogous to the Hua-yen Buddhist *dharmadhātu*, understood as the infinite background of causal relations which ontologically supports each particular dharma or determinite form (located at the core of the perceptual field) as perceived by an act of *prajñā*. Nishida Kitarō provides a similar account of the felt background or relational fringe of immediate experience, which he explicitly identifies as the "place" (*basho*) of *zettai mu* or Absolute Nothingness, or as it were, the "negative space" of experiential immediacy, arguing that it signifies an absolute, all-embracing reality, in that this fringe datum is *infinite* in scope. Nishida states: "William James wrote of a 'fringe of consciousness', but the world of the present has in fact an infinite fringe. Therein exists the world of Absolute Nothingness."[2] Yet, in Whitehead's process metaphysics, the felt background of experiential immediacy perceived through perception in the primordial mode of causal efficacy reveals a radically *temporal* field of causal relatedness, a past rushing into the present and a present surging into the future, what William James termed the empirical datum of "felt transitions," or what in modern phenomenological discourse is called: the "protentive-retentive" structure of internal time-consciousness. Hence, the felt background of internal relatedness perceived through Whitehead's causal efficacy is not the felt totality described by F.H. Bradley in the West, or the all-embracing *dharmadhātu* perceived through *prajñā* as described by Hua-yen Buddhism in the East, but a primordial awareness of inrushing causal feelings or vector transmissions of emotional intensity pulsating from the ancestral past into the arising present within an ever-flowing stream of consciousness in the living immediacy of experience.

How is one to effect this transference of the gaze from the focal core of clear and distinct sense data to the felt background of causal feeling? As specified in previous segments of this work, such a dramatic shift of attention from core to periphery through an act of *noetic* reversal can only be animated by a process of "creative visioning," which phenomenological analysis has itself named: "free variation in imagination." The phenomenological praxis of imaginative variation, it should be recalled, functions to deconstruct sedimented focal-settings through a multiperspectival open possibility search for value-rich core/horizon gestalt environments. In Whiteheadian process theory, the creative visioning of value-rich gestalts through imaginative variation finds its theoretical basis in the metaphysical primacy accorded to creative synthesis over causal feeling or physical memory. For no occasion of experience is completely determined by its field of causal relations but ultimately constitutes its own definiteness through novel and spontaneous acts of creative synthesis. The primary role played by creativity at the level of human perception has been developed with great elegance by Robert C. Neville in terms of an axiological process cosmology of "imaginative synthesis." According to Neville's theory, the primary function of imagination as synthesis is to gather otherwise merely causal components into the contrast between background and focus, which he argues is the elementary structure of beauty. In his remarkable work entitled *Reconstruction of Thinking*, Neville writes:

> Experience is distinguished by virtue of involving a synthesis of otherwise merely causal components. . . . The most elementary form of this is synthesis of the components into a field that serves as a background for focused attention.

Neville continues:

> The contrast between background field and foreground focus of attention is the elementary form of beauty. The gathering of otherwise merely causal components of human processes into imaginative experiential synthesis is thus a primary form of valuation. In fact it employs valuation in a primary sense to constitute the field of experience.[3]

Neville's process theory of imaginative experiential synthesis, following Whitehead's complete reversal of the Kantian doctrine of synthesis (i.e., as objectivity-into-subjectivity instead of subjectivity-into-objectivity), argues that each act of imaginative synthesis constitutes experience in the form of an objective world present to a subject. Imaginative synthesis is the primordial value of gathering causal presence into the beauty of harmonic contrast between focus and background. The decision as to what is constituted as focus and what is constituted as background through each act of imaginative synthesis is thus the primary form of aesthetic valuation in perceptual experience. And the value of causal presence is always secondary to the more primordial value of imaginative synthesis.

We can now formulate some general conclusions regarding the nature of enlightened perceptivity in the tradition of Whiteheadian process metaphysics. On the one side, it involves a return to perception in the primordial mode of causal efficacy through a *noetic* reversal, i.e., a dramatic shift of attention from foreground focus to the felt background of experiential immediacy; while on the other side this radical reconstitution of the perceptual field into a value-rich background/focus gestalt pattern involves a spontaneous process of creative visioning and free variation through imaginative experiential synthesis. What gives to each gestalt pattern its value-rich character is not only its wholeness of causal presence, but also its *irreducible harmonic contrast* between background and focus, and this is made possible only through a creative act of imaginative synthesis. The creative visioning of value-rich background/focus gestalts through imaginative experiential synthesis can be diagrammed as follows:

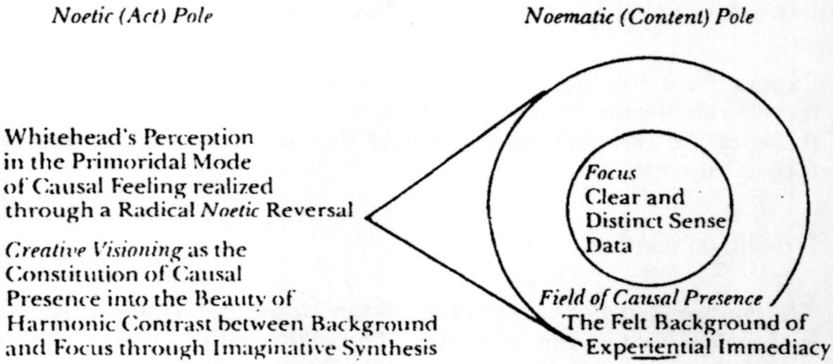

To conclude: the felt background of experiential immediacy is not a felt totality, as argued by Hua-yen Buddhism in the East or Bradley in the West; it is a felt past prehended through causal memory. Yet, the background of causal presence also contains an inner horizon of possible variations which can be actualized through future creative acts of imaginative synthesis. Through creative visioning, the field of otherwise merely causal presence is dramatically reconstituted into the beauty of harmonic contrasts between focus and background, which is the primary aesthetic-value realized by imaginative experiential synthesis. It is this physical embodiment of causal presence through primordial feeling as patterned into value-laden background/focus gestalt environments by means of creative visioning and imaginative synthesis which constitutes the essence of enlightened perceptivity in a metaphysics of cumulative penetration.

(ii) Universal Compassion as Sympathetic Concernedness

A common theme in Mahāyāna Buddhism at the moral level of

discourse is *śūnyatākaruṇābhinnam* or the "indivisibility of *śūnyatā* (emptiness) and *karuṇā* (compassion)." In terms of the Sinitic *t'i-yung* or essence-function construction governing Hua-yen Buddhist patterns of thought, emptiness or universal relativity is essence (*t'i*) and universal compassion or unconditional love is its dynamic and external function (*yung*). Again in terms of simile, this correlation of universal relativity with universal compassion is often compared with the relation obtaining between a lamp and its light, these representing *t'i* and *yung* or essence and function respectively. Or as described in the *Avataṁsaka Sūtra*, upon entering into Vairocana Buddha's non-obstructive dharma-realm of total interdependence and interpenetration, one thereupon simultaneously becomes transformed into bodhisattva Samantabhadra who performs inconceivable acts, inconceivable miracles and inconceivable vows, raining down his sea of compassion like a shower of jewels for the bliss and welfare of all sentient beings. Thus, the Hua-yen metaphysics of complete non-obstructed interpenetration and harmonization among all dharmas has significant ramifications of the highest order at the ethical level of discourse in so far as it involves a serious doctrine of "being-for-others," i.e., a doctrine of altruistic social engagement and benevolent rectification of affairs through compassionate saving activity and moral responsibility, as symbolized by Samantabhadra, and Hua-yen bodhisattva of universal love and compassion. For this reason, the *Avataṁsaka Sūtra* describes Samantabhadra as radiating potent rays, waves and beams of grace to all sentient beings throughout the ten realms of the *dharmadhātu* without obstruction, which upon striking them instantaneously illuminates their minds and fills their hearts with resolute faith. Bodhisattva Samantabhadra's universal compassion and mercy are given their deepest expression in his accomplishment of the Ten Vows: (1) To honor all Buddhas; (2) To praise all Buddhas; (3) To make offerings to all Buddhas; (4) To repent all sins; (5) To be sympathetically joyful for the merits accumulated by others; (6) To supplicate the Buddha to revolve the Wheel of Dharma; (7) To supplicate the Buddha to always remain living in this world; (8) To always emulate the Buddha's paradigmatic life; (9) To always look after the welfare of all sentient beings; and (10) To turn all of one's merits over to others. Indeed, Hua-yen Buddhism makes the claim that one's capacity to realize the supreme and infinite enlightenment of Vairocana Buddha rests precisely upon one's capacity to accomplish and hold the marvelous Sea of Vows of Samantabhadra bodhisattva.

In Whitehead's process metaphysics, this theme concerning the "indivisibility of emptiness and compassion" is discoverable as the "concern" structure of causal process, wherein each act of causal prehension or "feeling of feeling" is itself comprehended as an act of "sympathetic concernedness." Whitehead explicitly asserts that the object-into-subject pattern of causal transmission may be directly conceived as the "concern" structure of immediate experience when he writes: "The occasion as subject has a 'concern' for the object. And the 'concern' at once places the object as a component in the experience of the subject, with an affective tone drawn from this object and directed towards it" (AI, p. 176). Hence, Whitehead continues, "Concernedness is of the essence of perception" (AI, p. 180). This moral connotation of the object-into-subject structure of causal process is made still more patent when Whitehead formulates his theory of primordial perception in the mode of causal efficacy in terms of "sympathy" or "feeling of feeling." He writes:

> The primitive form of physical experience is emotional—blind emotion—received as felt elsewhere in another occasion and conformally appropriated as a subjective passion. In the language appropriate to the higher stages of experience, the primitive element is *sympathy*, that is, feeling the feeling *in* another and feeling conformally *with* another." (PR, p. 162)

Thus, concernedness or sympathetic feeling is virtually intrinsic to the object-into-subject structure of immediate experience as direct causal prehension and conformal appropriation. Again, compassion (deriving from the Latin verb root *compassio* meaning "to feel with") is built into the very structure of primordial experience as "feeling the feelings *of* another and feeling conformally *with* another." In other words, compassion, concern and sympathy are metaphysical in nature, not merely psychological achievements.

In his book *Creativity and Taoism*, Chang Chung-yuan develops at length the notion of *tz'u* or sympathy as it was utilized by the ancient Chinese Taoists and later by Chinese Buddhism to denote "Universal Compassion" or unconditional love and concern for all sentient beings. Chung-yuan asserts that the Chinese concept of "sympathy (*tz'u*) was primordial identification, interfusion and unification of subject and object, of one and many and of man and the universe," and again: "The dissolution of self and the interfusion among all individuals constitutes the metaphysical structure of sympathy (*tz'u*)".[4] However, again reflecting their divergent metaphysical commitments of symmetry as over against asymmetry, whereas the Chinese Buddhist concept of compassion or sympathy (*tz'u*) represents the total interpenetration and mutual fusion of subject and object or one and many, Whitehead's notions of sympathy and concern represent a cumulative fusion or one-way penetration of cause-into-effect, past-into-present or manyness-into-oneness, in concordance with the object-into-subject structure of immediate experience. Thus, whereas both Hua-yen Buddhism and Whiteheadian process theory recognize "universal compassion" as a logical correlate of "universal relativity," for the latter system of thought this always means one-way relativity or causation from the past, in that sympathetic concernedness is always a metaphysical function of some present subject's inclusion of an antecedent object into its own real internal constitution through an act of causal prehension or conformal appropriation.

There are persuasive and convincing arguments for adopting the asymmetrical structure of causal relations at the moral level of discourse. It is only the asymmetrically structured scheme of causality propounded by the metaphysics of cumulative penetration that allows for creative freedom through spontaneous self-constitution since relations are determinate or closed only at one end while being indeterminate or open at the other. Freedom of decision is a necessary component in any given moral act. For if one's act is to be judged morally responsible, one must have been free to act otherwise. Thus, the Buddhist notion of sympathy or compassion (*tz'u*) conceived as a function of metaphysical interpenetration and interfusion, seems incompatible with the concept of moral responsibility, and is more adequately interpreted in terms of a theory of cumulative penetration or processive fusion.

In his text *Hua-yen Buddhism: The Jewel Net of Indra,* Francis Cook quotes Fa-tsang's famous doctrine based on *Avataṁsaka Sūtra,* that the fifty-two stages of the bodhisattva's career entirely interpenetrate such that cause and effect as well as beginning and end are mutually identical. Fa-tsang writes:

> If one stage is acquired, all stages are acquired, because. . . of mutual interpenetration, because of mutual identity, and because of mutual interfusion. The *Avataṁsaka-sūtra* says, "One stage includes the qualities of all stages throughout." Therefore, what is meant here is the acquisition of all stages as well as the stage of Buddhahood as soon as one has reached that part (of the path) which is called "superior progress," which is the perfection of faith. Because all stages including the stage of Buddhahood are identical, then cause and effect are not different, and beginning and end interpenetrate. On each stage, one is thus both a Bodhisattva and a Buddha.[5]

Yet, if all fifty-two stages of the Bodhisattva's path simultaneously interpenetrate without obstruction such that each stage contains all future stages as well as all prior stages, then the act of taking vows of compassion and the resolute effort to cultivate the two perfections of merit and wisdom become wholly meaningless. Once again, for any one's act or decision to be morally responsible, including the acts of a Bodhisattva or Buddha, one must have been free to act or decide otherwise within a field of real alternatives. Hence, the Buddhist moral doctrine of karma (the inexhorable law of cause and effect) seems meaningful only within a framework of asymmetrical causation and cumulative penetration wherein the responsibility for future events at least partially rests on one's decisions made in the present, so that a Bodhisattva's vows and efforts make a real and significant difference. Of course, one can argue as did Chinul in his Hwaŏm/Sŏn system that sudden enlightenment (in the sense of initial insight) is fully present even at the first stage of a Bodhisattva's career in the mode of nascent *faith* (in one's own primordial attainment of Buddhahood), which is then cultivated through gradual practices, finally coming to full maturation in the state of ultimate wisdom, the non-regressive or non-backsliding stage of perfected faith. However, this kind of theory is more intelligible within the process framework of actualizing latent potentiality wherein awakened faith, the initial mode in which enlightenment is available to a practitioner, is gradually cultivated by accumulating wisdom and merit, finally culminating in perfect Buddhahood at the final stages of the path as is commonly expressed by the *upamā* or simile of a seed gradually coming to fruition as a fully blossomed flower.

Finally, as Hartshorne often argues, the process doctrine of asymmetrical inclusiveness functions just as efficiently as the doctrine of symmetrical inclusiveness to undermine the ego-centric theories of motivation and provide a firm basis for a truly altruistic morality based on universal love and compassion, although not at the expense of creative freedom as does this latter mode of thought.[6] For a self-interest theory of motivation seems tenable only in a substance cosmology positing simply-localized entitative units with independent self-existence and stable endurance. But in Whitehead's process theory, altruistic morality and sympathetic concern are established by the radically social structure of actuality wherein no unit-event can separate itself from other events or from the whole (MT, p. 111). Since no individual (i.e., a serially ordered society of events whose members are flashing into existence and instantaneously perishing) is wholly identical with itself in time (being an event-sequence through historical routes of causal transmission bound together by a recurrently inherited pattern) or wholly separate from others in space (being a creative synthesis of those others from a unifying perspective) a self-interest and ego-centric theory of motivation breaks down. Thus, universal love and compassion in the mode of sympathetic concernedness is indeed intrinsic to actuality itself as universal relativity; but again, this always means one-way relativity in accordance with the asymmetrical structure of social relatedness as established by the metaphysics of cumulative penetration.

(iii) *Ecstatic Bliss and Aesthetic-Value Feeling as Dipolor Contrast*

At the axiological level of speculative discourse it is of special interest to consider Hua-yen patterns of thought intrinsic to Tantric Buddhism such as Indo-Tibetan Vajrayāna or Kūkai's esoteric Shingon Buddhism in Japan. The Tantric tradition culminated the positive (*astivāda*) expression of the Buddhist Dharma through its construction of a radically value-centric metaphysics which explicitly identifies ultimate reality with *mahāsukha* (ecstatic pleasure) and *ānanda* (supreme bliss).[7] Yet, upon deeper analysis it is evident that *mahāsukha* and *ānanda* are a function of the microcosmic-macrocosmic structure of reality itself comprehended through such basic ontological categories as *yuganaddha* (union of opposites or polar fusion), *advaya* (non-dualism) and *sahaja* (togetherness) which are all essentially restatements of Hua-yen patterns of thought. Garma C. C. Chang has pointed out the deep structural proximity of Buddhist Tantrism to the interpenetrative vision of reality articulated by Hua-yen Buddhism in a discussion concerning the Tantric notion of "The Magic Manifestation Web or Net," stating:

> This is an important term, reflecting the basic Tantric view on the "Realm of Totality," which is strikingly similar to the philosophy of Hua-yen Buddhism. To explain it very briefly, all manifestations are unsubstantial. . . . Because of this very unsubstantiality or void nature, all manifestations can arise simultaneously in the same place without hindering each other—in fact each manifestation can arise in another's place in an interpenetrating manner.[8]

At the level of religious praxis, the so-called "secret" *upāya* or "skillful means" of the Tantric Vehicle in Buddhism is the imaginative visualization of oneself as a maṇḍala (with an indwelling god and goddess in *yuganaddha*) within the soteriological context of realizing the emptiness of inherent-existence. The maṇḍala is homologized with the whole universe and the entire Buddhist pantheon, representing a microcosm of the macrocosm, complete with the six elements (earth, water, fire, air, space, consciousness) and an inner zodiac (*kālacakra*) or astrological model of the psyche. Thus, through the ritual visualization of a maṇḍala in the creative imagination, the Tantric adept is reconstituted as a microcosm of the macrocosm in a manner at once analogous to the *li-shih-wu-ai* and *shih-shih-wu-ai* yogic meditations of Hua-yen Buddhist praxis. Through the visualization of oneself as a maṇḍala one achieves *yuganaddha* (union of opposites), *advaya* (non-dualism) and *sahaja* (togetherness), which in turn generate *mahāsukha* (ecstatic pleasure) and *ānanda* (supreme bliss). The fundamental conception of Tantric Buddhist metaphysics, namely, *yuganaddha,* signifies the coincidence of opposites. It is symbolized by the conjugal embrace (*maithuna* or *kāma-kala)* of a god and goddess or a Buddha and his consort (signifying *karuṇā* and *śūnyatā* or *upāya* and *prajñā,* respectively), also commonly depicted in Tantric Buddhist iconography as the union of *vajra* (diamond sceptre) and *padme* (lotus flower). Thus, *yuganaddha* essentially means the interpenetration of opposites or dipolar fusion, and is a fundamental restatement of Hua-yen theoretic structures. Indeed, the Tantric doctrine that *mahāsukha* and *ānanda* are a function of *yuganaddha* demonstrates a brilliant extension of the Hua-yen ontology of interpenetration over into the domain of value theory.

This Tantric conception of ultimate reality as ecstatic bliss, understood as a function of *yuganaddha* or dipolar fusion, is discoverable in Whitehead's process metaphysics wherein "aesthetic-value feeling" and maximum depth of intensity of satisfaction" are made intrinsic to actuality itself as a function of irreducible *dipolar contrasts.* The primacy of aesthetic experience and the fusion of facts and values in Whitehead's process metaphysics are proclaimed when he writes:

> The metaphysical doctrine here expounded finds the foundations of the world in the aesthetic experience. . . . All order is therefore aesthetic order, and the moral order is merely certain aspects of the aesthetic order, and the aesthetic order is derived from the immanence of God." (RM, p. 116)

Each unit-pulsation of emotional intensity is an aesthetic experience emerging out of the plenary creativeness at the base of actuality: "An intense experience is an aesthetic fact. . . .an actual fact is a fact of aesthetic exprience" (PR, p. 279–280). Elsewhere, Whitehead states that the intrinsic value in experience is beauty, which he defines as the perfection of harmony (AI, p. 252). He writes: "The teleology of the Universe is directed to the production of Beauty" (AI, p. 265). Furthermore, each actual occasion is described as an act of "self-enjoyment": "I have termed each individual act of self-enjoyment an occasion of experience" (MT, p. 325). Elsewhere he propounds the fusion of facts with values asserting: "'Value' is the word I use for the intrinsic reality of an event" (SMW, p. 93). Again, he uses the term satisfaction to denote that final phase in the creative process of experiential synthesis in which it completes itself as a single, determinate harmony of feelings: "The ultimate attainment is 'satisfaction.' This is the final characterization of the unity of feeling of the one actual entity. . . " (PR, p. 166).

Whitehead states that maximum depth of intensity of satisfaction in an aesthetic occasion of experience is achieved through irreducible dipolar contrasts, whereby antithetical data or mutually inhibitory feelings are entered as complementary *contrasts* of feelings, instead of eliminated through negative prehension as incompatible for synthesis within a single pattern of harmonic togetherness. The doctrine of "contrasts" in Whitehead's axiological metaphysics is part of the twentieth-century revolution in speculative thought that he instituted. A felt contrast is a binary or diadic tension of opposites which fit together into a harmonic pattern. Thus, dipolar opposites are not subsumed into some third reality, such as an absolute or all-embracing universal principle, which is the usual strategy for harmonizing contradictions in certain Buddhist modes of thought as well as in the absolute idealist theories of the West. Rather, dipolar opposites simply fit together into *irreducible* felt contrasts which in turn elicit maximum depth of intensity of emotion and heightened aesthetic-value feeling. Irreducible felt contrasts of dipolar opposites within harmonic patterns of experiential togetherness are therefore the intrinsic aesthetic-values discoverable at the base of actuality in Whitehead's axiological metaphysics. He writes:

> This "aim at contrast" is the expression of the ultimate creative purpose that each unification shall achieve some maximum depth of intensity of feeling. . . ." (PR, p. 249)
>
> [Massive diversity is shifted] into a harmony of contrasts, issuing into intensity of experience. The inhibitions of opposites have been adjusted into contrasts of opposites. (PR, p. 109)
>
> . . . the heightening of intensity arises from order such that the multiplicity of components in the nexus can enter explicit feeling as *contrasts*, and are not dismissed into negative prehensions as *incompatibilities*. (PR, p. 83)
>
> Contrast elicits depth, and only shallow experience is possible when there is a lack of patterned contrast. (PR, p. 114)

Whitehead seeks scientific and empirical confirmation for his doctrine of the primacy of aesthetic experience, arguing that the basic law of aesthetics, namely, patterned contrast, conceived as harmony-in-diversity or rhythm-and-novelty, is exhibited in the vibratory structure underlying all atomic phenomena:

In the physical world, this principle of contrast under identity expresses itself in the physical law that vibration enters into the ultimate nature of atomic organisms. Vibration is the recurrence of contrast under identity of type. (RM, p. 111)

Each occasion of experience is a cosmic togetherness of occasions harmonically patterned by irreducible *dipolar contrasts*. Thus, it is a supreme union of opposites or *coincidentia oppositorum*, both one and many, momentary and eternal, concrete and abstract, subjective and objective, physical and mental or emotional and conceptual (AI, p. 190). Whitehead writes: "Throughout the universe there reigns the union of opposites which is the ground of dualism" (AI, p. 190). It is precisely this matrix of irreducible dipolar contrasts which confers on each unit-experience its intrinsic intensity of aesthetic-value feeling and depth of final satisfaction in the consummatory phase of creative synthesis. However, as opposed to the interpenetration or polar fusion of *yuganaddha*, which is the central factor in generating *mahāsukha* or ecstatic bliss in Tantric Buddhism, the dipolar contrast generating aesthetic-value feeling is strictly characterized by a cumulative fusion or one-way penetration. Within any aesthetic pulsation, subject and object and one and many in no way simultaneously interpenetrate or interfuse into a state of mutual containment; rather, there is a cumulative fusion of manyness-into-oneness or object-into-subject, in accordance with the unidirectional cause-to-effect or past-to-present structure of immediate experience, which Whitehead also terms the "concern" patterning of causal transmission. Thus, the intrinsic values of *mahāsukha* or ecstatic pleasure and *ānanda* or supreme bliss, comprehended in Whiteheadian terms as the aesthetic-value feeling of experiential immediacy, can be fully sustained within a metaphysics of cumulative penetration, in terms of a theory of irreducible dipolar contrasts.

As argued in Neville's axiological process cosmology, the most primary mode of beauty in perception is the irreducible harmonic contrast between foreground focus and background field as constituted by a creative act of imaginative synthesis. Neville's cosmology of imaginative experiential synthesis thus provides us with a theoretic basis for the central form of meditative praxis in Tantric Buddhism, namely, the imaginative visualization of maṇḍala-palaces which enshrine resplendent Buddhas enhaloed by jewelled colored rainbow lights, while realizing the emptiness of all inherent-existence. Each imaginatively constructed maṇḍala, which represents a microcosm of the macrocosm, constitutes an indivisible form/emptiness or *shih/li* structure, i.e., a value-laden gestalt. In Tantric Buddhism, the imaginative constitution of microcosmic-macrocosmic maṇḍalas with indivisible form/emptiness structures is the primary means for generating the supreme aesthetic experience of luminosity adorned with bliss, i.e., *mahāsukha* or ecstatic pleasure. In such a manner then, we can interpret the imaginative constitution of form/emptiness maṇḍala structures as the constitution of harmonic contrast between foreground and background elements through imaginative experiential synthesis, which again, is the primary mode of beauty in perception. However, as explicated in the final chapters of this study, the Tantric Buddhist maṇḍala can be understood as an aesthetic-value pattern or lure for feeling (i.e., a Whiteheadian "eternal object") produced by the archetypal imagination which functions normatively in the process of concrescence to organize the manifold of inherited causal feelings into the beauty of harmonic contrasts between foreground and background. By repeated imaginative visualization of archetypal maṇḍala imagery one's ordinary physical perception comes to be wholly constituted by the microcosmic-macrocosmic structure of those maṇḍalas, thereby resulting in the experience of value-laden core/horizon gestalt environments. Yet, as has already been argued, the felt background or horizon of causal presence in the immediacy of experience is not a felt totality, but a felt past prehended by causal memory. Consequently, the primary beauty of harmonic contrast between foreground and background constituted through creative acts of imaginative synthesis, which comes to dominate our perceptual experience from the constant visualization of archetypal maṇḍala imagery, must ultimately be comprehended by a theory of cumulative penetration.

The cumulative or asymmetrical structure of Whitehead's axiological theory as over against the Buddhist symmetrical theory is made still more patent through an analysis concerning the notion of "togetherness." In Tantric Buddhism, *sahaja* (Tib: *lhan-cig-skyes-pa*) or "togetherness" is regarded as a symbol for ecstatic bliss. In his text *The Tantric View of Life*, Herbert V. Guenther describes the fundamental Tantric notion of *sahaja*, which he translates as "togetherness" or "togetherness-awareness" as follows: "Togetherness is the key to understanding the unitary character of whatever experience we have. . . togetherness-awareness in its intrinsic nature. . . is an aesthetically perceptive awareness of a plurality in terms of objective situation and owner of the objective situation."[9] Guenther continues: "This togetherness (*sahaja, yuganaddha*) is the fundamental original and pristine awareness (*ye-shes*) which we lose when we perform abstracting acts."[10] At once, the Tantric notion of *sahaja* or "togetherness-awareness" recalls the conception of experiential togetherness in Whitehead's metaphysics, which propounds that the whole universe stands indivisibly together as an aesthetic harmony of feelings within the awareness of each perspectival occasion of experience. However, the mode of togetherness is by no manner of speaking the total togetherness assumed in the Hua-yen or Tantric metaphysics, but the "production of *novel* togetherness" whereby the (antecedent) many become one and are *increased* by one in the course of creative advance. To repeat Whitehead's words: "'Creativity' is the principle of *novelty*. . . the 'production of novel togetherness' is the ultimate notion embodied in the term 'concrescence'" (PR, p. 21).

In conclusion then, both Whiteheadian process theory and Tantric Buddhism agree that aesthetic-value feeling is intrinsic to actuality itself and that this aesthetic-value is a function of dipolar fusion or dialectical penetration. However, according to process theory, this means a cumulative fusion or one-way penetration. The crux of the argument against interpenetration or total togetherness at the axiological level of discourse rests upon Whitehead's revolutionary notion of "dipolar contrasts." Aesthetic-value feeling and maximum depth of emotional intensity in the final satisfaction consummating an occasion of experience is always a function of *irreducible* dipolar contrasts; the As such, the irreducible dipolar contrasts are collapsed, which in turn tion. In a framework of interpenetration, there is a complete unobstructed mutual fusion and mutual identification between all dialectical opposites, such as one and many, subject and object, or cause and effect, thereby establishing a condition of perfect "sameness" (*samatā*). As such, the irreducible dipolar contasts are collapsed, which in turn precludes intensity of aesthetic-value feeling and final depth of satisfaction. Hence, the Tantric conception of ultimate reality as *mahāsukha* or ecstatic pleasure and bliss which is generated by *yuganaddha* or interpenetration of opposites, is better interpreted in terms of the Whiteheadian process hermeneutic as aesthetic-value feeling arising out of irreducible dipolar contrasts within a framework of cumulative penetration. Furthermore, this axiological polemic against interpenetration is further reinforced by the Whiteheadian analysis of aesthetic-value feeling as a product of creative synthesis. Due to the special significance of creativity in the production of aesthetic-value, not only at the artistic level, but the cosmological level as well in terms of the self-creativity of events, all dipolar fusion between dialectical opposites must be cumulative or asymmetrical in structure. For as has been argued at length in this work, creativity is tenable only in an asymmetrical framework of causal relatedness. Therefore, the aesthetic-value feeling intrinsic to each occasion of experience as a function of irreducible dipolar contrast and creative synthesis becomes most theoretically plausible within an asymmetrical system of cumulative penetration.

(iv) Final Deliverance through Transpersonal Peace

Buddhist soteriology rests upon a doctrine of *kleśas* (as do all Yogic religious doctrines of the East) which deals with the ultimate causes of human affliction and suffering as well as the means for their removal. One finds at the core of the Buddhist soteriological system the doctrine of the four noble truths as expounded by Gautama the Buddha. It is tantamount to a formula for the origin and cessation of human suffering. These four noble truths are as follows: (i) *duḥka* or suffering, (ii) *samudaya* or cause of suffering, (iii) *nirodha* or cessation of suffering, and (iv) *mārga* or the path leading to the cessation of suffering. The first noble truth asserts that *kleśas* (afflictions) and *duḥkha* (suffering) are intrinsic to actuality in the form of radical becoming and perpetual perishing due to the inevitable existential facts of aging, illness and death. The second noble truth identifies the root cause of suffering as thirsting (*taṇha*) or obsessive craving, perpetuated by karmically inherited *vāsanās* (habit-energies) and *saṃskāras* (mental tendencies). The third noble truth states that there is a cessation (*nirodha*) of suffering in the final peace of nirvāṇa. And the fourth noble truth elaborates the eightfold path which aims at the total transformation of life-experience culminating in the realization of supreme enlightenment in nirvāṇa.

As stated above, the cessation (*nirodha*) of suffering and affliction occurs in the Buddhist soteriological system with the realization of nirvāṇa. The word *nirvāṇa* is composed of the Sanskrit verb root *va* meaning "to blow" and the negative prefix *nir*, together implicating a "blowing out" of the flame of obsessive cravings and defiling impulses. It is the total cessation of all karmically inherited *vāsanās* (habit-energies) and *saṃskāras* (mental tendencies) underlying pathological and compulsive patterns of behavior, resulting in the abolition of human afflictions *(kleśas)* and suffering *(duḥkha)*. Hence, "nirvāṇa" signifies quiescence, tranquility, relaxation, calmness and repose in the deepest senses of these terms. Again, nirvāṇa is comprehended throughout the Buddhist world as resting in illumination with comfort and ease like a bright and brilliant lamp, with total non-effort and non-attachment, stabilized in perfect meditative equipoise on emptiness, like a waveless ocean or a cloudless sky. Or as articulated in the ancient Pali literature of Buddhism, *nibañña* is *śanta* (Skt: *śanti*), i.e., deep and abiding "peace". In the classic Pali text entitled *The Questions of King Milinda* it has thus been written: "If you ask: 'How is Nirvana to be known? It is by its freedom from distress and danger, by confidence, by peace, by calm, by bliss, by happiness."[11]

The conception of deliverance from suffering in final peace also crowns the metaphysical architectonic of Whitehead's speculative system. For Whitehead, as in Buddhism in general, suffering, affliction and tragedy is intrinsic to creative process as radical temporality and perpetual perishing: "Decay, Transition, Loss, Displacement belong to the essence of Creative Advance" (AI, p. 286). And at the very heart of the Buddhist theory of *kleśas* lies the proclamation: *sarvam duḥkam*, i.e., "all is suffering!" In consequence of this, both Whiteheadian process theory and Buddhism require a soteriological notion such as final peace in order to provide some mechanism for final deliverance and salvation from the tragic suffering inherent in actuality as perpetual perishing. Whitehead describes his notion of peace as a final deliverance from suffering when he writes: "This is the secret of the union of Zest with Peace: That the suffering attains its end in a Harmony of Harmonies. The immediate experience of this Final Fact. . . is the sense of Peace" (AI, p. 296).

Again, Whitehead describes his concept of peace in a manner consonant with the Buddhist notion of "detachment" when he writes: "Peace is the understanding of tragedy. . ." (AI, p. 286). The vaster experiential dimensions of the concept of peace begin to emerge when it is described as transpersonal feeling or self-transcendence, what Buddhism terms *anātman* or no-self: "Peace is. . . the width where the 'self' has been lost, and interest has been transferred to coordinations wider than personality" (AI, p. 285). Or again: "Peace carries with it a surpassing of personality" (AI, p. 285). Moreover, peace is articulated as a momentous expansion of feelings into oceanic experience when Whitehead states: "Peace. . . is a positive feeling. . . . It is a broadening of feeling due to the emergence of some deep metaphysical insight, unverbalized and yet momentous in its coordination of values" (AI, p. 285). He proceeds to identify the immediate experience of transpersonal peace with the "attainment of truth" (AI, p. 292), and even with "extreme ecstasy" (AI, p. 289). Thus, the picture of Whitehead's concept of peace which unfolds from his writing is that of a deep, harmonious, oceanic, transpersonal dimension of felt immediacy—ecstatic, final, and wholly released from the tragic suffering and affliction inherent in creative advance as perpetual perishing.

However, with respect to the specific doctrinal innovations formulated by the Hua-yen school of Buddhism, perhaps the most suggestive definition of peace provided by Whitehead is that of the conformation of appearance to reality (AI, p. 293). This definition may be interpreted as directly analogous to the Hua-yen Buddhist notion of enlightenment as *li-shih-wu-ai* or the unhindered interpenetration of reality with appearance, which is only to restate such fundamental Mahāyāna doctrines as the mutual identity of form with emptiness or of saṃsāra with nirvāṇa.[12] To repeat Nāgārjuna's famous proclamation: "There is nothing whatever which differentiates the existence-in-flux (saṃsāra) from Nirvāṇa. And there is nothing whatever which differentiates Nirvāṇa from existence-in-flux. . . . There is not the slightest bit of difference between these two."[13] Again, in what is perhaps the most celebrated statement in the whole of the voluminous *Prajñāpāramitā* literature, the *Heart Sūtra* propounds: "Form is Emptiness and Emptiness in Form."[14] *The Awakening of Faith in Mahāyāna,* which is a fundamental source for the Hua-yen theory of *li-shih-wu-ai*, restates this same Mahāyāna Buddhist formula for the identification of reality and appearance in terms of the mutual inclusiveness of the absolute (*tathatā*: suchness) and phenomena (saṃsāra: birth and death).[15] In Whiteheadian terminology, this concept could be restated to say: "Process is reality and reality is process." Or in Whitehead's own words: "Thus, nature is a structure of evolving processes. The reality is the process" (SMW, p. 72). This identification of appearances and reality thus stands in strong contrast to the traditional line of Western religious thought which is attached to conceptual models of dualism and transcendence, whereby God and nature, the sacred and profane and reality and appearance are strictly dichotomized. Rather, salvation is discoverable only in the profound social relatedness and union of opposites characterizing all events which are themselves the irreducible and ultimate matters of fact. However, in contradistinction to the Hua-yen doctrine of *li-shih-wu-ai*, Whitehead's identification of appearance with reality in the experience of final peace does not involve the realization of a static totality wherein past, present and future events all simultaneously interpenetrate into a single thought-instant; rather, it involves the realization that from the very beginning, ultimate reality has been the ongoing stream of novel and aesthetic occasions of experiential immediacy pulsating into momentary existence from out of the plenary creativeness at the base of actuality, forever without end. To conclude then, enlightened perceptivity through *noetic* reversal in the primordial mode of causal feeling, universal compassion through sympathetic concernedness, aesthetic-value feeling through dipolar contrast and final deliverance through transpersonal peace are all intrinsic to the structure of actuality itself as a dialectical interplay of one-into-many and many-into-one, but only in concordance with those strictly asymmetrical infrastructures underlying the metaphysics of cumulative penetration.

Part III

THEOLOGY OF THE DEEP UNCONSCIOUS: A RECONSTRUCTION OF PROCESS THEOLOGY

Preliminary Remarks

The present section endeavors to radically reconstruct Whitehead's revolutionary process theology by transforming its key notion of a dipolar or bimodal God-in-process into the collective unconscious. The notion of a collective unconscious as utilized in this context is designed to embrace not only the Jungian collective or transpersonal unconscious in contemporary Western depth-psychology, but also the *ālaya* (storehouse) consciousness of Buddhist depth-psychology in the East. As Jung argues in his epoch-making psychological commentaries on Eastern thought, Mahāyāna and Vajrayāna Buddhism are generally governed by the ontological commitment to avoid transcendent principles of any kind, and therefore reassign the divine faculties and cosmological roles which the West ordinarily attributes to a transcendent God to the collective unconscious at the depths of the psyche; thus, God is fully immanent in each occasion of experience. In his radically innovative process theology, Whitehead clarifies the various cosmological roles which must be performed in any ontology of momentary events, especially the envisagement and prescription of archetypal value-patterns to govern occasions of experience during creative synthesis and the preservation of all past events through cosmic remembrance. These functions Whitehead assigns to the "primordial" and "consequent" natures of the dipolar God, respectively. However, following the basic ontological commitments of Buddhist and Jungian depth-psychology, these cosmological roles are here entirely transferred to the collective unconscious. Whitehead's dipolar God is here virtually identified with each occasion of experience, whereupon "God" is now comprehended as the transpersonal and unconscious dimensions of each event in a manner similar to which one mind and the storehouse consciousness is identical to each dharma in Hua-yen Buddhism.

The motivation for transforming Whitehead's process theology in terms of various reconstructive categories derived from East-West depth-psychology is in part to remove certain fundamental inconsistencies besetting Whitehead's own categoreal scheme; but more ultimately, it is to provide theoretical expression for the immensity of vision and inexhaustible depth of feeling-tone cultivated through Buddhist religious praxis and yogic discipline, culminating with the realization of Ocean-Seal-Samādi, the supreme visionary experience of Hua-yen Buddhism, while yet remaining within the asymmetrical perimeters underscoring the metaphysics of cumulative penetration. I argue that the dipolar God represents the sort of psychical totality indicated by Ocean-Seal-Samādi as experienced by an enlightened Buddha in advanced phases of contemplation. For the dipolar God in his primordial nature mentally envisions all future possibilities while physically remembering all antecedent facts in his consequent nature. Thus he embraces past-present-future at once, although inside entirely asymmetrical boundaries, since the past is closed while the future is open within the immediacy of a creative present. The strategy here is to transfer the vastness of experience accorded the dipolar God to the occasions of experience themselves. And this, I argue, is possible by reinterpreting the dipolar God as the collective unconscious at the depths of the psyche. In this way the primordial and consequent natures of God may be conceived as the syntheses of imagination (the projection of future possibilities) and memory (the restoration of the past in the present) by means of which each event emerges into temporal actuality at every instant.

However, the concluding chapter of this work focuses on the primordial nature of God which is the atemporal mental envisagement of all possibilities or archetypal value-patterns, or what are termed "eternal objects" in Whitehead's categoreal scheme. God's primordial envisagement of eternal value-patterns is comprehended in terms of the Jungian imaginal psyche with its numinous contents, the eternal archetypes. The organizational principle of the collective unconscious or imaginal psyche, according to Jung, is not the cause-effect principle which regulates physical actuality, but "synchronicity", the principle of acausal order which stretches across time. Thus, the Hua-yen visionary experience of Ocean-Seal-Samādhi, a simultaneous, multidimensional reality wherein past, present and future happen at once, in fact refers to the primordial mental envisagement of eternal possibilities in the archetypal imagination as regulated by synchronicity, the noncausal principle of the collective unconscious. In this context, Kūkai's esoteric Shingon (Tantric) Buddhism of Japan is introduced. According to Kūkai, the Hua-yen (Jap. Kegon) theory of total non-obstructive interpenetration is the supreme doctrine of "exoteric" Buddhism; yet, it must still be "esoterically" realized through Shingon Tantric practice, namely, visualization of oneself as a maṇḍala-palace. The Tantric practice of visualization is what Jung conceives as a praxis of active imagination whereby one envisages archetypal images and enters into the imaginal dream processes of the collective unconscious at the depths of the psyche. Thus, it is argued here that through the visualization of oneself as a maṇḍala-palace with resident deity, one is radically reconstituted as a microcosm of the macrocosm, not in physical actuality, but in the mythical realm of the archetypal imagination, where Buddhalands the number of dustmotes all interpenetrate without obstruction and realms-embrace-realms ad infinitum.

CHAPTER 11

Whitehead's Dipolar God as the Collective Unconscious

Section I

Whitehead's notion of a dipolar or bimodal God-in-process is one of his most radically innovative conceptions and has initiated a major movement in contemporary religious speculation under the name of process theology.[1] The notion of a dipolar God with a "primordial" nature or absolute aspect and a "consequent" nature or relative aspect at once suggest parallels to certain fundamental Mahāyāna Buddhist religious conceptions, especially the notion of one mind with two aspects, as well as to the *ālaya vijñāna* or storehouse consciousness (with both an enlightened and nonenlightened aspect), these two notions often being regarded as synonymous in Mahāyāna patterns of thought.[2] *The Awakening of Faith in Mahāyāna,* which again, is one of the most seminal texts in all East Asian Buddhism in general and a major source text for Hua-yen Buddhism in particular, commences with a description of one mind with two aspects as follows:

> The revelation of the true meaning of Mahāyāna can be achieved by unfolding the doctrine that the principle of One Mind has two aspects. One is the aspect of Mind in terms of the Absolute (*tathatā:* Suchness) and the other is the aspect of Mind in terms of phenomena. Each of these aspects embraces all states of existence. Why? Because they are mutually inclusive.[3]

The *ālaya vijñāna* or storehouse consciousness is defined in similar terms by the text, having two mutually inclusive natures, an absolute enlightened aspect and a relative nonenlightened aspect. Again, *The*

Awakening of Faith in Mahāyāna asserts: "The Storehouse Consciousness. . . has two aspects which embrace all states of existence and create all states of existence. They are: (1) the aspect of enlightenment, and (2) the aspect of nonenlightenment."[4]

Although there are limitations to the analogy between Whitehead's dipolar God and the Mahāyāna Buddhist notion of the storehouse consciousness or one mind with two aspects, the point is that a rich dialogue between East and West is possible when one conceives of God in dipolar terms, with a consequent as well as a primordial nature, as opposed to the utterly transcendent notion of God maintained in traditional Western theology. However, the Mahāyāna notion of the *ālaya* consciousness bears perhaps an even more profound structural resemblance to the collective unconscious or transpersonal psyche posited by C.G. Jung in Western depth-psychology. *The Awakening of Faith in Mahāyāna* explicitly defines the *ālaya* as a subconscious mind which underlies all conscious mental processes in the psyche.[5] Moreover, the *ālaya* is regarded in general by Māhāyana Buddhist depth-psychology as that primordial stratum of the psyche existing anterior to the defiled "I" or ego consciousness *(kliṣṭomanovijñānas)* such as to represent a transpersonal or collective mode of psychical functioning.[6]

This structural proximity of the *ālaya* to the Jungian collective unconscious runs deeper still in terms of their respective contents, these being *vāsanās* or habit energies in the first case and the archetypes or primordial images in the second. For these archetypes are constitutive of experience in the sense of preformed organizational patterns by means of which the mind orders its contents; and second, these archetypes represent psychically inherited archaic vestiges or ancestral memories transmitted since antiquity, in the same sense in which *vāsanās* stored in the *ālaya*-consciousness have been karmically inherited since beginningless time. Jung's proximity to Buddhist depth-psychology is patent in the following summary statement of his theory as expounded in his famous "Commentary on the *Tibetan Book of the Dead*":

> We may accept the (Buddhist) notion of "Karma" cautiously if we understand it as "psychic heredity.". . . Among these inherited psychic factors there is a special class which is not confined to any race. These are the universal dispositions of the mind with which the mind organizes its contents. . . . I call them "archetypes.". . . The layer of the unconscious psyche which stores these universal dynamic forms I have termed the "collective unconscious."[7]

Jung's revolutionary depth-psychology functions as an interpretive framework to bridge Whitehead's process theology and fundamental religious conceptions at the base of Buddhism. Here, the *ālaya*-consciousness is understood in Jungian terms as the collective and unconscious dimensions of an occasion of experience whereas *vāsanās* are understood in the sense of karmically inherited archetypal patterns constitutive of experiential synthesis. Therefore, as employed within this context, the collective unconscious encompasses both the *ālaya* of Mahāyāna Buddhism and the Jungian notion of the transpersonal psyche. An effort is made to transpose Whitehead's theory of the dipolar God into the terms of the collective unconscious, so that now, the dipolar God is to be comprehended not as a transcendent deity, but the deepest dimension and highest potentiality of one's own psyche. Thus, what is ultimately aimed at here is a syncretic harmonization pattern of speculative thought incorporating Buddhist and Jungian depth-psychology as well as Whiteheadian process metaphysics into a single theological framework.

As the great Protestant theologian Paul Tillich states in his essay, "Two Types of Philosophy of Religion," there are two fundamental attitudes toward God, the first being God regarded in a dualistic way as the "Other," and the second being God regarded in a non-dualistic way as the "depth-dimension" at the ground of one's own being.[8] The first approach to God may be exemplified by Paul Weiss, for example, who defines God as the Absolute Other with respect to actualities.[9] The second approach to God may be best exemplified by Paul Tillich himself who comprehends God as the inexhaustible depth-dimension of one's own being. The fundamental existential crisis of contemporary man, according to Tillich, is that he has become estranged and alienated from the depths of existence, and now he must return to those depths. Tillich's conception of God as the depth-dimension of life-experience is given classic expression in his essay, "The Depth of Existence," wherein he writes:

> The name of this infinite and inexhaustible depth and ground of all being is "God." That depth is what the word "God" means. And if that word has not much meaning for you, translate it, and speak of the depths of your own life. . . . If you know that God means "depth" you know much about Him. You cannot then call yourself an Atheist or unbeliever. For you cannot think or say: Life has no depth! Life itself is shallow. . . . He who knows about depth knows much about God.[10]

When Whitehead's dipolar God in the sense of the Other is radically retranslated as the depth-dimension of one's own life-experience, at once the oceanic awareness as well as the various cosmological functions ordinarily attributed to the divine being, including the mental envisagement of all future possibilities in the primordial nature and the reaches of physical memory in the consequent nature, all become transferred to the transpersonal and subconscious phases of the psyche itself. Jung finds abundant empirical evidence for the existence of a kind of absolute knowledge in the collective unconscious, including a remembrance of all forgotten knowledge of the past as revealed by the extraordinary quantity of archaic vestiges and ancestral memories arising in dreams and fantasies, as well as a prodigious knowledge of the future revealed through anticipatory dreams and visions.[11] Jung emphasizes the strictly empirical and phenomenological foundations for his theoretical conclusions, which are based on a rigorous case study of dreams, interior visions and spontaneous fantasies (which he regards as the fundamental expressions of unconscious processes) wherein retrocognitive and premonitory dreams were frequently observed.

According to Jung, the key notion of depth-psychology, namely the collective unconscious with its dynamic contents, the archetypal images, i.e., psychically inherited archaic vestiges or ancestral memories, is grounded upon compelling experimental evidence and empirical data, especially the existence of transcultural archetypal patterns or universal symbolic images where migration as a means of transmission is highly implausible. Still more convincing is the enormous quantity of mythological imagery and archetypal symbolism spontaneously projected from the psyche during dreams, visions and fantasies, as well as during the psychotherapeutic praxis developed by Jung termed "active imagination," of individuals with no prior knowledge of such materials. In his commentary on the Tantric Buddhist text, *The Tibetan Book of the Dead*, Jung thus describes his methodological procedure as follows:

> Comparative religion and mythology are rich mines of archetypes as is the psychology of dreams and psychoses. The astonishing parellelism between these images. . . has frequently given rise to the wildest migration theories, although it would be far more natural to think of the remarkable similarity of the human psyche at all times and all places. Archetypal fantasy-forms are, in fact, reproduced spontaneously any time and anywhere, without there being any conceivable trace of direct transmission. . . . The archetypes are, so to speak, organs of the prerational psyche. They are eternally inherited forms and ideas which have at first no specific content.[12]

Jung's empiricism is complemented by the experiential foundations underlying the Buddhist notion of an *ālaya* consciousness and its karmically inherited *vāsanās* or habit-energies, realized through techniques of advanced yogic meditation. Jung interpreted yogic meditation in general as an arcane initiatory process of *descensus ad inferos*, i.e., as a descent to the underworld or a descent to the unconscious. Jung writes:

> Meditation. . . is therefore something like a descent into the fountainhead of the psyche, into the unconscious itself. . . the gaze of the meditator can penetrate into the depths of the psyche's secrets. Therefore he sees what could not be seen before, i.e., what was unconscious.[13]

In his history of Asiatic Buddhism entitled *Buddhism: The Light of Asia* the eminent Buddhologist Kenneth Ch'en provides a similar interpretation of meditation as a progressive lowering of the threshold of conscious lucidity such that one directly penetrates the depths of the *ālaya* consciousness:

> The *ālaya vijñāna* or storehouse consciousness is the storehouse of all the ideas and impressions experienced by mankind since the beginning of time. . . . It is common to all individuals, it is the ocean of consciousness out of which all ideas arise and to which all ideas return. During his waking moments the individual is conscious of but a small fragment of this repository; but by meditation he becomes aware of its profundity and depth.[14]

Jung was especially interested in the Indo-Tibetan Tantric Buddhist modes of yogic praxis such as the dream yoga and the technique of maṇḍala visualization, whereby one awakens into the imaginal dream process of the collective unconscious at the depths of the psyche, and thus integrates into normal wakeful consciousness the primordial archetypal images (i.e., peaceful and wrathful deities). Jung approximated both these Tantric Buddhist techniques through the direct observation of dreams and fantasies, as well as through the psychotherapeutic praxis of active imagination (the active evocation of interior images) in order to directly awaken into the imaginal processes of the collective unconscious.

Hence, the conception of the collective unconscious with its psychically inherited archetypal contents is a powerful explanatory notion resting on convincing and abundant empirical foundations in both its Eastern and Western theoretical formulations. Moreover, Jung argues that from the strictly empirical point of view, it is wholly impossible to distinguish manifestations of God (divine grace, inspiration, spiritual visions, prophetic dreams, etc.) from the unconscious psyche. If God and the collective unconscious are not identical, they are at least empirically indistinguishable. In Jung's words, since it is "only through the psyche that God acts upon us," then "we are unable to distinguish whether these actions come from God or from the unconscious. We cannot tell whether God and the unconscious are actually two different entities."[15] According to Jung, it is ultimately this very reason why in Buddhist depth-psychology, "the 'unconscious' is credited with all the faculties which in the West are attributed to God."[16]

Section II

What is now to be opened up for critical analysis is the question as to whether or not Whitehead's dipolar God can be sustained as a separate entity with transcendent status; or if the cosmological roles and faculties assigned to it would be more appropriately assigned to the collective unconscious at the depths of the psyche. According to Whitehead's theology of process, God is an actual entity, or if Hartshorne is right, a society of actual entities. And by analogy with all actual entities, God is dipolar, with both a physical pole and a mental pole. The mental pole of God constitutes his primordial nature, the physical pole his consequent nature. The primordial nature of God "... is his complete envisagement of eternal objects..." (PR, p. 44). The eternal objects or Platonic archetypes are the abstract value-patterns or ideal modes of togetherness by means of which any event in the process of self-creation can combine the antecedent many into a new one with harmonic contrast. Again, the eternal objects are comprehended by Whitehead as "forms of definiteness" or "pure potentials for the specific determination of fact" (PR, p. 22). God's envisagement of these Platonic archetypes or pure possibilities is variously described as "eternal" (PR, p. 345), "infinite" (PR, p. 345), "all-embracing" (PR, p. 348), "complete" (PR, p. 345), and finally as "omniscient", as when Whitehead writes that in the primordial nature, all eternal objects are "grasped together in the synthesis of omniscience" (RM, p. 147). However, this one infinite conceptual realization in God's primordial envisagement is still "actually deficient" (PR, p. 345), i.e., devoid of physical feelings, as well as completely "unconscious" (PR, p. 345.)

The specific cosmological role assigned to the primordial nature of God is to prescribe the eternal objects to each actual occasion in valuated grades of relevance. Thus, his function is to supply each occasion with its "initial aim," which is the organizational pattern governing the occasion through its various phases of integration toward maximum depth of intensity of final satisfaction. In Whitehead's words: "Each temporal entity... derives from God its basic conceptual aim. . . . This subjective aim, in its successive modifications, remains the unifying factor governing the successive phases of interplay between physical and conceptual feelings" (PR, p. 224).

Or again: "... God is the principle of concretion; namely, he is that actual entity from which each temporal concrescence receives that initial aim from which its self-causation starts" (PR, p. 244). In this context, the divine role of the primordial nature of God is that of a "persuasive" agency (the Platonic demiurge) i.e., a "lure for feeling" which urges each occasion towards creative advance, emergent novelty and adventure of experience. Moreover, it is the immanence of God in each occasion of experience by virtue of the latter's reception of an aesthetic-value pattern from his primordial nature which establishes the primacy of aesthetic experience in Whitehead's axiological metaphysics. To reiterate Whitehead's words: "The metaphysical doctrine here expounded finds the foundations of the world in the aesthetic experience. . . . All order is therefore aesthetic order. . . and the aesthetic order is derived from the immanence of God" (RM, p. 116).

However, in addition to the conceptual pole of God in his primordial nature, he also has a consequent nature, which is ". . . the weaving of God's physical feelings upon his primordial concepts" (PR, p. 345). If God's primordial nature represents omniscient envisagement of future possibilities, his consequent nature represents total remembrance of all history such that all antecedent events are everlastingly preserved in the divine memory: "The consequent nature of God is the fluent world become 'everlasting' by its objective immortality in God" (PR, p. 347). Thus, not only are all events saved as imperishable and everlasting data in God's divine memory, but in some sense, immediacy is retained: "In everlastingness, immediacy is reconciled with objective immortality" (PR, p. 351). Or to reiterate Hartshorne's words: "They [events] 'perish yet live forevermore' is the final word of *Process and Reality*, and to this I adhere, whether or not Whitehead did. The perishing, taken anything like literally, is an illusion occasioned by the hiddenness of deity from us" (see p. 147).

However, as argued earlier, what Hartshorne seems to intend with his denial of perishing and the retention of immediacy in the divine memory is that the depth of satisfaction attained by each occasion is preserved by God's infallible memory in its original vivacity and intensity. Yet, immediacy in the sense of agency, self-creativity and decision have clearly perished; it is the event in its emotional fullness that lives on forever in the immediacy of God's consequent nature, neither as a subject, nor as an object, but as a *transpersonal* cosmic fact in the divine memory.

It is here that one must consider the Jungian empirical polemic; if it is in fact only through the psyche that God acts upon us, then we cannot ascertain whether or not God and the unconscious are actually two different entities. God and the unconscious psyche, at the empirical level of analysis, appear to be indistinguishable. It is only by inference that one can postulate a separate or transcendent entity termed "God." Consequently, with Jungian and Buddhist depth-psychology, the more empirically valid theory is to reassign those faculties ordinarily attributed to God to the collective unconscious at the depths of the psyche. The inheritance of an archetypal pattern or eternal object as the initial aim governing experiential synthesis is a necessary cosmological function which must be accounted for in any theory of momentary process-events. But in accordance with the Jungian hermeneutic, this function is fulfilled not by a separate entity termed "God," but by the collective unconscious, as primordial archetypes or preformed organizational patterns surface from the depths of the psyche to govern the genetic process of nontemporal concrescence, the experiential synthesis by which each occasion emerges into determinate actuality. Moreover, insofar as the collective unconscious is itself the universal storehouse of psychically inherited archaic vestiges, the transpersonal bank of memory which infallibly records each event in the antecedent universe, it functions to fulfill the consequent role of God's nature, which is to preserve the past everlastingly as imperishable data through divine remembrance.

To conceive of the dipolar God as a separate and transcendent entity is to violate Whitehead's ontological principle which states: "the actual world is built up of actual occasions; and by the ontological principle whatever things there are in any sense of 'existence' are derived by abstraction from actual occasions" (PR, p. 73). Consequently, the primordial and consequent functionings of the dipolar God are to be comprehended as *abstractions* from the process of creative synthesis whereby actual occasions constitute themselves. Also, in concordance with the principle of Occam's Razor, which states that entities should not be multiplied beyond necessity, the notion of a collective unconscious is by far the simpler theory.

If Whitehead's notion of the dipolar God is pressed to its ultimate logical conclusions, it becomes increasingly difficult to sustain any sort of distinction between God and the plurality of events themselves. Whitehead says that God is the Alpha and Omega of each event: "But God, as well as being primordial, is also consequent. He is the beginning and the end" (PR, p. 345). Thus, each momentary event is precariously sandwiched-in, as it were, between the primordial and consequent natures of the dipolar God. God initiates each occasion by providing its basic organizational pattern and then everlastingly remembers it as his own past, such that it is relegated to the mere function of a divine role. Paul Weiss has criticized Whitehead on just this point, asserting that because God's consequent nature functions as the ground of the givenness of the past, prehension can only be of God. In a study of Paul Weiss's philosophy in relation to Whitehead's process theory concerning the reality of the past, one author has correctly assessed Weiss's critique of Whitehead as follows: "It is God in his consequent nature who sustains such actual occasions as objectively immortal, as sustained in him and consequently as able to be given as real potentiality. The past is one with the divine being."[17] Moreover,

> Since Whitehead refuses to identify creativity and the divine being, he cannot be accused of affirming a monistic position; but he cannot be said to affirm a pluralistic position which maintains the full-blooded character of finite entities. For finite actual entities in Whitehead's scheme function as divine roles, and insofar as they are roles, they are retained in the divine as its own past. To the extent that the past can be retained as the past of God in his consequent nature, finite actual entities must not only be conceived as, but also in fact be the divine in finite guise.[18]

According to Weiss, the past does not need God in order to be. For Weiss, the locus of Whitehead's problem is that actualities are momentary, and only God persists, so that the past can persist only through the agency of God. For Whitehead, according to Weiss's analysis, to be is ". . . to be a completed being at every moment of time, perishing with the passing moment because inescapably contained within the span of a moment."[19] Whereas for Whitehead only God persists, for Weiss, "realities persist while they change."[20] Weiss continues: "The fundamental temporal fact is not the passage of events, but the occurrence of changes in persistent substantial individuals."[21] For Weiss, the past is in no way immanent in the present but is wholly "other" to it. The past cannot be inside the present, because it has no causal efficacy; it is entirely exhausted. In Weiss's words:

> An actuality can have a temporal career only because there are other entities on which it is now dependent. . . . These entities cannot be in the past. The past is finished, impotent, powerless, dead. If an entity needed something of the past it could not obtain it, for the past is not available.[22]

In an event ontology such as Whitehead's, events emerge anew at each instant so they must utilize the past as material for synthesis; but since only God persists, it is God who must preserve the past through his consequent nature. However, Weiss repudiates Whitehead's event ontology and advocates a return to Aristotelian substance categories. Since for Weiss actualities are substances which persist through change, there is no need to account for either the transmission of the past into the present or the preservation of the past by the agency of a persisting God. Weiss's criticism of Whitehead's theory of the past is well taken. But the answer certainly does not seem to lie in a return to the substantialist categories of an Aristotelian ontology of enduring actualities. Such a theory is wholly alien to the quantization of reality which has occurred in contemporary physics and biology. It is also entirely alien to the experience of momentariness and felt transition characterizing the stream of consciousness in the immediacy of experience. Rather, the answer seems to lie in a pressing forward of Weiss's analysis of Whitehead's philosophy, and wholly identify the dipolar God with the actual occasions themselves. For if God is the ground for the givenness of the past in its real potentiality, then each event prehends only God as its efficient and material cause. Furthermore, if God initiates each event by providing its subjective aim, then God is also the formal and final cause. Moreover, according to the ontological principle, everything which in any way has existence, is derived by abstraction from actual occasions. Thus, God can only be regarded as an abstraction from the process of concrescence by which actual entities constitute themselves. The conclusion arrived at here is that the primordial function of envisioning and prescribing archetypal patterns for experiential synthesis and the preservation of the past through memory are all subconscient and transpersonal phases of the process of nontemporal concrescence itself. Therefore, there is no need, nor any warrant, for the attribution of these cosmological roles to some separately existing or transcendent principle, over and against the events themselves. And finally, as Jung argues following the Buddhist methodological procedure, there is no way to ascertain whether such functions as described above come from God or the unconscious psyche, such that if the dipolar God and the collective unconscious are not identical, they are at least empirically indistinguishable. Thus, according to the theology of the deep unconscious propounded in this work, the traditional interpretation of Whitehead's dipolar God-in-process is directly challenged and reconceived as the collective unconscious at the transpersonal and subconscient dimensions of the psyche. The primordial and consequent natures of God are understood to represent the syntheses of imagination (the projection of future possibilities) and memory (the restitution of the past in the present) by means of which each occasion of experience emerges into determinate actuality at every instant through nontemporal concrescence.[23] In the final analysis then, the Hua-yen visionary experience of Ocean-Seal-Samādhi or the timeless envisionment of past-present-future simultaneously, must be comprehended in its widest sense as the realization of the process of nontemporal concrescence or genetic self-constitution in its deepest internal subjectivity, which involves the mental prehension of all archetypal possibilities through the synthesis of imagination as well as the physical prehension of all antecedent actualities through the synthesis of memory in a seamless whole of past, present and future which occurs entirely outside of time. The Hua-yen enlightenment experience of Ocean-Seal-Samādhi will now be analysed in its specific relation to the "primordial" noetic functioning of the collective unconscious, which is its atemporal act of simultaneously envisaging all possibilities, past, present and future, through the archetypal imagination or creative image-making power of the transpersonal psyche.

CHAPTER 12

The Collective Unconscious and Synchronicity: Atemporal Envisagement in the Archetypal Imagination

Section I

This concluding chapter will focus upon the primordial nature of the dipolar God in abstraction from its consequent nature, not unlike the manner in which Hegel's system of Logic purports to analyze the structure of "God in His eternity prior to the creation of the world."[1] In terms of the psychological hermeneutic, which translates Whitehead's dipolar God in its sense as an "Other" into the "depth-dimension" of our own experience, we can now reinterpret God's primordial envisagement of all possibilities in terms of what Jung has named: the "archetypal imagination." When wholly demythologized, the dipolar God-in-process as the collective unconscious is simply the creative act of imaginative experiential synthesis itself, which combines an antecedent plurality into a new unity, whereas the primordial nature is its aspect as the archetypal imagination, which provides normative aesthetic-value patterns functioning to organize the manifold of causal feelings into harmonic contrasts, thus producing maximum depth of emotional intensity in each occasion of experience. Jung did not conceive of the collective unconscious as a reified entity, but as an archetypal imagination, understood as a dynamic image-making function. Jung methodologically conceived of his depth-psychology as being a "phenomenology of the imagination," which proceeded through a careful observation and description of imagery flowing from the unconscious psyche during dreams, fantasies and visions, or as manifest in the primordial symbolism of transcultural mythology. Naturally, since Jung is dealing with unconscious dimensions of reality, his project is beset with some of the same obstacles which presented themselves for Maurice Merleau-Ponty who attempted to phenomenologically describe the pre-conscious and impersonal dimensions of lived bodily perception, in its intersensory synaesthesia, at the level of "operative motor intentionality," which functions, according to Merleau-Ponty, beneath the level of conscious "act intentionality." Again, Jung's effort to perform a rigorous phenomenology of the unconscious imagination carries with it difficulties similar to those faced by Whitehead in his effort to give a radically empirical descriptive generalization of pre-conscious feeling or prehension in the primordial mode of perception termed causal efficacy, which itself arises anterior to the levels of sensation and cognition. According to Jung's phenomenology of unconscious psychic life, the archetypal imagination is an atemporal envisagement of archetypal symbols or primordial images. Jung identified the most potent archetypal image appearing in dreams, visions or cross-cultural myths as the God-image, particularly in the form of maṇḍalas, which he regarded as being empirically indistinguishable from archetypes of the Self. Hence, for Jung the archetypal imagination is a theophanic imagination, i.e., a polytheistic psyche which produces archaic pantheons of gods and goddesses without end. In this context then, I would like to consider Jung's theory of an archetypal imagination as a possible framework for interpreting the simultaneous, multidimensional visions of past, present and future reported by the patriarchs and sages of Hua-yen Buddhism, and particularly, those visions of innumerable Buddhas and bodhisattvas which radiate halos of jewelled colored lights as described at such length in the *Avataṁsaka Sūtra*.

According to Jung, the organizational principle regulating the collective unconscious is not the cause-effect principle that governs physical actuality, but what he has termed "synchronicity," conceived as an "acausal connecting principle" or a principle of "noncausal orderedness."[2] As Jung asserts: "Synchronicity is a phenomenon that seems to be primarily connected with psychic conditions, that is to say, with [archetypal] processes in the unconscious."[3] Jung conceives of synchronicity or acausal orderedness as a principle of simultaneity as opposed to the law of cause and effect regulative of physical actuality, which essentially represents a principle of chronological succession or linear seriality.[4] In terms of historical precursors to the concept of synchronicity, Jung especially points out Leibniz's principle of pre-established harmony in the West,[5] which insures a correspondence between the microcosmic and the macrocosmic orders of reality, as well as the principles of *tao* and *li* in Oriental thought, which are principles of universal harmony or pattern which stretch across time as acausal ordering factors.[6]

In his study entitled *Jung, Synchronicity and Human Destiny*, Ira Progoff expresses the importance of Jung's synchronistic principle as follows:

> The belief in cause and effect is one of the cardinal tenets of the Western view of life. . . The special contribution that Jung is making now is that through the hypothesis of Synchronicity that he has developed it becomes possible to include causality within the context of a more comprehensive view of the universe.[7]

However, Jung did not intend to replace the concept of causation with his synchronistic principle, but only to posit both of them as two *complementary* principles, each valid within its own framework.[8] As Progoff writes in his study on synchronicity:

> Jung presents Synchronicity as a principle equal in stature with causality, specifically formulated as a means of explaining the type of phenomena that may be attributed to the "acausal orderedness" found in the cosmos as a whole. In this respect, Synchronicity does not conflict with causality, but rather subsists side by side with it. . . . Its value specifically is that it affords a means of dealing with those phenomena for which causality is not sufficient.[9]

Thus, in addition to the causal transmission connecting events at the physical level of actuality, Jung posits the existence of a noncausal synchronicity in the unconscious processes of the transpersonal psyche at the level of the archetypes, such that both principles co-exist together within a framework of complementarity.

Whereas the "consequent" nature of the collective unconscious is its function as transpersonal memory, its "primordial" nature is its function as the archetypal imagination, i.e., the creative and purposeful image-making faculty of the psyche whose principal expressions are dreams, spontaneous fantasies and visions. It is primarily this sort of interior visionary data spontaneously produced by the transpersonal psyche that provided Jung with the empirical evidence for his synchronistic hypothesis. At once, a monumental advance has been made in the field of speculative metaphysics with the introduction of a radical dream empiricism, if it may be so called. James and Whitehead undertake a radical empiricism which directs awareness to new and fresh focal-settings, wherein psychic fringes, conjunctive relations, and transitive feelings arise as originary data in the field of experiential immediacy or primordial presence. Through this radically empirical methodology underlying the American tradition of process metaphysics, Buddhist modes of enlightened perceptual awareness such as *prajñā* which shifts attention to *śūnyatā* or the field of causal relatedness constitutive of phenomena is retranslated into the terms of the felt background of experiential immediacy observable at the periphery of the perceptual field. In such a manner, speculative discourse can proceed on firm empirical foundations without making recourse to extraordinary yogic trance states which often obstruct scholarly investigation by precluding those who have not entered into such trances. Similarly, with the introduction of Jung's radical dream empiricism, one may commence to advance the philosophical dialogue concerning synchronistic phenomena without making recourse to Ocean-Seal-Samādhi, which is the supreme trance state and visionary experience in Hua-yen Buddhism undergone only by those victorious practitioners who have passed through all ten *bhūmis* (stages) of Buddhahood as described by the *Avataṁsaka Sūtra.* In his essay entitled "Synchronicity: An Acausal Connecting Principle," Jung relates the concept of synchronicity to the "absolute knowledge of the unconscious, and to the presence in the microcosm of macrocosmic events."[10] Jung has provided this absolute knowledge of the collective unconscious with convincing empirical testimony from the significantly high degree of retrocognitive and premonitory visions recorded in his rigorous case study of over 100,000 dreams. For example, in his psychological commentary on the Tantric Buddhist text, *The Tibetan Book of the Great Liberation,* Jung writes:

> I have already explained this "timelessness" as a quality inherent in the experience of the collective unconscious. The application of the "yoga of self-liberation" (described by the text) is said to reintegrate all forgotten knowledge of the past with consciousness. The motif of restoration occurs in many redemption myths and is also an important aspect of the psychology of the unconscious, which reveals an extraordinary amount of archaic material in the dreams and spontaneous fantasies of normal and insane people. . . . It is also a fact that premonitory dreams are relatively frequent, and this substantiates what the text calls "knowledge of the future.". . . The unconscious certainly has its "own time" inasmuch as past, present and future are blended together in it.[11]

Due to this experience of archaic and premonitory materials in the timelessness of the collective unconscious as empirically testified to by well-documented dreams, fantasies, visions and other spontaneous manifestations of the collective unconscious Jung was ultimately compelled to formulate a synchronistic principle of acausal orderedness which co-exists in a relation of complementarity with the principle of cause and effect operant at the level of linear seriality.

Section II

The atemporal envisagement of eternal archetypes previously designated as the primordial nature of God may now be comprehended by means of the Jungian psychological hermeneutic as the collective unconscious which is the universal storehouse of primordial images or archetypal patterns regulated by a synchronistic principle of acausal orderedness. However, this atemporal envisagement of eternal patterns which occurs through the noetic functioning of archetypal imagination expresses *potential* reality alone, not historically completed physical fact. In Whitehead's phrase, the primordial nature of God is "actually deficient," i.e., devoid of physical feelings (PR, p. 345). Moreover the supreme visionary experience of Hua-yen Buddhism, namely, Ocean-Seal-Samādhi, is here interpreted as involving the realization of the primordial nature of God which is, according to Whitehead, the atemporal envisagement of archetypal patterns in an eternal "synthesis of omniscience." But once again, this atemporal envisagement realizes pure possibility alone and is wholly devoid of physical actuality which requires "the weaving of God's physical feelings upon his primordial concepts" (PR, p. 345). Or in Jung's words, the archetypal reality of the collective unconscious represents "a 'total vision' *in potentia*."[12] However, this does not imply that the domain of pure possibility is in any way less real than the order of actuality. For as Justus Buchler argues with such force in his *Metaphysics of Natural Complexes,* actuality and possibility must be understood as having complete ontological parity in Whitehead's categoreal scheme since neither category of existence is intelligible in separation from the other.[13] Nor should the archetypal realm be exalted as being "more real" than the order of physical actuality as is usually implicit in Platonic schemes of thought. Rather, while maintaining the irreducible dipolar contrast obtaining between actuality and possibility (which is central to the Whiteheadian axiological theory of aesthetic-value realization as the actualization of potentiality), the two categories of existence must yet be said to have equal ontological status. Thus, whereas the archetypal world of the collective unconscious is fully real, in the deepest meaning of the word "real," it is nonetheless actually deficient or devoid of physical feeling.

According to the theology of the deep unconscious then, Ocean-Seal-Samādhi is to be comprehended as an atemporal envisagement of all possibilities. It is a realization of the synchronically ordered archetypal reality of the collective unconscious, in an act which Platonic philosophy termed *anamnesis,* or the "recollection" of the realm of archetypes, which, according to the Jungian psychological hermeneutic, means precisely the archetypal imagination. Thus, the simultaneous interpenetration of all times and spaces and the infinite realms-embracing-realms occurring in the Ocean-Seal-Samādhi must not be attributed to physical actuality which is regulated by the principle of karmic inheritance or cause and effect, but only to the synchronistic archetypal reality of the archetypal imagination as empirically manifested in dreams, interior visions and other spontaneous expressions of the collective unconscious.

It is in such a manner that the synchronic realm of the collective unconscious and the diachronic realm of physical events co-exist within a balanced framework of complementarity. This view may be clarified still further in terms of Jung's psychological interpretation of the *trikāya* (three bodies of Buddha) doctrine of reality as propounded by such Tantric Buddhist texts as *The Tibetan Book of the Great Liberation.* Having cited the text as stating, "Therefore the Trikāya is the All-Englightened Mind itself," Jung writes: "Put into psychological language, the above sentence could be paraphrased thus: The unconscious is the root of all experience of oneness (*dharmakāya*), the matrix of all archetypes or structural patterns (*sambhogakāya*) and the *conditio sine qua non* of the phenomenal world (*nirmāṇakāya*)."[14] According to the text, one mind (i.e., Buddha) has three bodies (*trikāya*): death, intermediate state and rebirth, i.e., *dharmakāya* (the clear light of death), *sambhogakāya* (the matrix of all archetypes) and *nirmāṇakāya* (physical actuality).[15] In Indo-Tibetan Tantric Buddhism, the *trikāya* theory directly underlies a theory of bardos or intermediary states which articulates the various experiential dimensions of reality. According to Tantric bardo theory, whereas *nirmāṇakāya* is correlated with *skye-gnas bardo* (place of rebirth) and its corresponding state in the post-mortem period, *srid pa'i bardo* (seeking rebirth), *sambhogakāya,* which is explicitly identified by Jung as the "matrix of all archetypes or structural patterns," is correlated with *rmilam bardo* (the dream state) and its corresponding dimension in the post-mortem period, *chos-nyid bardo* (the realm of peaceful and terrifying visions). This system of correlations may be schematized as in the chart below:[16]

Trikāya	*Earth Life*	*After-Death Period*	*Theology of the Deep Unconscious*
I) Dharmakāya	Bardo of Meditation (bSamgtan bardo)	Bardo of Clear Light (Chi-kha'i bardo)	Psychic Radiance
II) Sambhogakāya	Bardo of Dreams (rMilam Bardo)	Bardo of Reality (Chos-nyid bardo) "Realm of Peaceful and Terrifying Visions"	Archetypal Imagination: Synchronicity and Acausal Orderedness
III) Nirmāṇakāya	Bardo of Place of Birth (sKye-gnas bardo)	Bardo of Rebirth (Srid pa'i bardo)	Physical Actuality: Cause-Effect and Cumulative Penetration

According to the schematic representation of reality being propounded here then, the principles of karmic inheritance, cause-effect and cumulative penetration are operative in *nirmāṇakāya*, the level of physical actuality; whereas simultaneous interpenetration in the sense of atemporal envisagement and acausal synchronicity apply specifically to *sambhogakāya*, the matrix of all archetypes, comprehended as the experiential dimension of dreams and inner psychic visions produced by the archetypal imagination. Beyond the bardos of physical actuality and the archetypal imagination, there is still the clear light of death (psychologically corresponding to the state of deep sleep), which is the indeterminate ground of all determinations and the formless source of all forms. Thus, ultimately the Whiteheadian process theory of cumulative penetration as well as the Hua-yen theory of simultaneous interpenetration are capable of harmonious co-existence within the threefold bardo cosmology posited by Indo-Tibetan Tantric Buddhism.[17]

Section III

In this concluding chapter, an effort is made to fuse Hua-yen and Tantric Buddhist speculation into a comprehensive syncretic harmonizing pattern. The Tantric bardo cosmology is brought to bear upon the Hua-yen speculative framework in order to make explicit the latter's psychological dimensions. I suggest that *sambhogakāya*, the matrix of all archetypes, as well as its correlated bardos or experiential dimensions, these being *rmilam bardo* (the dream state) and *chos-nyid bardo* (the realm of peaceful and terrifying visions) are all constitutive of the inner psychic reality of the collective unconscious. Moreover, I suggest that the collective unconscious is in fact identical to the dipolar God of Whiteheadian process theology, the primordial nature of God being the archetypal imagination, which is the atemporal envisagement of all possibilities, whereas the consequent nature is the transpersonal memory operative at the depths of the psyche composed of karmically inherited archaic vestiges. Indeed, the atemporal envisagement of all potentiality in God's primordial nature as well as the cosmic remembrance of all antecedent actualities in his consequent nature are but pale abstractions in separation from the experiential dimension of retrocognitive and premonitory dreams and inner visions emanating from the archetypal imagination and transpersonal memory of the collective unconscious at the depths of one's own psyche.

What is central to the present discussion is that the fundamental *upāya* or expedient means of the Tantra Vehicle, namely, the visualization of oneself as a maṇḍala, whereupon the practitioner is radically reconstituted as a microcosm of the macrocosm, does not in fact take place in physical actuality, but in the domain of the archetypal imagination. In Tantric maṇḍala contemplation, one noetically constitutes alternate interior psychical realities through creative visualization and imaginal holography. Like a three-dimensional and multi-colored holographic laser projection wherein each part contains an image of the whole, the practice of creative visualization in the active imagination constructs elaborate inner maṇḍala worlds, each one a microcosm of the macrocosm, each like a rainbow, beautiful and vivid, yet wholly transparent and non-substantial, such that all totally interpenetrate without obstruction in the dream reality of imaginal space and time.

Through the Jungian psychological hermeneutic, the Tantric Buddhist practice of visualizing or evoking deities within their respective maṇḍala palaces is comprehended as a process of active imagination, i.e., a method of actively imagining archetypal images emanating from the collective unconscious. Jung conceived of active imagination as a psychotherapeutic mode of praxis which animates a visionary transmutation process, alternatively termed "individuation," "centroversion" or "psychic transformation." It is a process whereby one's personality structure undergoes radical transformation, finally consummating in the establishment of psychic wholeness, which represents a state of equilibrium between the unconscious and conscious dimensions of the psyche. The praxis of active imagination is understood by Jung as analogous to the Medieval alchemical process of *imaginatio*, which he defined as "an image-making, form-giving, creative activity" in contradistinction to *phantasia* or "fantasy," which is a "subjective figment of the mind."[18] Again, Jung defines active imagination as "the real and literal power to create images,"[19] or as "the active evocation of inner images."[20] Thus, whereas *phantasia* is a random stream of subjective fictions, *imaginatio* signifies a creative and purposeful process of visionary exfoliation through the active evocation of archetypal images from the unconscious psyche. In Jung's psychotherapeutic praxis of active imagination, attention is focused upon a psychically charged archetypal image such as a dream-fragment or fantasy-picture, usually a maṇḍala-image (i.e., a circular motif with a quaternity structure, often including a deity or symbol of androgyny at its center, this being the basic archetype of psychic wholeness in Jung's psychology) so that one directly awakens into the imaginal dream processes of the collective unconscious. As has been developed at length by the Jungian psychologist Mary Watkins in her book entitled *Waking Dreams*, the psychotherapeutic praxis of active imagination in fact constitutes a procedure of controlled dreaming, in the sense of a waking dream, lucid dream or half-dream state, whereupon unconscious archetypal processes are integrated into ordinary wakeful ego-consciousness.[21] The Tantric Buddhist praxis of maṇḍala visualization represents an analogous methodology to the Jungian process of active imagination. One aims at the production of artificial dream states so as to awaken into *rmilam bardo* (the experiential dimension of dreams) at the level of *sambhogakāya,* which is the matrix of all archetypes.

According to the Jungian psychological hermeneutic, the Tantric Yoga of maṇḍala visualization or deity evocation is a cultural-historical variant of the praxis of active imagination, in the sense that it is a process of actively imagining archetypal presences as controlled by the traditional liturgical descriptions and iconographic imagery of a particular religious context. Or again, Tantric visualization in the active imagination may be seen as functioning analogously to the phenomenological praxis of imaginative variation as described earlier in this study, in that one's sedimented *ahaṃkāra* or self-image is radically reconstituted through dramatic free variations in imagination. Through the controlled visualization of microcosmic-macrocosmic maṇḍalas, which are the basic archetypal images of psychic wholeness and equilibrium projected from the collective unconscious, one directly awakens into *rmilam bardo,* the dream state, as well as into *chos-nyid bardo,* the realm of peaceful and terrifying visions, which emanates from the *ālaya vijñāna* or storehouse consciousness as a result of one's karmic inheritance of *vāsanās* or habit-energies. That the Tantric praxis of visualizing archetypal images in fact constitutes a procedure of controlled dreaming in the sense of a waking dream state has been articulated by the eminent Buddhologist Alex Wayman as follows:

> This theory of creating a dream state by repeated meditation thus to evoke a deity, implies that the bulk of Lamaist iconography—those fierce and mild deities—amounts to sets of controlled dreams. Indeed, the production of an artificial dream state is prevalent in the Buddhist Tantras.[22]

Thus, the praxis of visualizing archetypal images in the active imagination, comprehended as the production of a waking dream state tantamount to a direct awakening into *rmilam bardo* or the experiential dimension of dreams, is equivalent to the Platonic act of *anamnesis,* which is precisely the recollection of the realm of archetypes. As Edward S. Casey has written:

> Beyond the personal and collective past is a past which. . . is a timeless time, inchoate and antedating history or personal experience. It is a special case of Great Time, mythic in status, and its temporality is that of *in illo tempore:* in that time, a time before measurable, chronic time. Such a time *never was actual* and is hence not remembered as actual. This means that it is not remembered at all in the usual sense. Rather, the mythic past is re-collected in an act of reminiscence (*anamnesis*) whose content is impersonal. Re-collected from what? Not from perception, thought or personal memory, but from the *imagining* of archetypal presences.[23]

I am suggesting that the Hua-yen Buddhist visionary experience of Ocean-Seal-Samādhi involves the realization of the multidimensional dream reality of *rmilam bardo* at the level of *sambhogakāya,* the matrix of all archetypal images and structural patterns organized by synchronicity, the principle of acausal orderedness, and that this *anamnesis* occurs precisely through the controlled visualization of archetypal images in the active imagination. Yet, to repeat Casey's words, this mythic time of the archetypal realm "never was actual and is hence not remembered as actual." According to this interpretation then, the astonishing Hua-yen vision of Ocean-Seal-Samādhi as articulated by the *Avataṁsaka Sūtra,* wherein one envisages hundreds of thousands of millions of Buddhas all assembled within a single hair of the *Tathāgata's* head, all performing inconceivable acts, inconceivable vows and inconceivable miracles while absorbed in unutterable *samādhis* in indescribable pure lands, raining down their immeasurable compassion like a shower of jewels for the bliss and happiness of all sentient beings, thus decorating the whole *dharmadhātu* with a garland of flowers—all of this, indeed, cannot be said to occur in physical actuality, but is rather the complex holographic projection of a microcosmic-macrocosmic maṇḍala universe entirely visualized through the creative image-making power of the active imagination in the state of waking dream.

Such an unorthodox interpretation of Hua-yen Buddhism is strongly supported through a historical analysis of Yogācāra *citta-nātra* or mind-only theory. In his book, *The Buddhist Teaching of Totality,* Garma C.C. Chang points out that the mind-only theory which Hua-yen appropriated from Yogācācara Buddhism into its own syncretic harmonization pattern is an essential reason for the interpenetrative nature attributed to all dharmas, writing: "Ch'eng Kuan in his *A Prologue to Hua Yen* gave ten reasons for the all-merging Dharmadhātu. The first reads, 'It is because all things are merely manifestations of the Mind, that all dharmas can all merge through and through in the realm of Totality.'"[25] Chang then goes on to cite mind-only texts such as the *Saṃdhinirmocanasūtra* which he translates as follows:

> The Bodhisattva Maitreya asked the World-Honored One, "Should we say that the visions and images seen by the act of Samādhi are different, or are not different, from the Mind?" Buddha replied, "You should say that they are not different from the Mind. Why? Because these images. . . are all of the mind."[24]

However, in a scholarly work entitled *On Knowing Reality,* Janice D. Willis argues through well-documented evidence that the central notion of Yogācāra Buddhism, namely, *cittamātra* or mind-only, was not metaphysical or speculative in its original Yogācāra usage, but was employed in the strict context of meditative practice, or more specifically, in the visualization of an "image" (Skt. *ālambana; pratibimba*) of various Buddhas during contemplation in *samādhi*. Willis demonstrates that the earliest sūtra expounding the mind-only theory, the *Bhadrapāpalasūtra*, is primarily concerned with a meditation of visualizing images of Buddhas, and then comments on the sūtra as follows:

> Clearly then, in this work. . . the term cittamātra was first used within the context of meditative practice. What is "just mind" or "wholly mind"? The earliest answer seems to have been: "The image (*ālambana; pratibimba*) cognized during intense contemplation (*samādhi*)." It was an answer which intended to describe the "ideal" character of the *samādhi-image*, the object mentally visualized by the meditating yogin.[26]

Willis goes on to cite the key passages from other early Yogācāra texts such as the *Daśabhūmika* (later incorporated into the *Hua-yen Sūtra*) and the *Mahāyāna-samgraha* by Asaṅga and *Samdhinirmocana Sūtra*, demonstrating that in each case it is a *samādhi*-image visualized by the meditating yogin which is said to be *cittamātra* or mind-only.[27] Thus, in light of this edifying reexamination of the mind-only doctrine, one must inquire how this term was originally propounded in the ancient Sanskrit text, the *Avataṁsaka Sūtra*. For are not the incredible visions beheld during Ocean-Seal-Samādhi which are constantly proclaimed in the sūtra as being mind-only, also to be regarded as *samādhi*-images visualized by a meditating yogin? If such is indeed the case, then ultimately the visions appearing in Ocean-Seal-Samādhi must not be interpreted as representing already actualized physical events as is ordinarily done by Hua-yen scholars; rather, they must be conceived as being elaborate psychic visualizations having their reality in mythic time and space at the level of the archetypal imagination.

The view of the archetypal imagination as propounded by the theology of the deep unconscious has perhaps never been articulated with greater visionary force than by the great English Romantic poet, William Blake. To have recourse to the experiential testimony of the English Romantics is of special interest here, since Whitehead himself devotes an entire chapter to English Romanticism in his *Science and the Modern World*, citing the Romantic experience as providing some of the empirical and imaginative ground for his philosophy of organism. Blake boldly proclaimed the archetypal imagination to be God himself, as did his contemporary, Samuel T. Coleridge, with such verses as: "This Eternal body of Man is the Imagination, i.e., God."[28] The imagination was then specifically described by Blake as an eternal envisagement of archetypal forms in such a manner as follows:

> The world of Imagination is the world of Eternity; it is the divine bosom into which we shall go after death of the vegetable body. This world of Imagination is infinite and eternal, whereas the world of generation is finite and temporal. There exist in that eternal world the permanent realities of everything which we see reflected in the vegetable glass of nature. All things are comprehended in their Eternal Forms in. . . the vine of eternity, the Human Imagination.[29]

Here, Blake perfectly reflects the Platonic foundations of Whitehead's process theory of actuality wherein "The things which are temporal arise by their participation in the things which are eternal" (PR, p. 40). However, the difference is that whereas Whitehead attributes the atemporal envisagement of eternal archetypal patterns to a transcendent deity, i.e., to the primordial nature of the dipolar God, Blake, as does Jung, recognizes the true source of this atemporal envisagement in the archetypal imagination, i.e., the creative and purposeful image-making faculty of the transpersonal unconscious at the depths of the psyche. Finally, that the atemporal envisagement of eternal patterns in the archetypal imagination described by Blake represents the Hua-yen visionary experience of Ocean-Seal-Samādhi, is reflected in his most celebrated poem, wherein he states:

> "To see a World in a Grain of Sand,
> And a Heaven in a Wild Flower,
> Hold Infinity in the palm of your hand,
> And Eternity in an Hour!"[30]

Yet, here we can observe the indivisible relation that exists between the *sambhogakāya* realm of archetypal imagination and the *nirmāṇakāya* realm of physical feelings. By repeatedly visualizing archetypal maṇḍala-images in the active imagination, one's perceptual experience comes to be wholly constituted by the microcosmic-macrocosmic structure of those maṇḍalas, hence resulting in the vision of value-rich core/horizon gestalt environments. In process terminology, this means that such maṇḍala imagery emanating from the archetypal imagination function normatively in the process of imaginative experiential synthesis as aesthetic value-patterns or lures for feeling which organize the given multiplicity of physical prehensions into expanded horizons of experiential wholeness through the establishment of intense harmonic contrasts between foreground and background. Thus, it is in such a manner that one comes to perceive "a world in a grain of sand and a heaven in a wild flower," i.e., what Hua-yen Buddhism terms: *li-shih-wu-ai*.

Section IV

It would be appropriate to bring this work to a close with a consideration of Kūkai's esoteric Shingon Buddhism in Japan. For in fact, the explicit categoreal interpenetration and syncretic harmonization of Hua-yen (Jap. *Kegon*) and Tantric (Jap. *Shingon*) thought patterns has to some extent already been accomplished in Kūkai's extraordinary system of theory and praxis. Shingon (i.e., the Mantra Vehicle) is the Japanese version of Tantric Buddhism based principally upon the *Mahāvairocanasūtra* as systematized by Kūkai (774–835), who received the honorific posthumous name of Kōbō Daishi. Perhaps the best manner to exhibit the relation between Kegon and Shingon is through Kūkai's *p'an chiao* or doctrinal classification system. The Shingon *p'an chiao* system divides Buddhism into ten stages, including three worldly stages, two pre-Mahāyāna stages, followed by Yogācāra, Mādhyamika and T'ien-t'ai. Kegon or Hua-yen Buddhism, according to Kūkai's typological classification scheme, represents the ninth and culminating stage of what he terms *kengyō* or "exoteric" Buddhism. The Kegon teachings concerning the non-obstructive *dharmadhātu* of total interpenetrative harmonization and all-merging suchness is accepted by Kūkai as the supreme theoretical description of ultimate reality; yet, this reality must still be revealed through *mikkyō* or esoteric (i.e., Shingon) Buddhist practices. In his work *The Precious Key to the Secret Treasury*, Kūkai expresses the shift from the ninth stage, which he terms "The Profoundest Exoteric Buddhist Mind That is Aware of Its Non-immutable Nature" (the stage of Kegon) to the tenth and final stage, which he terms "The Glorious Mind, the Most Secret and Sacred" (the stage of Shingon) in the following manner: "The world of Dharma (*dharmadhātu*) is not yet ultimate. One must proceed further by receiving revelation. . . . When the medicines of Exoteric Buddhism have cleared away the dust, Shingon opens the Treasury. Then the secret treasures are at once manifested and one realizes all values."[31]

As Minoru Kiyota asserts in his text entitled *Shingon Buddhism: Theory and Practice*, "In Shingon, *Dharmadhātu* refers to the world of Mahāvairocana. Mahāvairocana is the creator of *Dharmadhātu*."[32] He continues:

> Vairocana, the Kegon Buddha, is a symbolic representation of the Kegon world of perfect harmony, which in turn is the Kegon concept of ultimate reality. But Shingon claims that the Kegon *Dharmadhātu* is not the ultimate, because Kegon only points to that world. It does not reveal that world. . . . The tenth and final stage is Shingon. . . . This stage reveals the *Mikkyō* (secret teaching) doctrine. The *Mikkyō* doctrine reveals the world of Mahāvairocana.[33]

In his work *Hua-yen Buddhism*, Francis Cook devotes an entire chapter to discussing the central importance of Vairocana, the supreme Buddha of Hua-yen, stating: "The dharmadhātu of identity and interdependence. . . is thus none other than the body of Vairocana."[34] Cook correctly determines the meaning of Vairocana Buddha when he writes: "'Vairocana' is merely a name given to the law of interdependent origination or interdependent existence,"[35] finally citing the *Avataṁsaka Sūtra* verse:

> "Clearly know that all *dharmas*
> Are without any self-essence at all;
> To understand the nature of *dharmas* in this way
> Is to see Vairocana."[36]

However, according to the Shingon perspective, although this understanding of the non-obstructive *dharmadātu* as the body of Mahāvairocana Buddha is theoretically accurate, it is not ultimate; for it must still be esoterically revealed through Shingon Tantric praxis. What precisely are these so-called "esoteric" Shingon practices? In Kūkai's Tantric system, as in the Indo-Tibetan Mantra Vehicle in general, the essence of practice is *tri-guhya* (Jap. *San-mitsu*) or the three mysteries, namely, *mudrā* (gesture), *mantra* (incantation) and *maṇḍala* (visualization of a mystic circle) whereby the yogin imitates the paradigmatic body, speech and mind of *Mahāvairocana*, the Kegon Buddha of total non-obstructive interfusion and mutual identification. Minoru Kiyota describes the *tri-guhya* practice of *mudrā*, *mantra* and *maṇḍala* as signifying

> . . . the three Tantric Buddhist "teaching-practices of the Buddha" theory, revealed through the functions of body, voice and mind of the Shingon Buddha, Mahāvairocana. The three *guhya* are characteristics of *Mahāvairocana*. (This) triad of characteristics is to be united through *adhiṣṭhāna* (compassionate power of saving grace), the instrument of integration, which is the Tantric idealization of the mystic power of Mahāvairocana as the universal source of Tantric enlightenment.[37]

In his text, *Kūkai: Major Works*, Y.S. Hakeda also describes the *tri-guhya* practice, stating:

> In a word, the essence of Kūkai's Esoteric Buddhist meditation is simply "imitating." This is technically called the practice of "entering self into Self." . . . The self is the individual existence and the Self is Mahāvairocana. To practice the samādhi of Mahāvairocana is to "imitate" it through one's total being. . . . the stage is the sacred ground (*maṇḍala*). . . . Here the

eternal and cosmic drama of the samādhi of self-enjoyment (*jijuyō sammai*) of Mahāvairocana is performed through rigidly prescribed activities of body, speech and mind, every step exactly as prescribed; how to move one's fingers (mudrā); what to think or 'visualize' or feel; and which mantra to recite at what moment and how many times.[38]

In order to comprehend the deeper significance of Kūkai's Tantric methodology of yogic praxis, we would do well to recollect here the Hua-yen meditation on the aura or halo of jewelled colored lights radiating from the personage of Vairocana Buddha, the Buddha of Universally Illuminating Light, as was described at length by Li T'ung-hsüan in his *Hua-yen ching lun*. In this meditative exercise, the yogin is instructed to follow the inexhaustible waves, beams and rays of jewelled colored lights emitted by Vairocana Buddha like rainbow lamp-clouds until they illumine the whole universe with their radiance, whereupon the practitioner's mind also becomes inexhaustible and thus realizes its identity with the *dharmadhātu* of non-obstructive interpenetration. Thus, through the visualization (and audialization) of the *Garbhkosadhātu Maṇḍala* housing Mahavāirocana Buddha, who shines rays of jewelled colored lights outward into infinity, one comes to directly envisage the reality which Hua-yen Buddhism terms: *li-shih-wu-ai*. From where do such astonishing visions of gods and goddesses out of the Tantric Buddhist pantheon emerge during Shingon meditative praxis? In accordance with the Jungian psychological hermeneutic, this multiplicity of maṇḍala-palaces with their resplendent deities are ultimately to be analyzed as emanating from the creative image-making faculty of the collective unconscious, i.e., the archetypal imagination. Thus, the archetypal imagination is a theophanic imagination, which through the creative potency of the polytheistic psyche produces *sambhogakāya* Buddhas and bodhisattvas without number, each symbolizing intrinsic psychical values of color, light and emotional tonality. And the organ of perception whereby these theophanic creations of the polytheistic psyche are visualized is precisely: the "active imagination." However, by repeated visualization of Mahāvairocana Buddha's maṇḍala-palace in the active imagination at the level of *sambhogakāya*, one's perceptual field of causal presence at the level of *nirmāṇakāya* or physical actuality itself becomes wholly transformed into the microcosmic-macrocosmic structure of that maṇḍala, while one's mundane self-image becomes transformed into the image of Mahāvairocana, thus resulting in the constitution of value-rich core/horizon gestalt environments as shaped by free variation in imagination. In such a manner then, the primordial image of Mahāvairocana Buddha's maṇḍala-palace may be understood as an aesthetic-value pattern supplied by the archetypal imagination which functions normatively in the process of imaginative experiential synthesis to organize the plurality of antecedent causal feelings into the primary beauty of harmonic contrast between background and focus. And in this way the causal presence of *nirmāṇakāya* is axiologically patterned by the archetypal images of *sambhogakāya* while at the same time shining outwards with brilliant light through the radiance of *dharmakāya.*

The Garbhakosadhātu Maṇḍala
Enshrining Mahāvairocana Buddha

Hence, through *tri-guhya*, the three secret Tantric modes of praxis extolled by esoteric Shingon Buddhism, these being mudrā, mantra and maṇḍala, one is said to imitate the physical, verbal and mental reality of Tathāgatahood, whereupon the body, speech and mind of the yogin are radically transformed into, and ultimately identified with, the paradigmatic Body, Speech and Mind of Mahāvairocana Buddha, who in fact represents the supreme personification of the Kegon *dharmadhātu*, which is the non-obstructed dharma-field of interpenetrative harmonization and all-merging suchness. Through the exercise of *creative visioning*, which designates the elaborate *Yoga of Imagination* animating the Mantra Vehicle of Buddhism, itself encompassing such diversified techniques as *active imagination*, i.e., the active evocation and spontaneous exfoliation of archetypal God-images or symbols of transformation, *free variation in imagination*, i.e., the open possibility search for value-rich gestalt environments through polymorphic variations, as well as *ritual visualization*, i.e., the controlled envisagement of sacred mental pictures in accordance with standardized iconographic imagery and liturgical description, the practitioner of esoteric Shingon Buddhism enters the microcosmic-macrocosmic *maṇḍala*-palace enshrining Mahāvairocana Buddha—beautiful, splendidly adorned, and vivid, yet wholly unsubstantial and translucent, radiating concentric bands of brilliant multi-colored auras and halos along with luminous orbs and satellite orbs of holographic rainbow lights, thus consummating in the supreme Kegon visionary experience of *li-shih-wu-ai* or the complete non-obstructed fusing of form with voidness. Yet, this microcosmic-macrocosmic maṇḍala-palace housing Mahāvairocana Buddha constructed through visualization cannot itself be said to exist in physical actuality at the level of *nirmāṇakāya*. which is characterized by causal memory and cumulative penetration, but rather at the level of *sambhogakāya*, which is the acausal and synchronistic realm of the archetypal imagination, i.e., the atemporal envisagement of all archetypal-images, manifesting itself in the bardos of dreaming and inner visions: and beyond which there is only the clear light of voidness, the transparent *dharmakāya* space of brilliant luminosity, the state which Western theological discourse has itself named: God above God.[39]

APPENDIX

A Translation of Ŭisang's Autocommentary on the Ocean Seal

As indicated in the Prologue of this work, the *Kyo* (doctrinal study) side of Korean Buddhism has been so completely dominated by the one vehicle round-sudden teachings of the Hwaŏm (Chi. Hua-yen) school that it is generally characterized by such apellations as *hwajaeng* or "harmonization of all disputes," *wŏllyung hoet'ong* or "interpenetrative syncretic harmonization" and *t'ong pulgyo* or "Buddhism of total interpenetration." Since the *Hwaŏm ilsŭng pŏpkye do* or "Diagram of the Dharmadhātu. According to the One Vehicle of Hwaŏm" is the only major extant work of Ŭisang (625–702), the First Patriarch of Hwaŏm Buddhism in Korea, it assumes a position of central importance in the history of Korean Buddhism. Ŭisang's *Hwaŏm ilsŭng pŏpkye do* (T. 1887A.45.711-716), which again, is comprised of his Ocean Seal accompanied by an autocommentary, subsequently inspired a whole Ocean Seal tradition in Korean Hwaŏm Buddhism, including various other Ocean Seals with autocommentaries emulating Ŭisang's prototype, as well as a number of voluminous sub-commentaries expositing Ŭisang's text. For example, the Unified Silla Dynasty scholar-monk Myŏngjŏng (date unknown) designed a splendid variation of Ŭisang's Ocean Seal entitled *Haein sammae non* or "Treatise on Ocean Seal Samādhi" (T. 1889.45.773-79). The two most significant subcommentaries on Ŭisang's Ocean Seal in Korea are the *Pŏpkye do ki ch'ong surok* or "A Comprehensive Record of Commentaries on the Diagram of the Dharmadhātu" (T. 1887 b. 45.716-767), an anonymous compilation of expository treatises, and the *Ilsŭng pŏpkye do wŏnt'onggi* or "Kyunyŏ's Commentary on the One Vehicle Dharmadhātu Map"

(Kim Ji-kyon, ed. *Kyunyŏ Taesa Hwaŏmgyung chŏnso*, Vol. I, Seoul Korea, 1977), composed by the Koryo Dynasty scholar-monk Kyunyŏ (923–973). In that neither Ŭisang's *Hwaŏm ilsŭng pŏpkye do*, nor any other major treatise from the tradition of Korean Buddhism has as yet been translated and published in a Western language, I have thus included a complete translation of Ŭisang's text in the form of an appendix.

In his autocommentary, Ŭisang employs his Ocean Seal or "Diagram of the *Dharmadhātu*" to illustrate numerous key doctrinal innovations of Hwaŏm Buddhism such as the Six Marks, Indra's Net, All-in-One/One-in-All, Simultaneous-Mutual-Establishment, and Unobstructed Interpenetration of the Three Times. The thematic inquiry pervading throughout the autocommentary is: "How can beginning and end or cause and effect (illustrated by the first and last characters of the seal, i.e., *dharma* and *Buddha*) remain distinct and yet both occupy the same position (in the center of the diagram)"? In such a manner, Ŭisang's Ocean Seal inquires into the fundamental structure of Hwaŏm Buddhism as articulated by the doctrine of Fifty-Two Stages (in the career of a bodhisattva), wherein the first stage of nascent faith contains all fifty-two stages of the path, including the last stage of wonderful enlightenment, although each stage remains successive and distinct. Thus, beginning and end (i.e., a first stage bodhisattva and the perfectly enlightened Buddha), as well as each of the intermediary stages, all occupy the same position while still retaining their own marks.

Ŭisang continues to clarify this relationship between beginning, middle and end through a lengthy discourse on the *Counting Ten Coins* analogy first expounded by his teacher Chih-yen (602-668), the Second Patriarch of Chinese Hua-yen Buddhism. According to the *Counting Ten Coins* analogy, due to the mystery of simultaneous-mutual-establishment, one coin is identical with all the other coins, including the tenth coin, although one and ten are not equal. Hence, first, last and in-between once again occupy the same position while retaining their own marks.

How does Ŭisang explicate this supreme mystery of simultaneous-mutual-penetration between beginning, middle and end? All three temporal periods occupy the same position while retaining their own marks due to the "great dependent coorigination law of universal *dhāraṇī*" whereby both one and many are free of self-nature, yet follow conditions inexhaustibly, thus establishing the middle way through non-discrimination and non-abiding in extremes. Indeed, a notable characteristic of Ŭisang's autocommentary on the Ocean Seal is its frequent explanation of the unobstructed interpenetration and harmonization between all phenomena in terms of the great dependent coorigination law of universal *dhāraṇī*, which according to Ŭisang, signifies "holding everything" in a state of "as you wish."

Hence, in this context it would be appropriate to establish the profound connection existing between the Korean Hwaŏm school and the *Chinŏn* or Secret Mantra Vehicle of Tantric Buddhism founded by Myŏngnang Pŏpsa (in 635 A.D.), which flourished in the Unified Silla Dynasty during the life of Ŭisang. In fact, when Ŭisang returned from T'ang China in 671 in order to warn King Munmu of the T'ang's intention of dispatching reinforcements against Silla (as described in the Prologue), the king, so tradition has recorded, immediately supplicated Myŏngnang Pŏpsa of the Chinŏn sect to ward-off the invaders with powerful *dhāraṇī* incantations. The Chinŏn or Secret Mantra Vehicle, which cultivated the inexhaustible dharma treasury of secret magical *dhāraṇī* spells, was also know in Unified Silla as the *Shinin* or "God-Seal" school, which cultivated the mysterious dharma treasury of visualizing secret maṇḍala diagrams or magical "seals" so to invoke deities of the Tantric Buddhist pantheon. Thus, as a final word of preparation, I would like to suggest that Ŭisang's employment of a "seal" or maṇḍala diagram to illustrate the key doctrinal formulas of Hwaŏm, as well as his frequent references to the great dependent coorigination law of universal *dhāraṇī* in his autocommentary on the seal, should both be understood against the background of the Chinŏn (Secret Mantra) or Shinin (God-Seal) Vehicle of Korean Tantric Buddhism, since in the final analysis, Hwaŏm and Chinŏn Buddhism must be viewed as inseparable dharmas.

Diagram of the Dharmadhātu According to the One Vehicle of Hwaŏm by Ŭisang

Generally, great sages do not have a single method but teach people according to their capacity and following their disease. Those who are deluded and attached to words do not know that they miss the essence [of the teachings] and, although they are diligent, they do not know how to return to the doctrine. Since we are in this dharma-ending age, according to the universal principle and relying on the teachings, I have composed this brief poem hoping that those who are attached to names will return to the true source which is nameless. As to the method of reading the poem, you should begin with the character *pŏb* (Skt. *dharma*) at the center, going through many curves, bends and meanderings, finally coming to the character *pul* (Skt. Buddha). Then read following the *tao* (path) of the seal through 210 characters and 54 curves.

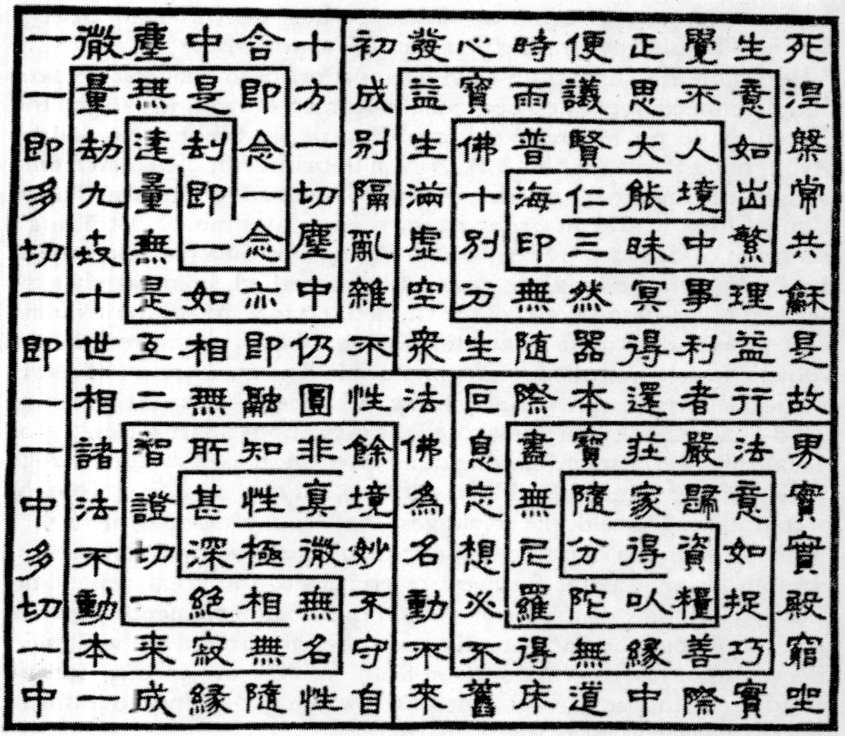

Now, interpreting the seal, I would like to have two separate sections: (i) a comprehensive interpretation of the seal's meaning, and (ii) a special analysis of the seal's marks.

[First Section]

Question: Why do you depend upon [the form of] a seal?

Answer: Because I wish to express that three kinds of worlds included in Sakya Tathāgata's teaching system are produced from ocean seal samādhi. These so-called three worlds are (i) the material world; (ii) the world of sentient beings; and (iii) the world of perfectly enlightened wisdom. Those who have perfectly enlightened wisdom are Buddhas and bodhisattvas. These three kinds of worlds include and exhaust all dharmas. For the deeper meaning of this discussion see the *Flower Adornment Scripture* (i.e., the *Hwaŏm-gyŏng*).

In the second section there are three subsections: (i) discussing the marks of the seal's sentences; (ii) clarifying the nature of the words; and (iii) interpreting the meanings of the text.

[First Subsection]

Question: Why does the seal have only one path?

Answer: Because it expresses the One Sound of Tathāgata, the so-called expedient means (*upāya kauśalya*).

Question: Why does it have so many meanderings?

Answer: To follow [all the] sentient beings whose capacities and desires are various. This is the teachings of the three vehicles (i.e., *śravakas*, *pratyekabuddhas* and *bodhisattvas* of Hīnayāna).

Question: For what reason does the one way have no beginning and end?

Answer: To manifest that [Tathāgata's] expedient means has no [fixed] method but should correspond to the world of dharma so that the ten (spatial and temporal) worlds are mutually corresponding and completely interpenetrating. This means the round teaching (of Hwaŏm).

Question: Why are there four sides and four angles?

Answer: To express the four inclusives (*catuḥ-saṁgraha vastu* or the four means of conversion, i.e., *dāna* or giving, *priyavādita* or kind words, *arthacāryā* or helpfulness and *samānārthata* or consistency between words and deeds) and four immeasurables (*catvāriaparamaṇa-cittāni)*or four infinite minds, i.e., *maitri* or friendliness, *karuṇā* or compassion, *muditā* or sympathetic joy and *upekṣā* or equanimity). This means that by depending on the three vehicles the text manifests the one vehicle. The marks of the seal are like this.

[Second Subsection]

Question: Why do the characters at the center have a beginning and end?

Answer: In order to manifest that cause and effect are not equal from the standpoint of expedient means in practice.

Question: For what reason do the characters have many meanderings and curves?

Answer: In order to manifest that capacities and desires of people in the three vehicles are different and unequal.

Question: Why are the two characters at the beginning and end put in the center?

Answer: So to express that the two positions of cause and effect or real virtuous function and essence in the dharma-nature (Hwaŏm) school are in the middle way. The marks of characters are like this.

Question: Previously it was said that cause and effect are not equal, but now it is being said that true virtuous function and essence in the one [vehicle] school are in the middle way. We still don't know its reason. What is the meaning of this?

Answer: Its meaning is truly difficult to explain. Nonetheless, according to debating master Vasubandhu, with the expedient means of the *six marks* he establishes the explanation of its meaning. Based upon the truth expounded in its meaning, one can understand according to one's capacity. If one holds *ten phrases* one can explain the six marks as is said below. When one holds the seal's image and clarifies the six marks then it shows that the one vehicle and three vehicles or main and subordinate [teachings] are mutually accomplished. Thus, the present dharmas have both division and equality. The so-called six marks are the universality mark and particularity mark, the identity mark and difference mark, the integration mark and disintegration mark. The universality mark is the foundation of the seal whereas the particularity mark is its various meanderings. The particularity [mark] fills the seal up. Then the identity mark enters the seal. In other words, the meanderings are differentiated and yet are still identical to the seal. The difference mark increases [the seal's] marks. The so-called first and second curves are different so that marks are increased. The integration mark generally speaking forms the seal. The disintegration mark broadly speaking is its many curves, bends, and meanderings. Everything is originally unproduced. In all dharmas of conditioned origination, there is none which is not formed by these six marks.

The so-called universality mark means the round teachings [of Hwaŏm]. The particularity mark means the three vehicles teaching [of Hīnayāna]. Therefore, the universality mark and particularity mark, the integration mark and disintegration mark, etc. are neither identical nor separate, neither same nor different, but are always in the middle way. The one vehicle and three vehicles are also like this, since main and subordinate marks are mutually dependent, being neither identical nor separate, neither same nor different. Even though they benefit all sentient beings, they are still only in the middle way. Main and subordinate marks mutually complete each other manifesting dharmas just as they are.

Based on this doctrine the special teachings in both the one vehicle and three vehicles can be understood. The meaning of the question you raised before is also just like this. The first curve is like the cause while the last curve is like the effect. Even if beginnning and end are not equal, yet both are at the center. Even though the meaning of cause and effect are different, still they abide in their own positions. Depending on the three vehicles teachings on expedient means, superior and inferior are not equal. Depending on the one vehicle teaching, there is no before and after. Thus its reason should be known. As the (Hwaŏm) sutra says: "Also, all bodhisattva's clear explanation of unimaginable

Buddhadharmas lets people enter the stage (*bhūmi*) of wisdom (*prajñā*)."

The above may be explained as follows: "all bodhisattva's" refers to the [Hwaŏm stages of] faith, abiding, practice and *bhūmis;* "clear" refers to seeing wisdom and obtaining enlightenment; "explanation" means clarification of the contents; "enter" means that through joyful faith one obtains enlightenment; "stage of wisdom" indicates the wisdom of the ten *bhūmis.* As the interpretation of the main section, this is the fundamental entrance.

Like the [Hwaŏm] sūtra says: "Also, all bodhisattva's clear explanation of the unimaginable Buddhadharmas lets people enter the stage of wisdom." In this sūtra, it is said that there are nine kinds of entrance depending on the fundamental entrance. The first is the inclusive entrance. In the listening wisdom all good roots are included, just like the sūtra includes all good roots. The second is entrance by thinking. Wisdom by thinking is an expedient means in the dimension of *tao,* just like the sūtra shows all Buddhadharmas by means of good analysis. The third is entrance by dharma marks. In those doctrines there are immeasurable myriad wisdoms, just like the sūtra comprehensively knows all dharmas. The fourth is entrance by transformative wisdom. Following these thoughts, the names and words have all good teachings, just like the sūtra which is good for explaining all dharmas. The fifth is entrance by enlightenment. About all dharmas, one can hold wisdom of equality because one is really pure when seeing the *tao,* just like the sūtra [says] undifferentiated wisdom is pure and inseparable. The bodhisattvas' cultivating [all] sentient beings is their self-completion of the Buddhadharma. Therefore benefiting others is simply benefiting oneself. The sixth is entrance by diligence. When you practice *tao* you are completely free from all obstacles of defilement. Like the sūtra says all demonic dharmas cannot influence [you]. The seventh is entering by transforming all stages. In the dimension of supramundane *tao* the good roots such as non-desire are purified, just like the sūtra [says] good roots of the dharma are purified. Also, if there are good roots, they can become the cause of the supramundane *tao.* The eighth is entrance by exhausting bodhisattvas' stages at the tenth *bhūmi.* One enters all Buddhas' secret wisdom, just like the sūtra [says] that you obtain all unimaginable worlds. The ninth is entrance by exhausting all Buddhas' stages. At the place of all wisdom one enters all wisdom, like the sūtra [says] you finally obtain all wisdom and enter the world of wisdom.

All these entrances are [only] for comparing and measuring differences in the meaning of wisdom and one's gradual trasnformation into excellence, and are not the fundamental entrance. In all the ten phrases having been discussed, all have six sections of analytical marks. Since these are linguistic interpretations you should know the items eliminated from them such as clusters (*skandhas*), elements (*dhātus*) and sense fields (*āyatanas*), etc. There are six kinds of special marks, universality mark and particularity mark, integration mark and disintegration mark, etc. The universality mark is the fundamental entrance, and the particularity mark, which is the other nine [entrances]. By relying on the fundamental [entrance], they fill the [seal]. The identity mark means everything mutually enters; the difference mark increases [the seal's] marks; the integration mark means brief explanation; the disintegration mark means broad explanation, like the world which is formed and disintegrated.

All the other ten phrases are to be similarly known following this meaning. The treatise is like this. Only this is the truth of the doctrine established by the author. Therefore, you should know that although cause and effect [which respectively correspond to the Hwaŏm stages of] faith, understanding, practice, returnings, *bhūmis* and Buddha, each have their immovable self position, yet still there is no before and after. Why are all dharmas different? Because each stays in its own self-suchness. One may say one suchness or many suchnesses, yet marks of those suchnesses can never be obtained. Therefore the treatise says: "Question: What is deep faith in the Buddhadharma? Answer: All dharmas are known only by Buddha, not by my own experience. Being like this, it is named deep faith in Buddhadharma." This is my meaning.

Question: What meaning is manifested by the six marks?

Answer: It manifests the principle of non-differentiation which is expounded by the principle of dependent coorigination. Since there is the doctrine of the six marks, you should know that although the one sūtra (i.e., the *Hwaŏm-gyŏng*) with its seven places, 8 assemblies, and various kinds of chapters, etc. are not the same, still all are included in the chapter of *bhūmis*. Why is it so? Because this is the fundamental chapter which includes all dharmas exhaustively. In the chapter of the *bhūmis*, even though the ten *bhūmis* are not identical, still they are all only in the first *bhūmi*. Why is it so? Before one *bhūmi* arises, it universally includes all merits of all *bhūmis*. In one *bhūmi* although there are many unequal distinctions, still they are [all] only in one thought-instant. Why is it so? Because the three worlds and the nine worlds are identical to one thought-instant. All are identical to one, just as one thought-instant and many thought-instants are also just like this. One is identical to all, and one thought-instant is identical to many thought-instants, and so on.

In the case of such expressions, the previous part (i.e., the one) is changed and becomes identical to the second part (i.e., the many). Because of this truth, in the law of *dhāraṇī*, main and subordinate parts are mutually established. By means of raising one dharma, all [dharmas] are exhaustively included. If it is explained from the standpoint of assemblies (i.e., the 8 assemblies wherein the Buddha expounded the *Hwaŏm-gyŏng*), then each assembly exhaustively includes all [assemblies]. If it is explained in terms of chapters, then each chapter exhaustively includes all [chapters]. And finally, if it is explained in terms of sentences, then each sentence exhaustively includes all [sentences]. Why is it so? If there is no this (i.e., the one), then that (i.e., the many) cannot be established. [In the world of] *dhāraṇī*, every dharma is like this, as is explained below.

[Third Subsection]

Interpretation of the meaning of the sentences. There are thirty verses of seven characters in the seal. Among them, broadly speaking, there are three sections: (i) the first eighteen verses discuss the practice of self-benefit; (ii) the next four phrases are about the practice of benefiting others; (iii) the last eight verses clarify the expedient means of practice and the benefits they obtain. In the first section there are two subsections: (i) the first four verses [1-4] manifests enlightenment; (ii) the following fourteen phrases manifests dependent coorigination. Among these, the first two verses [5 and 6] indicate the essence of dependent coorigination. The next two verses [7-8] clarify the included dharmas and their classification from the standpoint of the principle and function of *dhāraṇī*. Third, the next two verses [9 and 10] manifest the included dharmas and their classification based upon particularity. Fourth, the next four verses [11-14] reveal the included dharmas and classifications in terms of dimensions. Fifth, the next two verses [15-16] show the included dharmas and classifications in terms of levels. Sixth, the next two phases [17-18] comprehensively explain the meaning of the above. Although these six gates are not equal, [they] still only manifest the law of *dhāraṇī*, which is the law of dependent coorigination.

As to the essence of dependent coorigination first mentioned, this is the law of *dhāraṇī* in the one vehicle. One is identical to all and all is identical to one, which describes the *dharmadhātu* of unobstructed events. Moreover, by holding one gate, one manifests the doctrine of dependent coorigination. As to so-called dependent coorigination, when the great sage takes care of all sentient beings, he wishes to cause people to understand universality and be free from [attachment to] particularity. However, when ordinary persons see the particular, they are immediately deluded [such as to neglect] universality. But when the sage obtains universality, he is already free from particularity. Therefore, by means of true universality [the great sage] penetrates all deluded people and lets them know that particularity is non-particularity, which is the understanding of universality. Thus, the great sage has produced this teaching.

For this reason the *daśabhūmika-śāstra* (i.e., the *Treatise on the Ten Stages* by Vasubandhu) says there are three kinds of self-natures: (i) first is the reward mark where name and form are co-produced with the storehouse (*ālaya*) consciousness. Like the [*daśabhūmika*] sūtra says, in the three worlds of *bhūmis* there is co-production. So-called name and form, they are co-produced with that [storehouse consciousness]; (ii) second is the causal mark of that [consciousness]. Name and form are not separate from that. Depending on that [consciousness] they are co-produced, just as in the sūtra they are not separate; (iii) third is the mark of the process of its effect. From the six sense organs finally you come to having *bhāva* (becoming). Like in the sūtra name and form have grown and have accomplished the assembly of six sense organs. Finally we reach *bhāva* which means causal conditions. Therefore, there are birth, old age, disease, and death, which are all afflictions, sorrows, sufferings and distresses. Thus, sentient beings produce much suffering. In this there is a separation of I and mine (i.e., subject and object). No perceiving and no awakening, just like the grass and trees. As to the expression here saying "separate from I and mine," these two show emptiness. As to the expression saying "not perceiving and not awakening," self-essence is free of self. As to "grass and trees," this shows the number of non-sentient beings. You should know that the twelve causal conditions, etc. are essentially empty of self-nature, all of which are co-produced depending on the storehouse consciousness. The storehouse consciousness itself is too subtle to have self-nature. Therefore, although the storehouse consciousness produces twelve causal conditions, still, twelve causal conditions show all things as devoid of selfhood.

Since conditioned co-production, etc. do not have any special dharma, based on the meditation on conditioned co-production, Buddha penetrates all dharmas. Then everything does not have discrimination and accomplishes true nature. The *daśabhūmika-śāstra* says, "By observing worldly truth one can immediately enter highest truth." This is exactly my point. This doctrine belongs to the three vehicles. It can also be applied to the one vehicle. Why? It is also aimed at the one vehicle. If one holds this special teaching of the one vehicle, briefly speaking, it has ten sections. They are: (i) [its] causal conditions have gradual steps; (ii) [it is] included in one mind; (iii) [it is] accomplished by self-karma; (iv) [it] cannot be mutually distinct; (v) [its] three paths cannot be cut; (vi) [it involves] observation of the before and after world; (viii) [it] consists of three sufferings; (viii) [it is] produced by causes and conditions; (ix) [it is] bound by arising and ceasing of causal conditions; (x) [it] exhausts all observations by means of following [all sentient beings]. Thus, the twelve causal conditions are included by the doctrine of the one vehicle. Why is it explained in ten numbers? Because I wish to manifest infinity.

Question: Do the ten causal conditions involve before and after or are they simultaneous?

Answer: Before and after are identical to no before and after. How do [I] know this? These gates are not the same, and thus, there are before and after. However, the six marks are accomplished and there is thus no before and after. What is meant by this? Although the ten numbers are distinct, still they are equally accomplished without self. Therefore, in the *ying le ching* ten numbers of causal conditions are included in the doctrine of the three vehicles. Why is it so? At the level of mere teachings, these are distinguished and made unequal. Details are seen in the *daśabhūmika-śāstra.* As is said in the twelve causal conditions, all dharmas of conditioned arising may also be understood according to this example.

Second, the law of *dhāraṇī* is as said below. Third, concerning particulars, all dharmas manifest both Indra's Net and the small. Details of this doctrine are seen in the sūtra. Fourth, as to the so called nine worlds, these are: (i) past of the past; (ii) present of the past; (iii) future of the past; (iv) past of the present; (v) present of the present; (vi) future of the present; (vii) past of the future; (viii) present of the future; (ix) future of the future. The three worlds [of past, present and future] are mutually interpenetrating and mutually identical, thus being accomplished in one thought-instant. Particularity (nine times) and universality (one time) are combined, thus to make ten worlds. One thought-instant is explained by the notion of particularity. Fifth, as to what is meant by dimension, with the expedient means of the six marks, the message of the doctrine is to be explained. As to the six marks, these are explained above.

Question: In one word of conditioned co-production, the non-duality of all dharmas are immediately manifested. Why do you then need so many sections.?

Answer: If essential wisdom is immediately present, then one need not seek anything elsewhere. Therefore, the sūtra says: "The nature of adultery, distress, and ignorance, are identical to wisdom." Such delusions are extremely remote. Thus, in Buddhism, besides seven kinds of suffering, there also exists wisdom. For three innumerable *kalpas* [deluded people] practiced as taught; and only then could they obtain salvation. For these deluded people many sections of explanation were required.

Question: If this is so, since dharma gates are innumerable, why are there only six sections given for explanations?

Answer: By means of six gates all dharmas are explained. According to this example, the rest should be understood. If, being explained like this, its truth must be in accord with the teachings. If six gates are completely non-differentiated, all dharmas of dependent coorigination are like this. Therefore, according to the above, you should contemplate this.

[Second Section]

About the practice of benefiting others. The seal obtains its name based upon simile. What simile? It is the great ocean which is extremely deep and clear so as to penetrate to the very bottom. When *devas* (heavenly gods) and *asuras* (angry gods) are fighting together, all soldiers and weapons reflect in the midst of the ocean very clearly, just like the seal manifests sentences and characters. Therefore it is named the ocean seal. Buddha's *samādhi* is also like this. Dharma-nature which is ultimately awakened does not have a source or bottom. By means of ultimate purification it became completely clear. Therefore, three kinds of worlds appear in the midst of Buddha's *samādhi*. Thus it is named the ocean seal.

The word "many" [in verse 20 of the seal] means numerous. The word "produce" means to spring forth inexhaustibly. The phrase "as you wish" obtains its name by analogy. A precious king acts according to his will with no mind but manifests all sentient beings like a shower of jewels, following conditions inexhaustibly. Tathāgata Śakyamuni Buddha's expedient means is also just like this. The [Buddha's] one sound responds to the world of sentient beings. The [one sound] destroys evil and produces good, benefiting sentient beings. No matter where [expedient means] is applied, there is nothing that one cannot do. Therefore it is named [the state of] "as you wish."

[Third Section]

The expedient means of practice has two subsections in it: (i) clarification of the practice of expedient means; (ii) clarification of attaining its benefits.

[First Subsection]

About practice in the first section. It is said that the universal law of the one vehicle which was seen and heard is now already gone and needs to be realized. This is the doctrine of the one vehicle based upon the special teachings. If we hold the doctrine of the one vehicle based upon expedient means, the five vehicles are comprehensively included in the one vehicle. Why is it so? Because [five vehicles] are flowing in one vehicle, seen in one vehicle and are the expedient means used by the one vehicle. If one holds this doctrine, he comprehensively includes five vehicles.

As to the phrase which says the one vehicle practitioner also obtains [five vehicles], that phrase is held by the principle of dependent coorigination. Expedient means refers to words based on wisdom. Why? Acting without attachment is called expedient means. The mind which is not detached cannot be called expedient means. Also, the [previous discourse on expedient means] is based on the teachings of the great sage. How so? By means of good expedient means [all sages] save sentient beings. In what way? Just as the five vehicles explain all dharmas including such doctrines as men and dharmas, cause and effect, understanding and practice, *li* (universal-principle) and *shih* (particular-phenomena), etc. According to this example, our topic must be understood.

Question: Should we say the five vehicles teachings are an active doctrine or a passive doctrine.?

Answer: All dharmas in either active teachings or passive teachings are only conceptual distinctions. Its meaning is like the passive teachings in which the dharma marks are all cut-off. All Buddhas, due to the strength of great compassion and primordial vows, and due to all dharmas of Buddhism which are like this, are established and taught for the sake of sentient beings. Because of this doctrine, all dharmas included in [Buddha's] teaching system are found in language. Therefore, the sūtra says all dharmas have only names. This is my meaning.

Question: Words cannot reach the world of enlightenment. Intellectual teachings are always found in particulars. Do the two dharmas of enlightenment and intellectual teachings always make the mistake of [establishing] two extremes?

Answer: If one says based on mere feeling that the two dharmas of enlightenment and intellect are always found in two extremes; whereas if based upon universal-principle, the two dharmas of enlightenment and intellect are both originally in the middle way. That is why one is able to know that *parikalpita* (discriminated nature) is devoid of its own marks, *paratantra* (interdependent nature) is unproduced and *parinispanna* (universal nature) does not have its own essence. These three kinds of self-nature are always in the middle way. Besides these three dharmas there is neither enlightened teachings nor intellectual teachings. Therefore you should know that there is no discrimination.

Since the perfected man attains this universality, names and marks fail to arise. Since they are said for sentient beings, words are always in the particular. Therefore the sūtra says: "All *tathāgatas* never speak Buddhadharma but follow after those needing to be transformed, yet still they lecture on the Dharma." This is its meaning. Therefore, the sage follows *parikalpita* and establishes the three natures theory, pacifying and clarifying the mind of sentient beings. Later, by gradually manifesting the three natures theory, the sage awakens deluded people. This is the sages great expedient means.

Question: As said in the *mahāyānasavigraha-sūtra, parikalpita* (discriminated nature) is the world of ordinary people, while *paratantra* (interdependent nature) and *parinispanna* (universal nature) are the world known by enlightened sages. Why then does the sage follow *parikalpita?*

Answer: All dharmas discriminated by sentient beings through *parikalpita* exist due to their perverted views. Therefore, the *śāstra* says that the ordinary person's world will be eventually empty. Hence, there is nothing to objectify. For this reason, in the treatise the profane world is not wisdom, emptiness or the sacred world. The sage's compassionate expedient means follows the disease [of sentient beings] without obstacle. This is its meaning. The mark of *paratantra* is originated from causal conditioning. It does not have self-nature and is free from the two extremes. Thus, it is identical to no-self. Dharmas of equality seen in *parinispanna* are completely interpenetrating and there is no discrimination. Originally of one taste because of this doctrine, distinctions are possible. Therefore, the world of sacred wisdom discussed in this treatise has a special meaning like this.

If one holds the true theory, three kinds of self-nature are all in the ordinary people's world. Why is it so? Following feelings of particularity establishes three kinds of self-nature and this is sacred wisdom. How so? Following wisdom manifests universality, and this universality is not artificially established. Therefore, the sūtra says outside of three natures, three no-natures cannot be established. Also, one can place oneself outside the three natures, separately establishing three no-natures. What is the reason? Following feeling something is established, since holding the intellectual perspective three no-natures are separately established. Following wisdom universality is manifested, because practice is adhered to. Besides these two (i.e., practice and theory), there is no truth. How can there be three self-natures outside of these three no-natures? Therefore one can know the manifestation of wisdom such as no marks. Finally, there is no dharma which can be objectified; they are only in the middle way. Thus, you ought to know why the doctrine is established.

Question: Concerning what was said in the above, is there any difference between dharmas of the enlightened level and dharmas of the dependent coorigination level?

Answer: There is difference and also there is no difference. What is meant by this? Dharmas of the enlightened level are described based on true marks because they are known only by enlightenment. Dharmas of the dependent coorigination level are originated from many conditions. Therefore they have no self-nature. Originally they are without distinctions. Thus, they [also] have no difference.

Question: If being so, self-enlightenment is spoken for the sake of sentient beings. With the end there are no differences. Is there any difference with ordinary people?

Answer: Attend this meaning. If enlightenment is in these words it is not different from the branches. If the words are in enlightenment, they are not different from the root. Since they are not different from the root, they are used but always quiet, they are spoken yet not spoken. Since they are not different from the branches, they are quiet yet also used, not spoken, yet spoken. Since not spoken yet spoken, not spoken is not non-spoken. Since spoken yet non-spoken, spoken is not spoken. Since both are not obtainable, both are mutually non-obstructive. Because of this meaning, spoken and non-spoken are identical with no difference. Producing and non-producing are [also] identical with no difference. Moving and not moving are [also] identical without difference. All are differentiated and relative teachings. According to this example, the rest should also be known. Therefore, the sūtra says: "All conditioned and unconditioned dharmas as well as having the nature and marks of Buddha and no Buddha are always present. There is no change." This is its meaning.

Also, in the right dharma, there is no special meaning apart from words. Taking words as doctrine, in the teaching of right doctrine, outside of the right doctrine, there is no special word. Since taking doctrine as language, language does not have no doctrine. Since taking language as doctrine, doctrine does not have no language. Since doctrine does not have no language, doctrine is not doctrine. Since language does not have no doctrine, language is not language. Since language is not doctrine, both cannot be obtained. Therefore, all dharmas are originally in the middle way. The middle way is interpenetration between both language and not language. Why is it so? True marks of all dharmas are not in language. Since it is free from the nature of all names, the dharma of language does not exist in true nature. Since it is made by people, a name does not have true nature. Since it is free from the nature of names, it is a name yet not a name. Since it is a name yet not a name by means of names seeking reality, the real cannot be attained. Its nature cannot be obtained, because of this doctrine, and therefore both cannot be obtained. This is to be known only by enlightenment, not by any other experience. Therefore the sūtra says: "All dharmas are to be known only by Buddha, not by my world."

Question: Is there any difference between the previous and later doctrines?

Answer: The previous doctrine takes roots and branches as being mutually interpenetrating and mutually identical, [thus] manifesting the middle way. The later doctrine takes name and doctrine as being mutually inclusive and manifesting the theory of no-self. The truth being manifested does not differ from the expedient means being used. This means that the roots and branches are mutually dependent. Name and doctrine are mutually inclusive [aspects] which guide sentient beings, cause people to return to the nameless true source. The doctrinal essence of transformer and transformed is seen here.

Question: The meaning of this doctrine corresponds to the doctrine of the sudden teaching. Why is it explained here?

Answer: As clarified above, explanation and non-explanation are identical and there is no difference. How so? Because all are real virtue and have no obstructions; also, because there is need for explanation, bodhisattvas are able to follow the theory of the three vehicles. Generally, this is the sage's excellent capacity. Doctrines of both the enlightened level and the dependent coorigination level as mentioned above correspond to the greatness of doctrine and the greatness of teaching mentioned in the treatise. Turning from discrimination, one obtains non-discrimination. It is named the unconditioned. Following truth without attainment, this is named expedient means. Practice as taught [alone] obtains the sages mind. Therefore it is named attainment "according to one's wishes" as described before.

What is meant by "returning home" [in verse 26 of the seal] is awakening to original nature. What is meant by home? It means to shelter; it means dwelling and abiding. So-called true emptiness of dharma-nature is the enlightened person's abode. Sheltering sentient beings with expedient means, great compassion is called home. This doctrine is in the three vehicles. However, the one vehicle is ultimate. Why is this so? Because it corresponds to the *dharmadhātu*. The so-called house of *dhāraṇī* in the *dharmadhātu*, the house of Indra, and many infinitesimal houses, etc. are all the abodes of sages. It is therefore named "home."

The phrase "according to one's capacity" [in verse 26 of the seal] means never being filled-up. The word "wealth" refers to helping wisdom. These are the two-thousand answers found in the end of the [Hwaŏm] sūtra in the chapter on "Leaving the World."

[Second Subsection]

The second subsection clarifying the obtainment of benefits [from expedient means] refers to *dhāraṇī*, meaning "holding everything," which will be discussed in the theory of *counting ten coins* explained below. By "true reality" [verse 29 in the seal] it is meant that dharma-nature is completely manifested. The phrase "middle way" indicates that all polarities are interfused. "Sitting in the bed" means all-inclusiveness. By peacefully dwelling on the vast and great jewelled bed of the ten kinds of *nirvāṇa* in the *dharmadhātu*, one includes everything. Therefore it is named "sitting in the bed." By the term "treasure" various valuable things are signified. By "bed" inclusiveness is meant. The "ten kinds of *nirvāṇa* are explained in the chapter on "Leaving the World" in the [Hwaŏm] sūtra as explained below:

By the phrase "originally not moving" [verse 30 in the seal] is meant "originally Buddha." The so-called ten Buddhas as specified in the [Hwaŏm] sūtra are: (i) Buddha of non-attachment, because he peacefully dwells in the world and achieves perfect enlightenment; (ii) Buddha of vows, because he has taken birth [in order to rescue sentient beings]; (iii) Buddha of karmic reward, because he has resolute faith; (iv) Buddha who receives, because he obediently serves [all sentient beings]; (v) Buddha of transformation, because he continually saves [sentient beings]; (vi) Buddha of *dharmadhātu*, because he is all-pervasive; (vii) Buddha of mind, because he peacefully abides; (viii) Buddha of samādhi, because he has no obstructions and no attachments; (ix) Buddha of nature, because he is determined; (x) Buddha of the "as you wish" state, because he universally embraces all. Why is there this ten number theory? Because I wish to manifest many Buddhas. Since this doctrine is the true source of all dharmas, the ultimate mysterious doctrine is extremely difficult to explain. You should contemplate this deeply.

Question: People in bondage [to *saṃsāra*] have never cut-off *kleśas* (defilements) and have never achieved bliss and wisdom. By what doctrine then have they originally achieved Buddhahood?

Answer: One who has never broken-off *kelśas* cannot be named a Buddha, but if *kleśas* are cut-off and exhausted, then bliss and wisdom are finally achieved. Since *kleśas* are already eliminated, [sentient beings] can be named originally Buddha.

Question: What is meant by cutting-off *kleśas*?

Answer: As the *daśabhūmika-śāstra* says, there is no before, middle or end. Because the division of before, middle and end are established, how can one cut-off [*kleśas*]? Like empty space! Since cutting-off is like this, your future cutting-off has not yet come, and so this is not called cutting-off. The present cutting-off is already gone, and so this is named originally cut-off, just like enlightenment and dreaming or sleeping and waking are not identical. Therefore, the difference between accomplished and not accomplished or cutting-off and not cutting-off has been established. But the true principle and true marks of all dharmas are neither increasing nor decreasing as well as originally not moving. Hence, the sūtra says: "In the dharma of *kleśas*, there hasn't been seen a single dharma decreased; in the dharma of purity there has not been a single dharma increased." This is my point.

One might say that such sentences quoted from the sūtras are spoken from the standpoint of *li* (universal-principle) not from the standpoint of *shih* (particular-phenomena). If one holds the expedient teachings of the three vehicles it fits this doctrine. If one depends upon the true teachings of the one vehicle, its principle cannot be explained. *Li* (universal-principle) and *shih* (particular-phenomena) are mysteriously without distinction. *T'i* (essence) and *yung* (function) are completely interpenetrating and always in the middle way. Outside of *shih* (particular-phenomena), where can you find *li* (universal-principle)?

Question: In the teachings of the three vehicles there is also found such doctrines as "quiescent yet always functioning," "functioning yet always quiescent." Why then did you say in the above that [the teachings of the three vehicles] are based only upon *li* (universal-principle) and are not based upon *shih* (particular-phenomena)?

Answer? There can be such doctrines [in the three vehicles] because *li* (universal-principle) and *shih* (particular-phenomena) are mutually identical. Yet this does not mean the mutual identity of *shih* (particular-phenomena) and *shih* (particular-phenomena). Why is it so? Because the three vehicle teachings want to cure the illness of discrimination holding as their key doctrine the interpenetration of *shih* (particular-phenomena) and *li* (universal-principle). However, if one depends upon the special teachings of the one vehicle, there is a mutual identity of *li* (universal-principles) and *li* (universal-principles); also, there is a mutual identity *shih* (particular-phenomena) and *shih* (particular-phenomena); also there is a mutual identity of *li* (universal-principle) and *shih* (particular-phenomena).

Furthermore, each is both not mutually identical and also mutually identical with the other. Why is it so? Because the middle way is based on non-equality. Also, there is the dharma-gate of universal-principle causation *dhāraṇī* and particular-phenomena causation *dhāraṇī*. In the house of *dharmadhātu* of the ten Buddhas and Samantabhadra bodhisattva, there is also the dharma-gate of the completely liberated and non-obstructed dharma-world. Other dharma-gates such as forward and backward of main and subordinate are mutually accomplished.

If one wishes to observe the dharma of true marks *dhāraṇī*, then one should first understand the theory of *counting ten coins*, i.e., from one coin to ten coins. The reason there are said to be ten coins is that I wish to manifest infinity. There are two subsections: (i) first, one is ten, ten is one; (ii) second, ten is one, one is ten.

[First Section]

In the first section, there are two kinds: the first means counting upward while the second means counting downward. In the words expressing counting downwards there are ten different gates. [First] it is one. Why is it so? Because it is the primordial number which is achieved by conditions. . . Thus, finally we come to the tenth, where in one there are ten. Why is it so? If there is no one, ten cannot be achieved. Yet, ten is not one. The rest are also like this.

According to this example all particulars can also be known. When one speaks of counting downwards there are also ten gates. [First] it is ten. Why so? It is established by dependent coorigination. . . Thus finally we come to the tenth, where in ten there is one. Why is it so? If there is no ten, one is not established, yet one is not ten. The rest are also like this, such as arising and ceasing. Through investigation this can be immediately known. In each coin, ten sections are established. In the first and last coins ten sections are [also] established. The other eight [coins] can be known according to this example.

Question: How can you state that in one there are ten?

Answer: In the dharma of great dependent coorigination *dhāraṇī*, if there is no one, many cannot be established. You must definitely know this aspect. One, as was said, is not one in terms of self-nature but one in terms of dependent coorigination. . . Thus, finally we come to ten. This is not self-nature ten but dependent coorigination ten. In all dharmas of conditioned co-production, there is no dharma which has definite marks and a definite nature. Since there is no self-nature, there is no freedom. Such a statement immediately produces non-producing production. As to non-producing production, this means non-abiding. Non-abiding means the middle way. Middle way means the interpenetration of production with non-production. For this reason Nāgārjuna says: "The way of production by causal conditions, I call this emptiness. It is also said, this is provisional truth and also termed the middle way." This is my meaning.

The doctrine of the middle way is the doctrine of non-discrimination. Since the dharma of non-discrimination doesn't attach to self-nature, it follows conditions inexhaustibly. This is non-abiding. Therefore, you should know that in one there is ten and in ten there is one. Both are mutually inclusive without obstruction. Nonetheless, there is [still] no confusions. In the present section there are ten gates. In this manner the wisdom of the middle way is to be clarified.

Question: In one section are ten sections exhaustively or non-exhaustively included?

Answer: Exhaustively and non-exhaustively. Why is it so? If need is exhausted, then it is exhausted. If need is not exhausted, then it is not exhausted. What is meant by this? Because one particular clarifies one and many therefore it is exhaustive. Because different phenomena clarify one and many, it is called non-exhaustive. Again, in one particular there is the doctrine of one and many without confusion. Immediately these are the many and one. Since it is a particular, there are many. These fourteen phrases argue [only] mistakes, and do not reveal virtues. Based on this, one can understand. Different phenomenal events are just identical.

Question: What is meant by "need"?

Answer: "Need" means "dependent coorigination." Why is it so? In the law of causal conditions, there is not one single difference. Hence, there are numerous particular phenomena in this section. According to this example it can be understood. The mysterious principle of dependent coorigination should be known like this.

[Second Section]

In the second section there are two subsections: (i) first, counting upwards; (ii) second, counting downwards. In the first section ten sections are not the same. First, it is one. Why so? Because it is established by conditions. . . Thus, finally we arrive at ten. One is ten. Why so? If there is no one, ten is not established, because it is established by conditions. In the second section there are also ten sections. The first is ten. Why so? Because it is established by conditions . . . Thus finally we arrive at ten. Ten is one. If there is no ten, one is not established. The rest are also like this example. Because of this doctrine, you should know that in every coin, the ten sections are established.

Question: Are the above plurality of sections completed simultaneously or are before and after differentiated?

Answer: Simultaneous completion *is* before and after. How is this so? If you wish completion, then there is completion; if you wish before and after, then there is before and after. How is this so? Virtue and function in the dharma-nature school is omnipotent without obstruction, because it is accomplished by conditions. All things are established like this.

Question: What is the mark of the doctrine of coming and going as explained above?

Answer: Self-position is not moving, yet it is always coming and going. Why? This is the meaning of causal conditions. Non-moving refers to the doctrine of origins. This is the doctrine of dependent coorigination.

Question: What is the difference between causal conditions and dependent coorigination?

Answer: They are different and also identical. [First], about the meaning of being different.

"Causal conditions" means that following marks and secularity are different. This is because cause and conditions are mutually dependent and manifest the doctrine of no self-nature. Moreover, this is the essence of right truth. "Dependent coorigination" means following nature without discrimination. This is mutual identity and mutual interpenetration which manifests the doctrine of equality. It is exactly the essence of the highest truth. Since secular truth does not have its own nature, it follows the highest truth. Therefore the sūtra says: "By following and observing worldly truth, one can immediately enter the highest truth." This is precisely my message. The meaning of being different is like this. [Second], the meaning of being identical is found as in Nāgārjuna's explanation before.

In each coin at the same time one completely has all ten sections. The rest can also be understood like this. All ten sections are explained as before. All coins, from the first up until the tenth, are not the same, yet they are mutually identical, and mutually interpenetrating without obstruction. Although doctrines such as cause and effect, *li* and *shih*, persons and dharmas, understanding and practice, as well as many other gates like main and subordinate, etc. are all different, yet by explaining one section, all sections are exhaustively included. The other doctrines should be known according to this.

About the theory of counting coins described above, again, by depending on particular coins belonging to *parikalpita* (discriminated nature), one can manifest the coin of causal conditions and dependent coorigination of the *paratantra* (interdependent nature) level. All dharmas produced by distinctions cannot be obtained. By attaching to discriminated entities one is deluded to the law of dependent coorgination. Manifested dharmas are completely distorted. The sūtra says: "One meritorious thought produced by a first stage bodhisattva cannot be exhausted." This teaching is just like the first coin. How so? Because holding one section it manifests inexhaustibly. How much more the immeasurably boundless merit of all dharmas! This is also to be applied to the second coin thereafter. Why is it so? Because it is explained in terms of different sections.

As to the phrase, "As soon as you aspire with your heart, instantly perfect enlightenment is attained" [in verse 15 of the seal], this is just like the case when one coin is ten coins. Why is it so? Because this is stated from the perspective of the essence of practice.

Question: A first stage bodhisattva means a bodhisattva of the [nascent] faith stage. If so, this is the position of the disciple. However, one who has achieved right enlightenment is in the stage of Buddha. This is a great teacher. Superior and inferior are not equal. Positions and stages are also different. Why then are head and feet placed in the same position?

Answer: The dharma and function of the three vehicle law of expedient means and the one vehicle law in the round teachings are different. Both of them should be distinguished without confusion. What is meant by this? In the three vehicle law, head and feet are different. The years and months of an old man and a baby are not the same. Why so? Because it is said based on marks. Because of producing the heart of [nascent] faith in the one vehicle round teachings, head and feet are comprehensively one. [Now] the years and months of an old man and a baby are the same. How? Because they are [both] established by causal conditions and based upon universal-principle.

Question: What is meant by one?

Answer: Identity means identical to non-abiding. Since non-discrimination means non-abiding, beginning and end occupy the same position. Teacher and disciple are therefore put together.

Question: What is the meaning of putting together the positions of teacher and disciple?

Answer: Putting together these positions of teacher and disciple means not knowing each other. Why? Because there is no discrimination.

Question: What is meant by non-discrimination?

Answer: Non-discrimination means conditioned co-production. This means beginning and end have no distinction. Why is it like this? All dharmas of conditioned co-production do not have a maker. Therefore, nothing is achieved. There is nothing known. Stillness and function are one mark. Superior and inferior are one taste, just like empty space. All dharmas are originally just as they are. Therefore, the sūtra says: "See all dharmas as neither arising nor ceasing; yet they exist by causal conditions." This is exactly my point.

Question: How can you recognize that a faith stage bodhisattva and Buddha both occupy the same place?

Answer: Like the [Hwaŏm] sūtra says below: "As soon as you aspire with your heart, instantly perfect enlightenment is attained." Also, like the *daśabhūmika-śāstra* explains: "A faith stage bodhisattva and Buddha are [both] accomplished through the six marks." You should clearly understand this doctrine. The six are explained above. These words enter the essential teaching of the dharma-nature school, opening the treasury of *dhāraṇī* like a key. What is being clarified in the above is only the great dependent coorigination law of the one vehicle *dhāraṇī*. Also, it discusses the non-obstruction of the one vehicle as well as clarifying the great essence which cannot be explained by the three vehicles.

Question: Since the first teaching has been established, all dharmas are empty and identical, and there is not a single difference. Why did you say in the above that head and feet are separate?

Answer: There is such a meaning because of immaturity [of understanding]. This will be explained below·

Question: How can you know that there separately exists the round [teachings] of the one vehicle outside of the three vehicles?

Answer: As the sūtra says below. All kinds of living beings are in the world, but few have a desire to follow the *śravaka's* way; those seeking the *pratyekabuddha's* way are even much smaller; those seeking the *mahāyāna* are rarer still. Seeking *mahāyāna* is rather easy. However, having faith in this dharma is extremely difficult. If sentient beings are inferious, and their minds are dull, [Buddha] shows them the *śravaka's* way so that they can escape all afflictions. Again, if sentient beings have faculties that are a little sharp, [Buddha] explains to them the world of *pratyekabuddhas.* If one has faculties that are sharp, along with great compassion for all sentient beings, [Buddha] teaches them the *bodhisattva's* path. If one has an unexcelled mind and enjoys great works, they are shown the Buddha's body, and instructed on inexhaustible Buddhadharmas. The sage's words are always like a bright pearl, and thus one need not be alarmed.

Question: How can I know the special difference between the one vehicle and the three vehicle doctrines?

Answer: Again, depending on the ten gates immediately you can understand this.

First, the gate of simultaneous and complete correspondence. In these there are ten marks. They are: (i) people; (ii) dharma; (iii) *li* (universal-principle); (iv) *shih* (particular-phenomena); (v) doctrine; (vi) meaning; (vii) understanding; (viii) practice; (ix) cause; (x) effect. These ten gates are mutually corresponding. There is no distinction between before and after.

Second, the gate of the world of Indra's Net. In this gate, the complete doctrine of ten gates is explained as before. From simile the difference is understood. The rest can be known based on this.

Third, the gate of mutual accomplishment between exoteric and esoteric. This gate also has all ten marks of the previous section. From conditions there is no difference.

Fourth, the gate of establishing mutual inclusion between all atoms. This also has the meaning of all ten gates explained before. From conditions there are mutual differences.

Fifth, the gate of accomplishing differences among dharmas of the ten worlds. This also has the meaning of all ten gates explained before. Differences come from the world.

Sixth, the gate of having all virtues from all treasuries. This also has the meaning of all ten gates explained before. Differences come from particularity.

Seventh, the gate of non-equality in which one and many are mutually inclusive. This also has the meaning of all ten gates explained before. Differences come from universality.

Eighth, the gate of freedom where all dharmas are mutually identical. This also has the meaning of all ten gates explained before. Differences come from function.

Ninth, the gate of achieving goodness by transformation of mind. This also has the meaning of all ten gates explained before. Differences come from mind.

Tenth, the gate of understanding based on particularity and manifesting dharmas. This also has the meaning of all ten gates explained before. Differences come from wisdom. The rest can be known according to this.

The above ten mysterious gates are all different. If the clarification of the doctrine corresponds to this then it is the one vehicle round teaching and is included in the sudden teaching. If all doctrines are corresponding with this yet are still not completed, then that is the three vehicles gradual teachings. You should understand it like this. Those who satisfy the ten gates perfectly are as is explained in the [Hwaŏm] sūtra. For more extensive explanations see the various treatises and commentaries on the sūtra such as *K'ung-mu* (the *Hua-yen ching nai chang-men teng tsa-k'ung-mu chang* by Chih-yen, T. 1870), and *wen-ta* (the *Hua-yen wu-shih wen-ta* by Chih-yen, T. 1869).

My *Diagram of the Dharmadhātu According to the One Vehicle* along with the poem in the *Ocean Seal* depends upon the *Flower Adornment Scripture* (or *Hwaŏm-gyŏng*) and the *Treatise on the Ten Stages* (or *daśabhūmika-śāstra*) in order to manifest the doctrinal essence of the round teachings. It is recorded in the fifteenth day, seventh month and first year of *tsung chang*.

Question: Why do you not record the name of the author?

Answer: In order to manifest that all dharmas produced by conditions do not have an author.

Question: Why then do you record the year and month of writing?

Answer: So to manifest that all dharmas depend on conditioned co-production.

Question: From what place do conditions come?

Answer: [Conditions] come from out of the perverted mind.

Translation of Ŭisang's Autocommentary on the Ocean Seal

Question: From what place does the perverted mind come?

Answer: It comes from beginningless ignorance.

Question: From where does beginningless ignorance come?

Answer: It comes from suchness.

Question: Where is suchness?

Answer: Suchness is self dharma-nature.

Question: How is dharma-nature characterized?

Answer: It is characterized by non-discrimination. Therefore, all mundane events are in the middle way which has nothing that is not non-discrimination. Because of this, at the beginning of the poem [in the seal] it says, "Dharma-nature is round and interpenetrating without duality," coming finally to "That which is originally not moving is named Buddha." My point is precisely here. Therefore by means of the poem, all becomes immediately empty and manifests reality. For this reason I made a vow by means of seeing, hearing, cultivating and collecting the name and doctrine of universal dharma in the one vehicle school. By returning these good roots to all sentient beings may they all be universally benefited and simultaneously accomplish Buddhahood. The *Diagram of the One Vehicle Dharmadhātu* ends here.

Notes

Prologue

1. T1887A, vol. 45, pp. 711-716
2. Ibid, p. 714b, line 16
3. T2039, vol. 49, pp. 1006c-1007a
4. T1887A, vol. 45, p. 711a, lines 3-5
5. Ibid, lines 5-7
6. Ibid, lines 24-25
7. The "ten worlds of the *dharmadhātu*" refer to the following realms: Hell Beings, Hungry Ghosts, Animals, Men, Asuras, Gods, Arhats, Pratyekabuddhas, Bodhisattvas, Buddhas. In the Hua-yen cosmology, all ten worlds of the *dharmadhātu* mutually contain each other through the mysteries of *shih-shih-wu-ai* (the unobstructed interfusion of particular-phenomena with particular-phenomena) and *chung-chung-wu-chin* (realms-embracing-realms ad infinitum). Ultimately, all ten worlds of the *dharmadhātu* are said to be identical to a single thought instant, i.e., the thought of the present moment.
8. T1887A, vol. 45, p. 711b, lines 5-11

Introduction

1. Garma C.C. Chang, *The Buddhist Teaching of Totality: The Philosophy of Hwa Yen Buddhism* (University Park and London: Pennsylvania State University Press, 1977), p. 121.
2. Ibid., p. 122.
3. Francis H. Cook, *Hua-yen Buddhism: The Jewel Net of Indra* (University Park and London: Pennsylvania State University Press, 1977), p. 73.
4. Chang Chung-yuan, *Creativity and Taoism* (New York: Harper and Row, 1963). See especially Chapter Two: "Immeasurable Potentialitis of Creativity," pp. 55–58.

PART I

Chapter 1. The Syncretic Harmonization Pattern of Hua-yen Dialectical Thought

1. The *locus classicus* of the Hua-yen metaphysics of interpenetrative harmonization and non-obstructed mutual containment between particular

and particular is the voluminous Indian Sanskrit text, the *Avataṁsaka Sūtra* or "Flowery Splendour Scripture." The first complete translation of the Sūtra into Chinese was introduced into China in 60 fascicles by Buddhabhadra in 418 A.D., where it was distilled and disseminated by the traditional Five Patriarchs of the Hua-yen School, Tu-shun (558–640), Chih-yen (602–668), Fa-tsang (643–712), Ch'eng-kuan (738–840) and Tsung-mi (780–841). It traveled to Korea 668 A.D. by the Korean monk, Priest Ŭisang (625–702), the First Patriarch of Korean Hua-yen (Kor. Hwaŏm) Buddhism. Shen-hsiang, one of the three reknown pupils of Fa-tsang brought the Hua-yen (Jap. Kegon) doctrine to Japan in 740 A.D. The *Avataṁsaka Sūtra* (Tib. *phal-po-che mdo*) was translated into Tibetan by three scholars, two Indians named Jina Mitra and Surendrabodhi, and one Tibetan, Ye-shes-sde. According to the indigenous Hua-yen tradition, it is said that the *Avataṁsaka Sūtra* was inwardly preached by the Buddha while in *sāgara-mudrā-samādhi* (Ocean-Seal-Samādhi) during his attainment of supreme enlightenment beneath the Bodhi Tree.

2. See Alfonso Verdu, *Dialectical Aspects in Buddhist Thought: Studies in Sino-Japanese Mahāyāna Idealism* (Lawrence, Kansas: Center for East Asian Studies, The University of Kansas, 1974), especially Chapter Four, Part II, "The Wu-chiao (Five Doctrines) Scheme," pp. 103–106.

3. Hence, while discussing the Hua-yen doctrine of the *ālaya* consciousness as a system of "twofold permeation" as over against the Yogācāra *ālaya* which represents a one-way world-projecting center through causation by mind-only *(wei-shih yüan-ch'i),* Garma C.C. Chang writes: "No more is the Mind-Only doctrine a one-way projection, but it becomes a kaleidoscope of multidimensional mutual projections and interpenetrations." (See Chang, *The Buddhist Teaching of Totality* (University Park and London: Pennsylvania State University Press, 1977), p. x.

4. The Yogācāra absolute is said to be *vijñaptimātratā* or consciousness-only, i.e., pure consciousness as entirely divested of the subject-object (*grāhaka-grāhya*) dualism or an undivided continuum of psychic radiance with no inner-outer division. Nonetheless, the subject has a definite ontological primacy over that of the object. As A.K. Chaterjee states: "The Absolute is defined by the subject-object duality. . . the two terms are however not on par. The Subject is not unreal. Only its relation to the object is negated. . . . The Absolute is reached by the total negation of phenomena. . . . The object is totally rejected; it is absolutely unreal. The Subject on the other hand is real, and as such, it cannot be negated. It is only purified, i.e., purged of the idea of the unreal object. The Subject, when not confronted by an 'other' to it, is the Absolute." See Ashok Kumar Chaterjee, *The Yogācāra Idealism* (Varanasi: Motilal Banarsidas, 1975), p. 142.

5. Verdu, *Dialectical Aspects of Buddhist Thought,* op. cit., p. 56. The symbolic circles depicted here were frequently used by Fifth Patriarch Tsung-mi to illustrate the interpenetrative nonimpededness of the Ch'an sudden enlightenment (Chi. *tun-wu;* Jap. *tongo*) experience, although they have been rearranged into diagrams by Verdu throughout his book, often in extraordinarily complex ways.

Chapter 2. Intercausation and Interpenetration

1. Gottfried Wilhelm Leibniz, "Discourse on Metaphysics," in *Leibniz: Basic Writings,* trans. G.R. Montegomery (La Salle, Ill: Open Court Pub. Co., 1968), pp. 14, 15.

2. Fa-tsang, "On the Golden Lion," trans. Garma C.C. Chang in *The Buddhist Teaching of Totality (*University Park and London: Pennsylvania State University Press, 1977), p. 229

Third patriarch Fa-tsang's "Treatise on the Golden Lion" is the most popular summary exposition of the Hua-yen teachings. Using a gold statue of a lion in the royal courtyard of Empress Wu, Fa-tsang expounds the quintessence of Hua-yen philosophy concerning the relation between *li* and *shih* or universal-principle and particular-phenomena (corresponding to gold and lion, respectively) through the use of ten principles.

1. dependent arising: The lion arises into non-inherent existence due to causes and conditions; it has no self-nature, own-being or intrinsic reality.
2. form and emptiness: The form of the lion is unreal; only the gold is real. Yet, emptiness has no characteristics of its own and is manifested only through form.
3. three natures: The lion has (i) imagined existence of false concreteness (*parikalpita*); (ii) dependent existence or true concreteness (*paratantra*); and (iii) immutability or true universality *(parinispanna).*
4. non-existence of characters: Since the gold completely constitutes the lion, apart from the gold there are no independent characteristics.
5. not-coming-into-existence: There is nothing apart from the gold. If we see the lion come into existence, it is still only the gold. Thus, neither the gold nor the lion truly comes into existence, since the gold does not increase or decrease but is immutable.
6. five teachings: Fa-tsang's *p'an chiao* or doctrinal classification system wherein Buddhist teachings on the universal and particular are ranked according to five schools: (i) Hīnayāna teaching; (ii) Elementary teachings of Mahāyāna (Yogācāra and Mādhyamika); (iii) Final Teachings of Mahāyāna (T'ien-t'ai); (iv) Sudden teachings of Mahāyāna (Ch'an); (v) Perfect teaching of Ekayāna (Hua-yen).
7. ten mysteries: The ten principles of unobstructed interpenetration and mutual containedness between all phenomena.
8. six characteristics: The lion manifests six characteristics of wholeness-diversity, universality-particularity and integration-disintegration, which interfuse without obstruction in the relation of whole to part.
9. achievement of *bodhi* or wisdom.
10. entrance into *nirvāṇa.*

3. Ibid., p. 23.

4. See Louis O. Gomez's *Selected Verses from the Gaṇḍavyūha* (Ann Arbor, Mich.: University Microfilms Press, 1967).

5. Nāgārjuna, "Fundamentals of the Middle Way: Mūlamadhyamika-Karikas." trans. Fredrick J. Streng in his work, *Emptiness: A Study in Religious Meaning* (New York: Abingdon Press, 1967) 24:18, p. 213.

6. Ibid., 24:19, p. 213.

7. Ibid., 7:16, p. 191.

8. Ibid., 1:1, p. 183.

9. Fa-tsang, "Hundred Gates to the Sea of Ideas of the Flowery Splendour Scripture," comp. and trans. Wing-tsit Chan in *A Source Book in Chinese Philosophy* (Princeton, N.J.: Princeton University Press, 1963), p. 414–20.

10. Ibid., p. 420.

11. Ibid., p. 421.

12. Ibid., p. 423.

13. Ibid., pp. 421, 422.

14. Ibid., pp. 423, 424. It is fascinating to note here the structural proximity of Fa-tsang's principles of "contraction" and "expansion" to a similar doctrine formulated by Nicholas de Cusa, the great Medieval Christian mystic who propounded the first systematic microcosmic-macrocosmic metaphysics in the West. In his work entitled *Of Learned Ignorance* Nicholas writes: "All things are 'contracted' to form each creature. . . . To say that 'everything is in everything' is the same as to say that God, by the intermediacy of the universe is in all things. . . . How God is without any diversity in all, since everything is in everything, and how all is in God, because all is in all, are truths of a very high order which are clearly understood by keen minds. The entire universe is in each creature. . . with the result that in each individual the universe is by 'contraction' what the particular individual is." [See Nicholas Cusanus, *Of Learned Ignorance,* trans. G. Heron (New Haven: Yale University Press, 1954), pp. 83, 84.] Nicolas terms the reality of God wherein "everything is in everything" the "Maximum," a concept analogous to the Hua-yen *dharmadhātu,* writing: "The Maximum is in everything and everything is in the Maximum; and what is in the Maximum is itself the Maximum. Though this Maximum embraces all things in its universal unity, so that all is in it and it is in all, yet it could not subsist outside the plurality in which it is contained" (Ibid., p. 10). Nicholas frequently characterized the Maximum as an infinite sphere wherein "the circumference is nowhere and the center is everywhere," (Ibid., p. 47), a metaphor often used by Nishida Kitarō to describe the Kegon universe of interpenetration and mutual fusion.

15. Fa-tsang, "Hundred Gates to the Sea of Ideas of the Flowery Splendour Scriptures," op. cit., p. 422.

16. Tu-shun, "On the Meditation of Dharmadhātu," trans. Garma C.C. Chang in *The Buddhist Teaching of Totality,* op. cit., p. 208.

17. Ibid., p. 217.

18. Ibid., p. 214.

19. Ibid., p. 219.

20. Ibid., p. 219

21. Ibid., p. 213.

22. Ibid., pp. 214, 215.

23. Ibid., p. 218.

24. Ibid., p. 219.

25. Fa-tsang, "Hundred Gates to the Sea of Ideas of the Flowery Splendour Scripture," op. cit., p. 243.

Chapter 3. Linguistic Analysis and Hua-yen Buddhism on the Simultaneous-Mutual-Establishment of Meanings

1. Fredrick J. Streng, *Emptiness: A Study in Religious Meaning* (New York and Nashville: Abingdon Press, 1967).

2. Ludwig Wittgenstein, *The Blue and Brown Books,* (New York: Harper and Row, 1965), p. 1.

3. Ludwig Wittgenstein, *Philosophical Investigations,* trans. G.E.M. Anscombe

(New York: Harper and Row, 1953), p. 43.

4. Ibid., p. 48.

5. Fa-tsang, "Treatise on the Five Doctrines" (Abstract), trans. Garma C.C. Chang in *The Buddhist Teaching of Totality* (University Park and London: Pennsylvania State University Press, 1977), p. 229. Also, see Francis Cook's edifying study of Fa-tsang's House and Beams analogy in *Hua-yen Buddhism: The Jewel Net of Indra* (University Park and London: Pennsylvania State University Press, 1977), especially Chapter Six, pp. 75–90.

6. Ibid., p. 169.

7. Chih-Yen, "Ten Mysteries of the One Vehicle of Hua-yen" (Abstract), in Chang, *The Buddhism Teaching of Totality*, op. cit., p. 158.

8. Charles Hartshorne, "Ontological Primacy: A Reply to Buchler," *The Journal of Philosophy* 67, no. 23 (Dec. 10, 1970), p. 980.

Chapter 4. Interpenetration as Openness, Presence and Nonconcealment: A Phenomenological Interpretation

1. Herbert V. Guenther, *Kindly Bent to Ease Us*, 3 vols. (Emeryville, Calif.: Dharma Pub., 1975).

2. Tu-shun, "On the Meditation of Dharmadhātu," trans. Garma C.C. Chang in *The Buddhist Teaching of Totality*, (University Park and London: Pennsylvania State University Press, 1977), p. 208.

3. Ibid., p. 211.

4. Ibid., p. 211.

5. Ibid., p. 217.

6. Ibid., p. 219.

7. Herbert V. Guenther, *The Tantric View of Life* (Boulder and London: Shambhala Publishers, 1975), p. 150.

8. See Martin Heidegger "Being and Time: Introduction" in *Martin Heidegger: Basic Writings*, ed. D.F. Kreel (New York: Harper and Row, 1977), pp. 73–82.

9. Edmund Husserl, *Ideas: General Introduction to Phenomenology*, trans W.R. Boyce Gibson (New York: Collier-Macmillan Publishers, 1975), p. 266, sec. 98.

10. Edmund Husserl, *Experience and Judgement*, trans. J.S. Churchill and K. Ameriks (Evanston, Ill.: Northwestern University Press, 1973), p. 48.

11. Husserl, *Ideas*, op. cit., p. 102, sec. 27.

12. Ibid., p. 351, sec. 119.

13. Martin Heidegger, *Discourse on Thinking*, trans J. Anderson (New York: Harper and Row, 1966), p. 63.

14. Herbert V. Guenther and Chogyam Trungpa, *The Dawn of Tantra* (Boulder and London: Shambhala Publishers, 1975), p. 27.

15. Ibid., pp. 26, 27.

16. Ibid., pp. 27–30.

17. Edmund Husserl argued that the essential and invariable structure of all mental life is its intentionality or directedness. All perceptual acts intend or point towards something. Intentionality is the correlation-apriori of consciousness expressed as *noesis*→*noema* or *cognito*→*cogitatum*. The *noema* is characterized by its core/horizon pattern which is directly organized or constituted by *noetic* acts. Husserl specifies that the *noesis* constitutes the *noema* in a radically

temporal pattern whereby retentions constitute a pastward horizon and protentions constitute a futural horizon, which surround the primal impression of a now-point. Maurice Merleau-Ponty later elaborated a more dialectically balanced doctrine termed the "intentionality arc" wherein *noesis* and *noema* are reciprocally constitutive through the intermediacy of the "lived body", although this intentionality arc operates within radically temporal lines.

18. Guenther and Trungpa, *The Dawn of Tantra*, op. cit., p. 27.

19. Don Ihde, *Experimental Phenomenology* (New York: G.P. Putnam's Sons, 1977), p. 129.

20. Martin Heidegger, *Discourse on Thinking*, op. cit., p. 72.

21. Don Ihde, "Phenomenology and the Later Heidegger," in *Philosophy Today* (Spring 1974), vol. 18, p. 28.

22. Maurice Merleau-Ponty, *Phenomenology of Perception*, trans. Colin Smith (New Jersey: The Humanities Press, 1962), p. 130. Also, see p. 30.

23. Martin Heidegger, "On the Essence of Truth," in *Martin Heidegger: Basic Writings*, op. cit., p. 127.

24. Martin Heidegger, "Aletheia," in *Early Greek Thinkers* trans. D.F. Kreel and F.A. Capuzzi (New York: Harper and Row, 1967), p. 103. Heidegger often points out that the German adjective *licht* or "open" is the same as the word "Light" in order to emphasize the connectedness between openness and luminosity or brilliance.

25. T1739: 36. 818b

26. Maurice Merleau-Ponty, *Phenomenology of Perception*, trans. Colin Smith (New York: Humanities Press, 1962), p. 67.

27. Ibid., p. 68. The word "inhabitation" is a key term in Merleau-Ponty's description of the "primordial spatiality" of the "lived body." Whereas the "objectified body" (at the level of conscious "act" intentionality) is "in" space and occupies a localized position, the "lived body" (at the level of pre-conscious "motor" or "operative" intentionality) is said to "inhabit" space, i.e., to be "opened-out" onto the synaesthetic perceptual field of global presence. Thus, at the level of the lived body, inner and outer or subject and object are completely "intertwined" in what Merleau-Ponty calls the "chiasm" through various "intentional arcs" or "circuits of existence."

28. Martin Heidegger, *Poetry, Language and Thought*, trans. A. Hofstadter (New York: Harper and Row, 1971), p. 107.

29. Ibid., p. 106.

30. Maurice Merleau-Ponty, *Phenomenology of Perception*, op. cit., p. 70.

31. Martin Heidegger, "Letter on Humanism," in *Martin Heidegger: Basic Writings*, op. cit., p. 229.

32. Martin Heidegger, "What Is Metaphysics," in *Martin Heidegger: Basic Writings*, op. cit., p. 210.

33. Ibid., p. 233.

34. In his revolutionary work entitled *Avatāra*, Antonio T. de Nicolas has elaborated a radical reinterpretation of the *Bhagavad Gītā* which in certain respects is analogous to H.V. Guenther's phenomenological reinterpretation of Tibetan Tantric Buddhism, based upon the primacy of "fields" (Skt. *kṣetras*) in

perceptual experience and ethical conduct. As de Nicolas reads the *Gītā*, the highest wisdom imparted by Arjuna to Kṛṣṇa is to become a *Kṣetra-jñanin*, i.e., a "knower of the field in all fields". Of course, the perception of *Kṣetras* is one of the basic themes of the *Avataṃsaka sūtra*. In the *Gītā*, the substance/field distinction is represented by Arjuna/Kṛṣṇa. Arjuna symbolizes the language of sensation, substance, invariance, karma (habitual interpretations) whereas Kṛṣṇa symbolizes the language of "fields" (*kṣetras*) or "context-wholes" (dharmas). A third language is that of movement, temporality, re-embodiment, sacrifice, detachment, i.e., imaginative variation. The *Kṣetra-jñanin* must possess *yajña-vidaḥ* or "sacrifice knowledge", the knowledge of detachment from and sacrifice (*yajña*) of frozen perspectives for the continuous re-embodiment of new circumstances, what is described in this chapter as the multiperspectival open possibility search for value-rich gestalt variations. Due to this primacy of field-structures in perception, the *kṣetra-jñanin* must dynamically act in accordance with dharma (context-wholes) instead of karma so as to "bind together" (from *dhṛ*, the Sanskrit verb root of dharma, meaning "to bind" or "to support") one's entire circumstance with every decision. Thus, deNicolas comes to reinterpret the *Gītā* in terms of Ortega Y Gasset's intercultural theme of Man and Circumstance, governed by the dictum: "I am I plus my circumstance—to save myself I must save it." The genius of deNicolas's interpretation is that he traces this liberating yogic knowledge of the *Kṣetra-jñanin* to its epistemological genesis in the *musical* cosmology and correlate "tuning theory" of the Ṛg Vedic pre-literary culture in ancient India, which he argues functioned to structure all future Eastern philosophical discourse, including Hinduism and Buddhism alike, long after this musical model itself had passed into oblivion. See Antonio T. deNicolas, *Avatāra: The Humanization of Philosophy Through the Bhagavad Gītā* (New York: Nicolas Hays Ltd., 1976). Also, see his *Meditations through the Ṛg Veda* (Boulder and London: Shambhala, 1978).

35. Heidegger, M., Poetry, *Language and Thought*, op. cit., p. 124.

36. Ibid., p. 123.

37. See especially Heidegger's *Identity and Difference*, trans. Joan Stambaugh (New York: Harper and Row, 1969) where he develops at length his notion of "ontological difference" between Being and beings or Presence and that which is present.

38. Martin Heidegger, "What is Metaphysics," in *Martin Heidegger: Basic Writings*, op. cit., p. 111.

39. Martin Heidegger, "The Origin of the Work of Art," Ibid., p. 175.

40. Martin Heidegger, *On Time and Being*, trans J. Stambaugh (New York: Harper and Row, 1972), p. 14.

41. Merleau-Ponty, *Phenomenology of Perception*, op. cit., p. 420.

42. Martin Heidegger, *Being and Time*, trans. J. Macquarrie and E. Robinson (New York: Harper and Row, 1962), p. 460, section 408.

43. Edmund Husserl, *The Phenomenology of Internal Time Consciousness*, trans. J.S. Churchill (Bloomington, Ind.: University Press, 1964), pp. 110–111, section 40.

44. Merleau-Ponty, *Phenomenology of Perception*, op. cit., p. 423.

Chapter 5. Interpenetration and Sudden Enlightenment: The Harmonization of Hua-yen Theory and Ch'an Praxis.

1. Chinul, *Wondon Sŏngbullon,* ed. T'anho Kim (Pŏpbowŏn: Seoul, 1963), pp. 91–120.
2. Chinul, *Hwaŏmnon Chŏryo,* ed. Chigyon Kim (Seifū Gukuin: Ōsaka, 1968),
3. Ŭich'ŏn (1055–1101) or Taekak, the fourth son of King Munjŏng (1019–1083), was known as a great child prodigy and became ordained as a monk at age eleven. Ŭich'ŏn established the T'ien-t'ai (*Ch'ontae*) sect in Korea. Ŭich'ŏn is known as the rediscoverer of Wŏnhyo's thought, and he even supplicated his father King Munjong to give Wŏnhyo a posthumous order, the Great Venerable *Hwajaeng* (the word "hwajaeng" meaning the harmonization of all disputes or reconciliation of all factional struggles). Ŭich'ŏn's greatest achievement was perhaps his supplementary extension of the Korean Buddhist Canon, which was a comprehensive collection of East Asian Commentaries on canonical literature, published in his monumental *Shinp'yon Chejong Kyojang Ch'ongnok* or *A Newly Compiled General Catalogue of Scriptural Commentaries in All Buddhist Schools* making reference to 1,010 titles in 4,740 fascicles.
4. Chinul, *Chim shim jik sŏl,* T. 2019, Vol. 48, p. 999.
5. Li T'ung-hsüan (635–730), a layman contemporary of Fa-tsang (643–712), was known during his life primarily as a contemplative yogin, who from the age of seventy-four lived as an ascetic hermit for the last twenty-one years of his life near T'ai-yuan in Shansi. Today, only four of Li's writings on the *Hua-yen sūtra* are still extant, the foremost work being his *Hua-yen ching lun* (T. 1739, Vol. 36, pp. 721–1008) or *Exposition of the Hua-yen Sūtra* in 40 fascicles. Although essentially unknown in his own time, Li exerted powerful influence on Sung Dynasty Buddhism, especially Ta-hui's line of Ch'an Buddhism. After Chinul's exaltation of Li T'ung-hsüan's work, the latter became especially preeminent in Korean *Hwaŏm* and *Sŏn* thought. In Japan, the Kegon master Kōben (1173–1232) was particularly influenced by Li's work. Although Li has in general received little attention from orthodox Hua-yen scholarship, one particularly significant and auspicious fact concerning him is that his writings were the first Chinese doctrinal works to be accepted into the Buddhist canon in the history of East Asian Buddhism. They are included in the *Hsu-chen-yüan lu* edition of the canon compiled in 938 A.D. only 210 years after Li's death.
6. Jae Ryong Shim, "The Philosophical Foundation of Korean Zen Buddhism: The Integration of Sŏn and Kyo by Chinul," *Journal of Social Sciences and Humanities* 50 (December 1979), p. 137.
7. Ibid., p. 135.
8. Ibid., p. 137.
9. Ibid., p. 138.
10. Ibid.
11. Ibid., p. 139.
12. This identification of Hua-yen interpenetration with Ch'an sudden enlightenment which stands at the very heart of Li T'ung-hsüan's and Chinul's respective systems of theory and praxis is also central in the work of Tsung-mi, although not in the context of an explicit theory of faith (*hsin*). Alfonso Verdu

develops Tsung-mi's equation of interpenetration or *yung-t'ung*, intuitively symbolized by Tsung-mi as  , with sudden enlightenment or *tun-wu* symbolized as  , in his work entitled *Dialectical Aspects in Buddhism Thought* (Lawrence, Kansas: Center for East Asian Studies, University of Kansas, 1974).

13. Jae Ryong Shim, "The Philosophical Foundation of Korean Zen Buddhism: The Integration of Sŏn and Kyo by Chinul," Journal of Social Sciences and Humanities 51 (June 1980), pp. 50, 51.

14. Ibid., p. 50.

PART II

Chapter 6. Creative Synthesis and Emergent Novelty

1. Fa-tsang, "Hundred Gates to the Sea of Ideas of the Flowery Splendour Scripture." in *A Source Book in Chinese Philosophy,* trans. Wing-tsit Chan (Princeton, N.J.: Princeton University Press, 1963), p. 423.
2. Ibid., p. 423.
3. F. Th. Stcherbatsky, *The Conception of Buddhist Nirvāṇa* (Leningrad: Public Office of the Academy of Sciences of the USSR, 1927), p. 42.
4. Charles Hartshorne, *Creative Synthesis and Philosophic Method* (LaSalle, Ill.: Open Court, Pub. Co., 1970), p. 53.
5. Ibid., p. 213.
6. Ibid., p. 211.
7. Ibid., p. 219.
8. Ibid., p. 5.
9. Nishida Kitarō, "Towards a Philosophy of Religion with the Concept of Pre-Established Harmony as Guide," trans. David Dilworth, *The Eastern Buddhist* 3, no. 1 (June 1970), p. 36.
10. Yoshinori Takeuchi, "The Philosophy of Nishida," *Japanese Religions* 3 (1963), p. 21.
11. Charles Hartshorne, *The Logic of Perfection,* (La Salle, Ill: Open Court Pub. Co., 1973), p. 233.
12. Charles Hartshorne, "Introduction: The Development of Process Philosophy," in *Philosophers of Process,* ed. Douglas Browning (New York: Random House, 1965), p. xviii.

Chapter 7. Causality as the Vector Transmission of Feelings

1. William Christian, *An Introductono to Whitehead's Metaphysics* (New Haven: Yale University Press, 1959).
2. Some East-West scholars have suggested that the issue of symmetry vs. asymmetry of temporal relations might be resolved through Whitehead's distinction between temporal transition and nontemporal concrescence, the first asymmetrical and the latter symmetrical in structure. For example, summarizing an East-West conference on Whitehead and Buddhism, the eminent process theologian John Cobb writes: "From the perspective of 'transition,' a determinate past becomes objectified in the becoming of the present, which perishes

into a condition for an as yet unactualized future. This is the unidirectional flow of time. From the perspective of 'concrescence,' however, past and future are realized as felt relations. Physical feelings feel the past, anticipatory feelings feel the future; and these feelings are symmetrically unified in the becoming of subjective experience. Thus, from the perspective of transition, time is asymmetrical, from that of concrescence, it is symmetrical." See John Cobb, "Introduction: Conference on Mahāyāna Buddhism and Whitehead," *Philosophy East and West* 24, no. 4 (October 1975), p. 402.

3. Eternal objects are Platonic forms, i.e., harmonic value-patterns or ideal modes of togetherness, whereby a multiplicity of data can be combined into a single pattern of aesthetic contrasts within a given occasion of experience. Technically, Whitehead defines eternal objects as "Forms of Definiteness" or "Pure Potentials for the Specific Determination of Fact" (PR, p. 22).

4. William James, *Some Problems of Philosophy* (London, New York, Toronto: Longmans, Green and Co., 1948), p. 218.

5. Charles Hartshorne, "Bell's Theorum, H.P. Stapp, and Process Theism," *Process Studies* 7 (1979), p. 185.

6. Stephen C. Pepper, *Concept and Quality: A World Hypothesis* (LaSalle, Ill.: Open Court Pub. Co., 1967), pp. 340, 341. Pepper then proceeds to identify Whitehead's position with Bergson's accusing him of only repeating Bergson's error regarding the status of the past. Pepper, however, rejects Whitehead's theory of prehension or direct perception of a past object in the present and opts for what he calls an "indirect" theory of perception. (Ibid., p. 341). But as the present analysis demonstrates, Whitehead's doctrine of the past is different from Bergson's in important respects: for Bergson the past is present as subjectively immediate whereas for Whitehead it is present in the mode of objective immortality. The crux of this difference is that whereas for Bergson time is purely *continuous,* for Whitehead it is pulsatory or quantized, i.e., epochal, such that the past must be conformally reproduced in each new unit-pulsation.

7. Ibid., pp. 339, 340. According to Stephen Pepper's typological classification schema as developed in *World-Hypotheses* (Los Angeles: University Pub., 1957) there are four basic world-hypotheses and underlying root metaphors which may be diagrammatically represented as follows:

World-Hypotheses	*Root Metaphors*
I. Formism (Plato, Aristotle)	I. Similarity
II. Mechanism (Descartes, Locke, Hume)	II. The Machine
III. Contextualism (Peirce, James, Dewey, Bergson)	III. The Historic Event
IV. Organicism (Hegel, Bradley, Royce)	IV. Organism

In later works Pepper asserts that Whitehead introduces a new world-hypothesis based on the root metaphor of a "creative act" whereas previously Pepper had classified him as a "contextualist".

8. Ibid., p. 340.

9. Dōgen, "Shōbōgenzō," in *Zen Is Eternal Life,* trans. Roshi Jiyu Kennett (Emeryville, Calif.: Dharma Pub. 1976), p. 168.

10. Ibid., p. 169.

11. Charles Hartshorne, *Creative Synthesis and Philosophic Method* (LaSalle, Ill.: Open Court Pub. Co., 1970), p. 118. Whitehead's process theology centers

around his revolutionary notion of a dipolar or bimodal God, which by analogy to actual occasions has both a mental pole, termed the "primordial nature," and a physical pole, termed the "consequent nature." The primordial nature is God's omniscient envisagement of eternal objects and functions to provide the initial aim or lure for feeling for each concrescent occasion. The consequent nature everlasting preserves all events as imperishable data in the divine memory. It sounds as if Whitehead intends that all events be preserved everlastingly in their *immediacy* in God's memory when he makes such statements as: "In everlastingness, immediacy is reconciled with objective immortality" (PR, p. 351). And as Hartshorne notes above, the closing words of *Process and Reality* are that in God's consequent nature, events "perish and yet live forevermore."

12. Whitehead asserts that events are creative acts which make decisions as to their own ultimate definiteness, such that an element of free self-constitution or emergent spontaneous self-creativity is always the final factor in the causal process of concrescence. But Whitehead specifies: "The word 'decision' does not here imply conscious judgement, though in some 'decisions' consciousness will be a factor" (PR, p. 43).

13. In his study of Whitehead's philosophy, William Christian isolates yet another important sense in which events "transcend" each other with respect to his doctrine of "regions". As geometrically extended, they occupy a definite and novel spatiotemporal region or extensive spread, and in this sense are also mutually exclusive and non-overlapping. See Christian's *An Introduction to Whitehead's Metaphysics,* op. cit.

14. See David A. Dilworth's interpretive analysis of Nishida Kitarō's syncretic thought system in his article, "Nishida Kitarō: Nothingness as the Negative Space of Experiential Immediacy," *International Philosophic Quarterly* 13, no. 4 (December 1973).

15. See Robert E. Doud, "Whitehead and Merleau-Ponty: Commitment as a Context for Comparison" in *Process Studies,* vol. 7, 1977, pp. 145–160.

16. Maurice Merleau-Ponty, *Phenomenology of Perception,* trans. by Colin Smith (New Jersey: The Humanities Press, 1978), p. 429.

17. Ibid., p. 214.

18. Ibid., p. 140.

19. Ibid., p. 100.

20. Ibid., p. 30.

21. Ibid., p. 421.

Chapter 9. A Process Theory of Substance

1. Fa-tsang, "A Commentary on the Heart Sūtra," trans. Garma C.C. Chang in *The Buddhist Teaching of Totality* (University Park and London: Pennsylvania State University Press, 1977), p. 201.

2. Ibid., p. 201.

3. Ibid.

4. Ibid., Fa-tsang "Treatise on the Golden Lion," Ibid., p. 225.

5. C.L. Tripathy, *The Yogācāra Theory of Knowledge* (Varanasi, India: Oriental Publishing, 1979), pp. 309, 310.

6. Ibid., p. 310.

7. See Nāgārjuna's "Fundamentals of the Middle Way," trans. F.J. Streng in *Emptiness: A Study of Religious Meaning* (Nashville and New York: Abingdon Press, 1967), I: 1-25, p. 185.

8. Gottfried Wilhelm Leibniz, *Leibniz: Selections,* ed. P. Wiener (New York: Charles Scribner's Sons, 1951), p. 536.

9. F.Th. Stcherbatsky, *Buddhist Logic,* Vol. 2 (New York: Dover Publishing, 1962), p. 87.

10. Ibid.

11. Tu Shun, "On the Meditation of Dharmadhātu," trans. Garma C.C. Chang in *The Buddhist Teaching of Totality* (University Park and London: Pennsylvania State University Press, 1977), p. 220.

12. Thomas Kuhn, *The Structure of Scientific Revolutions* (Chicago: University of Chicago Press, 1972).

13. Sir Isaac Newton, *Optiks* (New York: Dover Publishing, 1952), p. 375.

14. Michael Faraday, "A Speculation Touching Electric Conduction to the Nature of Matter", in *Experimental Research Electricity,* No. 2, 1844, p. 294.

Upon the basis of the "field" theory introduced in Faraday's classical electrodynamics, Whitehead abandoned the concept of "simple location" for that of spatiotemporal quantum-events which both house and pervade the whole cosmos. However, the American process philosophers, Charles S. Peirce and John Dewey, also rejected simple location in favor of a primacy of fields. For instance, Peirce writes:

> The proposition that we can immediately perceive only what is present seems to me parallel to that other vulgar prejudice that "a thing cannot act where it is not". . . experience shows that attractions and repulsions are the universal types of forces. A thing may be said to "be" wherever it acts; but the notion that a particle is absolutely present in one part of space, and absolutely absent from all the rest of space is devoid of all foundation." See Peirce's *The Collected Papers,* eds. Charles Hartshorne and Paul Weiss (Cambridge: Cambridge University Press, 1932), 1.38.

Similarly, John Dewey, who postulates a metaphysics of relational "situations" or "events" which are unified by what he terms "pervasive qualities" explicitly abandons simple location for a primacy of fields when he states:

> The source of the difficulty is failure to make a critical analysis of the conception of the "where" of (a situation). Where, for example, is an explosion? Where is an echo? Where is the magnetism that causes a sensitized needle to assume a certain directional position? Wherever there is an event, there is interaction, and interaction entails the concept of a field. No field can be precisely delimited; it extends wherever the energies involved in the interaction operate. . . . The field can be limited practically as can all matters of degree; it cannot be existentially located with literal exactness. The place of the most intense disturbance in an earthquake may be located with sufficient seismographic apparatus, the boundaries of its appreciable presence may be mapped out. But the boundaries are set practically. . . they are not absolute in any existential sense. One may say that existentially the field of the earthquake is the entire universe since the redistribution of energies extends indefinitely. . . specific location is always a relationship to a further event; it is additive in character." See Dewey's article entitled "The Naturalistic Theory of Perception by the Senses" in *Journal of Philosophy,* vol. 22, 1925, pp. 603–604.

However, the critical philosophic question which must be raised at this point is: how extensive are such fields, both spatially and temporally? The results of future experimental evidence arising in the physical sciences will have much bearing upon the problematic generated between Whiteheadian process metaphysics and Hua-yen Buddhism, i.e., interpenetration vs. cumulative penetration.

15. Albert Einstein and Leopold Infeld, *The Evolution of Physics* (New York: Simon and Schuster, 1938), p. 242.

16. F.H. Bradley, *Appearance and Reality* (Oxford: Charendon Press, 1968), p. 127.

17. Hsüan-tsang, "The Treatise on the Establishment of Consciousness-Only" in *A Source Book in Chinese Philosophy*, trans. and ed. Wing-tsit Chan (Princeton, N.J.: Princeton University Press, 1963), p. 392.

18. Ashok Chaterjee, *The Yogācāra Idealism* (Delhi, India: Hindu University Press, 1975), p. 45.

19. Bradley, *Appearance and Reality*, op. cit., pp. 128, 129.

20. Kitarō Nishida, *A Study of Good*, trans. V.H. Viglielmo (Tokyo: Maruzen Co., Ltd., 1960), especially Chapter One, "Pure Experience."

21. See Dilworth's Introduction to his translation of Nishida's *Fundamental Problems of Philosophy* (Tokyo: Sophia University Press, 1970).

22. David A. Dilworth, "Nishida Kitarō: Nothingness as the Negative Space of Experiential Immediacy," *International Philosophic Quarterly* 13, no. 4 (December 1973), p. 476.

23. Ibid.

24. In his essay entitled "Affective Feeling," Nishida Kitarō, like Whitehead, identifies true reality and concrete experience with immediate feeling. Nishida undertakes a phenomenological exploration of the various dimensions or horizons (*tachiba*) of experience, describing a hierarchy of experiential concreteness ranging from the more abstract planes of thought and sensation to the more concrete planes of will and aesthetically immediate feeling, what he calls the "apriori of apriori" and the noetic "act underlying all acts." See Nishida's "Affective Feeling," trans. David A. Dilworth in *Analecta Husserliana: The Yearbook of Phenomenological Research*, Vol. 8, *Japanese Phenomenology*, eds. Y. Nitta and H. Talematsu (Boston: R. Reidal Publishing Co., 1979), pp. 223–33.

25. In his *Modes of Being* (London: Southern Illinois University Press, 1958) Paul Weiss also provides a probing internal critique of Whitehead's event ontology, but he argues for the reinstitution of an Aristotelian substance cosmology in order to account for the experience of personal identity and stable endurance in what he regards as a more coherent manner. Weiss's critique of Whitehead's event ontology is examined at greater length in Part Three, Chapter Two of this work.

26. See David A. Dilworth's article, "Whitehead's Process Realism, the Abhidharma Dharma Theory and the Mahayana Critique," *International Philosophic Quarterly* 18, no. 2 (June 1978).

27. Nāgārjuna, "Fundamentals of the Middle Way," op. cit., 7:16, p. 191.

28. Ibid., 24:18, p. 213.

29. Justus Buchler, "On a Strain of Arbitrariness in Whitehead's System," *Journal of Philosophy* 66, no. 19 (October 1969), p. 590.

30. Justus Buchler, *Metaphysics of Natural Complexes* (New York: Columbia University Press, 1966), p. 49.

31. Ibid., p. 50.

32. Buchler, "On A Strain of Arbitrariness in Whitehead's System," op. cit., p. 592.

33. Buchler, *Metaphysics of Natural Complexes*, op. cit., p. 18.

34. Ivor Leclerc, "A Rejoinder to Justus Buchler," *Process Studies* 1 (1971), pp. 58, 59.

35. Charles Hartshorne, "Ontological Primacy: A Reply to Buchler," *Journal of Philosophy* 67, no. 23 (December 10, 1970), p. 980.

36. Charles Hartshorne, Chapter Six, "A Logic of Ultimate Contrasts" in *Creative Synthesis and Philosophic Method* (LaSalle, Ill.: Open Court Pub. Co. 1970).

37. Hartshorne, "Ontological Primacy: A Reply to Buchler", op. cit., p. 983.

38. See Robert C. Neville's article entitled, "Metaphysics," in *Social Research*, Winter, 1980, Vol. 47, No. 4.

39. Justus Buchler, *Metaphysics of Natural Complexes*, op. cit., p. 14

40. Stephen Ross, "The Inexhaustibility of Nature," in *The Journal of Value Inquiry* (Vol. VII, No. 4, Winter, 1973), p. 253.

Chapter 10. Metaphysics of Cumulative Penetration

1. F.H. Bradley, *Essays on Truth and Reality* (London: Clarendon Press), pp. 160–178.

2. Kitarō Nishida, *Fundamental Problems of Philosophy*, trans. D. Dilworth, (Tokyo: Sophia University, 1970), p. 177.

3. Robert C. Neville, *Reconstruction of Thinking* (Albany: State University of New York Press, 1981) pp. 17, 18.

4. Chang Chung-yuan, *Creativity and Taoism* (New York: Harper and Row, 1970), p. 21; also, p. 36.

5. Francis H. Cook, *Hua-yen Buddhism: The Jewel Net of Indra* (University Park and London: Pennsylvania State University Press, 1977), p. 112.

6. See Charles Hartshorne's *Creative Synthesis and Philosophic Method* (Illinois: Open Court Pub., 1970), pp. 198, 199.

7. For extensive treatment concerning the equation of ultimate reality with *mahāsukha* or ecstatic pleasure in Tantric Buddhism, see S.B. Dasgupta's *An Introduction to Tantric Buddhism* (Berkeley and London: Shambhala Pub., 1974), pp. 128–143.

8. Garma, C.C. Chang, *The Hundred Thousand Songs of Milarepa* (Boulder and London: Shambhala Pub., 1977), Vol. II, p. 372.

9. Herbert V. Guenther, *The Tantric View of Life* (Boulder and London: Shambhala Pub., 1976), pp. 28–31. Also, for general discussion on *sahaja* as togetherness see pp. 15, 17, 52, 100.

10. Ibid., p. 17.

11. *The Questions of King Milinda*, ed. Max Müller, Vol. 2 (New York: Dover Publications, 1963), p. 196.

12. In his book, *Creativity and Taoism* (New York: Harper and Row, 1963) Chang Chung-yuan develops at length the proximity of Whitehead's concept of peace as the "conformation of appearance to reality" not only to the Hua-yen doctrine of *li-shih-wu-ai* but also to the ancient Taoist conception of *ho p'ing* or

"harmonious tranquility". See especially Chapter Three, "Peace as identification of reality and appearance," pp. 89–122.

13. Nāgārjuna, "Fundamentals of the Middle Way," trans. Fredrick J. Streng in *Emptiness: A Study in Religious Meaning* (New York and Nashville: Abingdon Press, 1967), 24:19, p. 20.

14. "The Heart Sūtra," in *Buddhist Wisdom Books*, trans. Edward Conze (New York: Harper and Row, 1972), p. 81.

15. *The Awakening of Faith in Mahāyāna*, trans. Yoshito S. Hakeda (New York: Columbia University Press, 1967), p. 31.

PART III

Chapter 11. Whitehead's Dipolar God as the Collective Unconscious

1. The fountainhead of Process Theology is Whitehead's monumental last chapter of *Process and Reality* entitled "God and the World" wherein he articulates his notion of the dipolar God in visionary terms. Some other works which have now become standard reading in the field of Process Theology are Charles Hartshorne's *The Divine Relativity: A Social Conception of God* (New Haven: Yale University Press, 1948), John B. Cobb Jr.'s *Christ in a Pluralistic Age* (Philadelphia: Westminster Press, 1975), David R. Griffin's *A Process Christology* (Philadelphia: Westminster Press, 1973) and Lewis S. Ford's *The Lure of God* (Philadelphia: Fortress Press, 1973).

2. *The Awakening of Faith in Mahāyāna* not only identifies One Mind with the *ālaya* consciousness but also with the *tathāgatagarbha* or latent Buddha nature, as well as the *dharmakāya* or Buddha mind as fully actualized. See Yoshito S. Hakeda's translation (New York: Columbia University Press, 1967), p. 67.

3. Ibid., p. 31.

4. Ibid., pp. 36, 37.

5. Ibid., p. 89.

6. The Yogācāra depth-psychology stratifies the psyche into eight consciousnesses or *vijñānas*. The *Vijñāptimātratātrimsika (Thirty Verses on Consciousness-Only)* by Vasubandhu states: "They are the consciousness (the eighth or Storehouse consciousness) whose fruits (retribution) ripen at later times, the consciousness (the seventh or thought-center consciousness) that deliberates, and the consciousness (the sense-center consciousness and the five sense consciousness) that discriminate spheres of objects." See Wing-tsit Chan, *A Source Book in Chinese Philosophy* (Princeton, N.J.: Princeton University Press, 1963), p. 374. The Yogācāra schema of the eight consciousnesses may be diagrammatically represented as follows:

The Eight Consciousnesses

1) cakṣur vijñānas	(eye consciousness)—	(1) rūpam (form)
2) śrota vijñānas	(eye consciousness)—	(2) śabda (sound)
3) grahna vijñānas	(nose consciousness)—	(3) gandha (scent)
4) jihva vijñānas	(tongue consciousness)—	(4) rasa (flavor)
5) kaya vijñānas	(skin consciousness)—	(5) sprastavya (touch)

The Eight Consciousnesses cont.

6) manas vijñānas	(sensory-motor consciousness)
7) kliṣṭomanas vijñānas	(mental consciousness: ego-center)
8) ālaya vijñānas	(Storehouse consciousness and *vāsanās* or habit-energies)

7. Carl Gustav Jung, *Psychology and the East,* trans. R.F.C. Hull (Princeton, N.J.: Princeton University Press, 1978), p. 118.

8. Paul Tillich, "Two Types of Philosophy of Religion," in *Theology of Culture,* ed. Robert C. Kimball (New York: Oxford University Press, 1959), pp. 10–29.

9. Paul Weiss, *Modes of Being* (London and Amsterdam: Southern Illinois University Press, 1968), p. 473.

10. Paul Tillich, "The Depths of Existence," in *The Shaking of the Foundations* (New York: Charles Scribner's Sons, 1948), p. 57.

11. Jung, *Psychology and the East,* op. cit., p. 131.

12. Ibid., p. 68.

13. Ibid., p. 170.

14. Kenneth Ch'en, *Buddhism: The Light of Asia* (New York: Barron's Education Series, 1968), p. 78.

15. Carl Gustav Jung, *Collected Works,* trans. R.F.C. Hull, Vol. 2 (Princeton, N.J.: Princeton University Press, 1970), p. 468.

16. Jung, *Psychology and the East,* op. cit., p. 134.

17. Robert L. Caglione, *The Reality of the Past: A Comparison of the Philosophy of A.N. Whitehead and Paul Weiss* (Ann Arbor, Mich.: University Microfilms International Press, 1971), p. 209.

18. Ibid., p. 209.

19. Paul Weiss, *Reality* (Princetón, N.J.: Princeton University Press, 1938).

20. Ibid., p. 209: In his most systematic work, *Modes of Being* (London: Southern Illinois University Press, 1958), Weiss develops a "modal ontology" which describes reality as the togetherness of four irreducible and interlocked modes of being, namely: (I) Actuality, (II) Ideality, (III) Existence, and (IV) God, or (I) Substance, (II) Possibility, (III) Creativity, and (IV) Unity. Weiss's actualities are Aristotelian substances in that they are concrete individuals which persist through change. Weiss charges that Whitehead's ontology of momentary events is wholly unable to account for the experience of personal identity and the stability of nature, and endeavors to reframe reality in substantialist terms derived from Aristotle, having entities remain numerically the same while undergoing modifications.

21. Weiss, *Reality,* op. cit., p. 208.

22. Ibid., p. 210.

23. The first rigorously argued challenge to Process Theology, which nevertheless basically accepts the Whiteheadian cosmological view, was Robert C. Neville's *Creativity and God: A Challenge to Process Theology* (New York: The Seabury Press, 1980). Here, Neville articulates God as utterly transcendent and indeterminate apart from the relative nature He gives Himself as creator of the world. God creates *ex nihilo* every finite determination, actual or possible. He creates the novel determinations of an event's subjective form and all its phases

of coming into being. Thus, God is intimately present to each creature as creator in the act of conferring determinate being, even in the subjectivity of the creature's self-constitution. God is therefore "undetachable" from his creation. He represents the level of *ontological creativity*, which creates both the one and the many, along with the "cosmological creativity" which correlates them. But the latter is the only mode of creativity recognized by Whiteheadian Process Theology. Thus, Neville directly challenges Whitehead's separation of God from creativity at the ontological level, while still allowing for self-creativity at the cosmological level of analysis. Ultimately, Neville's theory involves an extension of Whitehead's ontological principle, wherein all unification and synthesis calls for reference to a *decision*, either that of events or God's primordial decision *ex nihilo*.

Chapter 12. The Collective Unconscious and Synchronicity: Atemporal Envisagement in the Archetypal Imagination

1. Hegel writes: "The absolute, eternal Idea in its essential existence, in and for itself, is God in His eternity before the creation of the world." G.W.F. Hegel, *Lectures on the Philosophy of Religion*, trans. E.B. Speirs and J. Sanderson, Vol. 3 (New York: Humanities Press), p. 69.

2. Carl Gustav Jung, *Collected Works*, trans. R.F.C. Hull, Vol. 2 (Princeton, N.J.: Princeton University Press, 1970). See Chapter Seven, "Synchronicity: An Acausal Connecting Principle," pp. 417–531.

3. Ibid., p. 511.

4. Ibid., p. 485; p. 520.

5. Ibid., p. 489.

6. Ibid., p. 498.

7. Ira Progoff, *Jung, Synchronicity and Human Destiny* (New York: Dell Publishing Company, 1973).

8. Jung, *Collected Works*, op. cit., p. 514.

9. Ira Progoff, *Jung, Synchronicity and Human Destiny*, op. cit., p. 147.

10. Jung, *Collected Works*, op. cit., p. 489.

11. Carl Gustav Jung, *Psychology and the East*, trans. R.F.C. Hull (Princeton, N.J.: Princeton University Press, 1978), p. 131. Jung goes on to explicitly identify the basic notion of the text, the concept of One Mind, (attributing to it an omniscient knowledge of past, present and future events) with his own concept of the collective unconscious, stating: "This section (of the text) shows very clearly that the One Mind is the [collective] unconscious, since it is characterized as eternal, unknown, not visible, not recognized" (p. 124).

12. Ibid., p. 151.

13. Justus Buchler, *Metaphysics of Natural Complexes* (New York: Columbia University Press, 1970). See especially Chapter Four, "Possibility and Actuality."

14. Jung, *Psychology and the East*, op. cit., p. 123.

15. Literally translated, *nirmāṇakāya* = the transformation body, *sambhogakāya* = the enjoyment body and *dharmakāya* = the truth body.

16. This chart is based on the excellent study of the *Bardo Thödol* by Ingo

Detlief Lauf entitled *Secret Doctrines of the Tibetan Book of the Dead* (Boulder and London: Shambhala Publishers, 1976).

17. The Indo-Tibetan bardo cosmology with its three experiential dimensions, Physical Actuality, Archetypal Imagination and Clear Light (which correspond to the three states of waking, dream and sleep, respectively) is analogous to the Western Neo-Platonic world-view, corresponding roughly to Plotinus's Three Hypostases, the Physical World, the Archetypes, and the One.

18. Jung, *Collected Works*, op. cit., Vol. 13, pp. 167, 168.

19. Ibid., Vol. 12, p. 219.

20. Ibid., Vol. 12, p. 219.

21. Mary Watkins, *Waking Dreams* (New York: Harper and Row, 1976), p. 31.

22. Alex Wayman, "The Significance of Dreams in India and Tibet," *History of Religions* 7 (May 1968), p. 11.

23. Edward S. Casey, "Time Out of Mind," in *Dimensions of Thought: Current Explorations in Time, Space and Knowledge*, Vol. 1 (Berkeley: Dharma Publishing, 1980), p. 151. In this article, Casey phenomenologically analyzes the protentive-retentive structure of internal time consciousness as constituted by imagination and memory, respectively, through the following diagram:

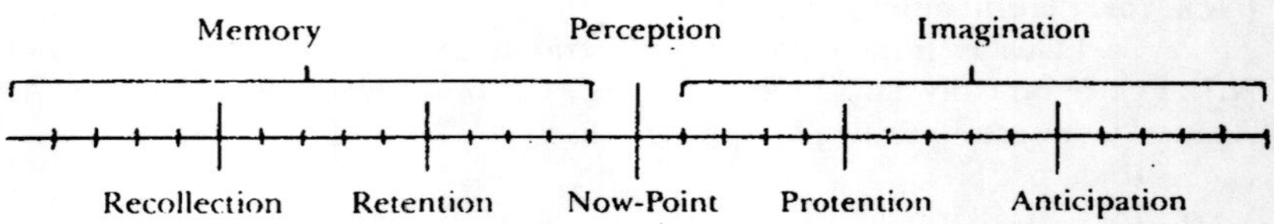

Casey then proceeds to show how at the level of the collective unconscious, retention and recollection phase-off into transpersonal memory, whereas protention and anticipation phase-off into archetypal imagination as Platonic *anamnesis*.

24. Garma C.C. Chang, *The Buddhist Teaching of Totality*, (University Park and London: Pennsylvania State University Press, 1977), p. 172.

25. Ibid., p. 180.

26. Janice D. Willis, *On Knowing Reality* (New York: Columbia University Press, 1979), p. 28.

27. Ibid., pp. 27–29.

28. William Blake, "The Lacoön," in *The Poetry and Prose of William Blake*, ed. D.E. Erdman (New York: Doubleday and Co., 1970), p. 271.

29. Ibid., p. 639.

30. Ibid., p. 118.

31. Kūkai, "The Precious Key to the Secret Treasury," in *Kūkai: Major Works*, trans. with commentary by Yhoshito S. Hakeda (New York: Columbia University Press, 1972), pp. 163, 164.

32. Minoru Kityota, *Shingon Buddhism: Theory and Practice* (Los Angeles and Tokyo: Buddhist Books International, 1978), p. 32.

33. Ibid., p. 55.

34. Francis H. Cook, *Hua-yen Buddhism: The Jewel Net of Indra* (University

Park and London: Pennsylvania State University Press, 1977), p. 91. See Chapter Seven, "Vairocana," pp. 90–188.

35. Ibid., p. 91.

36. Ibid., p. 104.

37. Minoru Kiyota, *Shingon Buddhism,* op. cit., p. 176.

38. Yoshito S. Hakeda, *Kūkai: Major Works,* op. cit., p. 98.

39. The eminent twentieth-century Christian theologian Paul Tillich ends his book *The Courage To Be* (New Haven and London: Yale University Press, 1952) with a section entitled "The God Above and the Courage To Be" (see pp. 186–90). Tillich himself in part derived his notion of a "God above God" from the speculative mysticism of Meister Eckhart (1260–1328) who distinguished "God" with His various dynamic functions as Creator of the universe from the unmoving "Godhead," writing: "Therefore I pray God that he may quit me of god, for his unconditioned being is above god and all distinctions." See *Meister Eckhart,* trans. R.B. Blakney (New York: Harper & Row, 1941), p. 231.

Glossary

Ch'eng-kuan Fourth Patriarch of Chinese Hua-yen: 738-840 A.D.
澄觀

ch'ung-ch'ung wu-chin realms-embracing-realms ad infinitum
重重無盡

chung tao middle way 中道

fa-chieh Skt. *dharmadhātu;* dharma-world 法界

Fa-tsang Third Patriarch of Chinese Hua-yen: 643-712 A.D. 法藏

fo Buddha 佛

hai-yin san-mei ocean seal samādhi 海印三昧

hsiang-chi mutual identity 相卽

hsiang-ho mutual harmonization 相和

hsiang-ju mutual inclusiveness 相入

hsiang-yu mutual causation 相由

hu-jung mutual containment 互容

Hua-yen ching Skt. *Avataṃsaka-sūtra; Flower Adornment Scripture*
華嚴經

Hwaŏm ilsŭng pŏpkye do *Diagram of the Dharmadhātu According to the One Vehicle of Hwaŏm,* by Ŭisang 華嚴一乘法界圖

hwajaeng harmonization of all disputes 和諍

i ch'eng yüan chiao One Vehicle Round Teachings 一乘圓教

i hsin one mind 一心

kung Skt. *śūnyatā;* emptiness, openness, voidness, nothingness, or relativity 空

Glossary

li universal-principle 理

li-shih wu-ai non-obstruction of universal-principle and particular-phenomena 理事無礙

liu hsiang Doctrine of the "Six Marks" 六相

1. *tsung hsiang* universality mark 總相
2. *pieh hsiang* particularity mark 別相
3. *t'ung hsiang* identity mark 同相
4. *i hsiang* difference mark 異相
5. *ch'eng hsiang* integration mark 成相
6. *huai hsiang* disintegration mark 壞相

shih particular-phenomena 事

shih-shih wu-ai non-obstruction of particular-phenomena and particular-phenomena 事事無礙

t'i-yung essence-function 體用

t'ong pulgyo Buddhism of total interpenetration 通佛教

Tu-shun First Patriarch of Chinese Hua-yen: 558-640 A.D. 杜順

Tsung-mi Fifth Patriarch of Chinese Hua-yen: 780-841 A.D. 宗密

t'ung interpenetration 通

Ŭisang First Patriarch of Korean Hwaŏm: 625-702 義湘

wei shin mind-only 唯心

wŏllyung hoet'ong syncretic interpenetrative harmonization 圓融會通

wu li/yu li lacking power/having power 無力・有力

wu shih erh chien tzu doctrine of the "Fifty Two Gradual Stages" 五十二漸次

(10)*shih hsin* Ten Faiths 十信

(20)*shih chu* Ten Abodes 十住

(30)*shih hsing* Ten Practices 十行

(40)*shih hui hsiang* Ten Returnings 十迴向

(50)*shih t'i* Ten *Bhūmis* or Stages 十地

(51)*teng chüeh* Equal Enlightenment 等覺

(52)*miao chüeh* Wonderful Enlightenment 妙覺

yüan ch'i conditioned origination 緣起

yüan yung complete interpenetration 圓融

Name Index

Name Index

Subject Index